Colonel Saunderson, M. P.: A Memoir – Primary Source Edition

Reginald Lucas

COLONEL
THE RT. HONBLE. EDWARD SAUNDERSON
M.P.

Edw H Saunderson

COLONEL SAUNDERSON

M.P.

A MEMOIR

BY REGINALD LUCAS

SOMETIME M.P. FOR PORTSMOUTH

AUTHOR OF "A OCTETS POINT OF VIEW"

WITH PORTRAITS AND ILLUSTRATIONS

LONDON

JOHN MURRAY, ALBEMARLE STREET, W.

1908

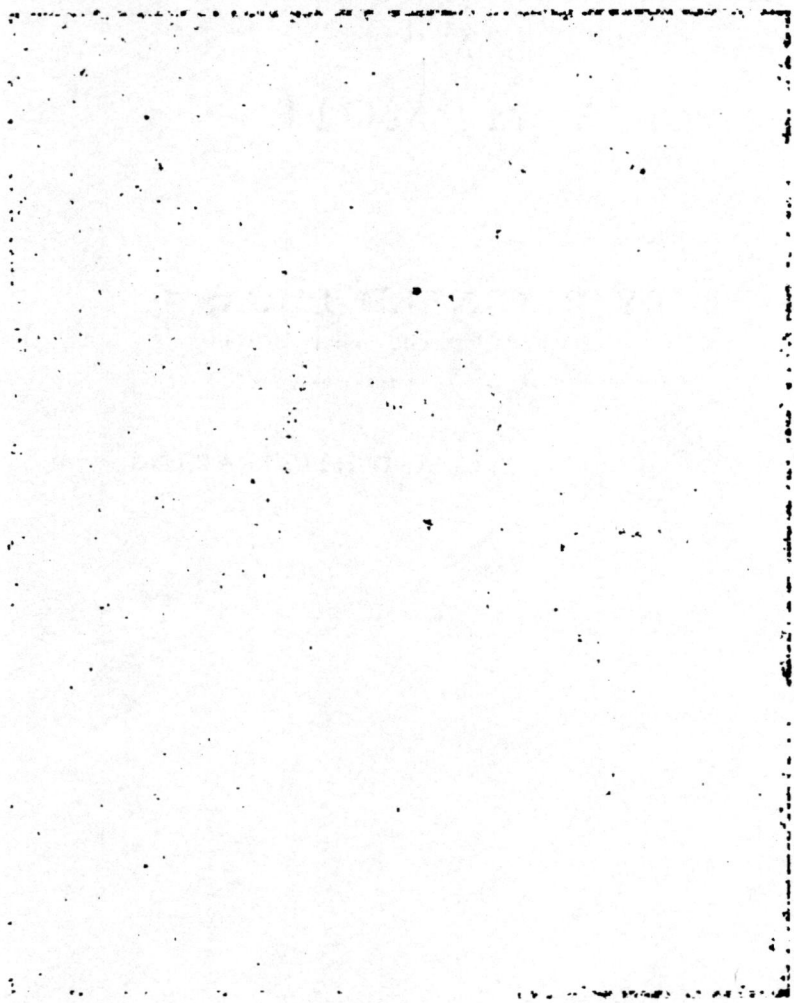

COLONEL SAUNDERSON

M.P.

A MEMOIR

BY REGINALD LUCAS

SOMETIME M.P. FOR PORTSMOUTH

AUTHOR OF "ANOTHER POINT OF VIEW"

WITH PORTRAITS AND ILLUSTRATIONS

LONDON

JOHN MURRAY, ALBEMARLE STREET, W.

1908

PRINTED BY
HAZELL, WATSON AND VINEY, LD.,
LONDON AND AYLESBURY.

PREFACE

I AM aware that the first duty of a biographer is to keep himself out of the story, and that in this respect I have deliberately broken rules. But it must be remembered that this does not aspire to be an historical work: it is a personal memoir, and therefore the personal element must of necessity be admitted.

The book has been written with the authority and under the inspiration of Mrs. Saunderson; consequently it would be superfluous to thank her for her assistance.

I have to make my grateful acknowledgments to all those who have given me permission to print the letters which appear; also to the proprietors of *The Times* for leave to publish the Primate's poem.

I have received valuable assistance and advice from many of Colonel Saunderson's friends in private as well as in political life. They are too numerous to name, but I must particularly mention, amongst the former, the Earl of Erne, K.P., the Bishop of Down (Dr. Crozier), and Mr. H. Gartside Tipping; amongst the latter, the Right Hon. W. E. Macartney and Mr. J. B. Lonsdale, M.P., past and present secretaries of the Irish Unionist party in the House of Commons. All these gentlemen have been good enough to read and criticise portions of my proofs.

To Mr. John Saunderson, Royal Artillery, I am

indebted for much information upon family matters. Mr. Burdett-Coutts, M.P., an intimate friend of Colonel Saunderson's, has made it a labour of love to promote the execution of the work. Little remains that is exclusively my own, except the faults.

In order to indicate the spirit in which my subject should be approached, I cannot do better than borrow a sentence from the Bishop of Down's preface to the Colonel's little volume of sermons. After speaking of "the faith that fired his heart in life, and comforted his soul in death," the Bishop goes on: "It was to this he owed that captivating and sunny gladness of almost child-like simplicity which made life so happy for all who came much in contact with him, coupled with a ceaseless desire to share with others the knowledge of the love of God."

In introducing this book to the public I have much pleasure in adding the following words which Mrs. Saunderson has asked me to include in my preface:

"As you know, I am anxious to have a record of the life of the bravest and truest man I have ever met. I am fortunate in finding in you one who knew Colonel Saunderson both in public and private life, and for whom he had a sincere regard; and feel you can present to the world an unembellished picture of one whose simple faith and trust in the guidance of God enabled him to do what he considered to be his duty to his country, notwithstanding failing health, from which he suffered for the last seventeen years of his life. Truly this was leaving footprints on the sands of time:

> Footprints that perhaps another,
> Sailing o'er life's solemn main;
> A forlorn and shipwrecked brother,
> Seeing, shall take heart again."

The task with which I had the honour to be entrusted I accepted gladly, but not without diffidence. I have endeavoured to avoid panegyric; and, without ignoring the infirmities from which the Colonel was no more exempt than any other human being, to represent him as he will be remembered by those who knew him best.

R. L.

ALBANY, PICCADILLY.
April, 1908.

CONTENTS

CHAPTER I

1837—1857

CHAPTER II

1857—1865

CHAPTER III

1865—1868

CHAPTER IV

1869—1874

CHAPTER V
1874—1884

CHAPTER VI
1884—1885

CHAPTER VII
1885—1886

CHAPTER VIII
1886—1887

CHAPTER IX
1887

CONTENTS

CHAPTER X

1887—1888

CHAPTER XI

1889—1890

CHAPTER XII

1890—1892

CHAPTER XIII

1892—1893

CHAPTER XIV

1893—1894

CHAPTER XV

1894—1895

CHAPTER XVI

1895—1897

CHAPTER XVII

1897—1898

CHAPTER XVIII

1899

CHAPTER XIX

1900—1901

CONTENTS

LIST OF ILLUSTRATIONS

COLONEL SAUNDERSON

CHAPTER I

1837—1857

THE biographer of Colonel Saunderson is confronted by an obvious embarrassment. In many
cases a memoir may be satisfactorily produced by
diligent transcribing from collected material—speeches
and letters tell a complete tale. With Colonel
Saunderson it is otherwise. It is true that during
twenty years his was a conspicuous figure in politics;
that he played a leading part in critical and dramatic
scenes; but to reproduce his speeches and relate his
opinions would afford a poor and inadequate record
of his career.

It is said that when Carlyle was engaged upon his
"Life of Frederick the Great" he kept some portraits of
the king hanging before his eyes so that he might
be continually imbued with the spirit of his theme.
To compare small performances with great, it is much
to be desired that here at the outset Colonel Saunderson could be as clearly portrayed for the inspiration
of what is to follow. His personality gave value and
significance to all his words and works: to appreciate
what he did, it is necessary to comprehend to some
extent what he was.

Nature had given him a prodigal endowment: his presence was imposing; his features were manly; his eyes possessed that peculiar keenness which every schoolboy remembers as γλαυπῶκις; he spoke in a sonorous tone, and at one time sang with charm; and he had the habit of compelling laughter in an unrivalled degree. He was profoundly and sincerely religious, yet the gayest and least austere of men. He was a zealous officer of militia. He was a talented artist and a'noted caricaturist. He could shoot as well as most men, and was once a daring and accomplished horseman. He was a practised billiard-player, and prided himself not a little on achieving some proficiency at golf in his later days. He was an expert yachtsman; and from the first stroke of the design planned in his billiard-room, to the moment of steering a winning boat upon the water, his was the executive and controlling hand. As we shall learn, he was a singularly effective speaker, and a winning and impressive preacher. Moreover, he was gifted with that inscrutable quality, which is difficult to define in personal communion and almost impossible to describe on paper.

It is vain to record that he was a lovable man and a remarkable character unless some evidence be adduced to make this manifest. A fond appreciation might give pleasure to his kindred and intimate friends; but something more is needed if an appeal is to be made to the wider circle of those who knew him only or principally in his public capacity. To satisfy the latter, without disappointing the former class of those who may read these pages, is at once the duty and desire of the present writer.

The Saundersons trace their origin to one Alexander de Bedic, who dwelt in Durham in the year 1333.

It may be surmised that he was familiarly known, *more Scotico*, as Sandy; however that may be, his son undoubtedly went by the name of Alexander's son; hence Sanderson, which in process of time was enriched with the letter *u*, and so produced the patronymic Saunderson. From this stock various branches grew, and with two of these we are concerned: one made its way into Lincolnshire; the other to Scotland, whence it turned to Ireland early in the seventeenth century.

The Lincolnshire Saundersons flourished. Settling at Saxby, they acquired property and position. In 1612 Nicholas Saunderson, M.P., was created a baronet, and in 1628 was raised to the Irish peerage as Viscount Castleton. Sir James, the sixth viscount, was created Baron Saunderson of Saxby in the peerage of Great Britain in 1714; in 1716 the viscountcy of Castleton was revived in his favour as an English title, and in 1720 he was promoted to an earldom; but this rapid progress was arrested three years later when he died without issue. Baronetcy and peerage were both extinguished, and his property passed by will to his cousin on his mother's side, Thomas Lumley, third Earl of Scarbrough, in whose family it remains to this day. Lord Scarbrough assumed the surname of Saunderson but he did not adopt the Saunderson arms—paly of six argent and azure, over all a bend sable; of which we shall have occasion to speak again.

Meanwhile Alexander Saunderson had settled in Ireland. His second son, Colonel Robert, served under Gustavus Adolphus, greatly distinguishing himself in the disastrous Russian campaign. His eldest son Robert married a Leslie of Glaslough: he was sometime M.P. for Co. Cavan, and was expelled by an order of Parliament in 1696 because his political opinions were not sufficiently accommodating. He left no issue, and the property went to his nephew Alexander. This man's grandson, another Alexander, was a notable character. He sought advancement by making an unsuccessful claim in the Irish House of Lords to the viscountcy of Castleton. To give colour to this pretence he adopted the *u* in the spelling of Saunderson and appears to have appropriated the Castleton arms. These, as we have seen, were paly of six argent and azure over all a bend sable. The researches of a member of Colonel Saunderson's family have revealed the fact that originally the Irish branch bore a variation on this, namely, bendy of six argent and azure charged with a mullet or; and so the coat appears above the door of Castle Saunderson to this day, albeit an unobservant carver has allowed himself to blazon the whole in reverse sinister. But succeeding generations retained the Saxby or Castleton coat and bear it now, with a difference of three annulets or on the bend.[1]

This Alexander was the black sheep of the family; he squandered his property in gambling and racing. His racecourse exists at Castle Saunderson to this day. His wife, Rose Lloyd, was of another temper. In sending her son Francis some "light volumes" of Plutarch's Lives, she warns him against "those fatal weaknesses which dig an early grave and which are only the result of confined and limited education." This Francis, succeeding in due season, profited by her wholesome counsel. He was a discreet man, M.P. for Cavan, and married Anne White, heiress

---

[1] Castle Saunderson was twice burnt during disturbed times in the seventeenth century. The present house was built at the beginning of the eighteenth century.

to the Bassett property in Glamorganshire, through her mother. Her sister was Lydia White, a shining light in the literary society of the day, whose name is enshrined in the pages of " Pelham." Anne herself was a lady of considerable attainments and no little eccentricity. So much occupied was she with her intellectual pursuits that she found a nursery extremely inconvenient ; consequently she proceeded to distribute her children amongst the neighbouring cottagers to be " walked," as the custom was with puppies and game-cocks. It is not improbable that her versatile and adventurous spirit entered into her descendants. A picture of her hangs now in Castle Saunderson. The heir of Francis and Anne was Alexander, born in 1783. Another son, Francis, became a clergyman, and married a sister of the Earl of Erne, thus allying the family with the neighbouring house of Crichton.[1] Alexander married the Hon. Sarah Juliana, daughter of the sixth Baron Farnham. He was in turn M.P. for Co. Cavan, and became the father of the subject of this memoir.

His eldest son Francis died young. Whether this or other causes were responsible for his decision, Colonel Saunderson[2] elected to leave home and spend the remainder of his life abroad. From motives which again we need not too closely examine he thought fit to pass over his second and third sons, Alexander de Bedic and Somerset, and leave Castle Saunderson to his fourth son, Edward. This implies nothing sinister. Alexander de Bedic chose to go to America, where he died in 1860 ; but to Somerset his father

---

[1] There were also (3) Hardress, Lt.-Col. Grenadier Guards : married Lady Maria Olmius, daughter of last Earl of Carhampton ; (4) James, Lt. R.N. : married daughter of Colonel and Lady Anne Fox ; (5) William Bassett, Lt.-Col. in the Army.

[2] Alexander Saunderson became Colonel of the Cavan Militia.

left his Welsh property. Llewellyn,[1] the fifth son, who survives, inherited, in the same way, Drumkeen, Co. Cavan.

Edward James Saunderson was born on October 1, 1837. There is no need to fear that this biography will be overlaid with trivial stories of his childhood and early days. The family archives are scanty, and owing to the circumstances, there can be no local traditions. Edward Saunderson was by no means indifferent to the value of record-keeping: in an undated fragment he writes as follows:

"It is a cause of unfailing regret to me that I did not keep a journal in past years of the different events and occurrences of which I was either a witness or an actor. Every one who can write ought to keep some sort of memorial of the kind; otherwise passing years are like an inscription engraved in sandstone, which gradually wears away: one word gets effaced, one disappears, and only here and there can sense be made out. So it is with years: one becomes intermixed with another and none but the most prominent events stand the test of time. How many trivial things—things which we thought of no account —would afford in after years a mine of amusement, if not a source of instruction, had they been written down!"

Very excellent precept. Unhappily Saunderson did not practise what he preached, and his journalising through life was but fitful and spasmodic. His salient memories of childhood are a droll commentary on the theory above enunciated. He squarely faces the beginning of things: "I was born in a big room over the Hall at Castle Saunderson . . . after which I suppose I squalled, yelled, and slobbered like other babies."

[1] Mr. Llewellyn Saunderson, a gentleman of various attainments, including a knowledge of Hebrew, joined the 11th Hussars, and saw service as a volunteer under General Lee in the American Civil War. He married Lady Rachel Scott, daughter of the 3rd Earl of Clonmell.

Then comes a "prominent event." "The very earliest event I can recollect is being carried down to be scolded by my father in an old grey cloak. I was then under two." It is not quite clear which of them wore this garment; but whether the child was critical of his own attire, or observant of what his father wore, the fact either way is significant. One may even suggest that it must have been an exceptional two-year-old for whom the discipline of the nursery was inadequate, and in whose case the parent's influence had to be so impressively invoked.

"The next event which I remember," he proceeds, "was my great-grandmother, Lady Carrick,[1] giving me a box of steel pens." One need not be surprised that a child should have suffered lasting astonishment on the receipt of such an extraordinary gift. More human is the next entry: "In the autumn of 1844 we all went to Dublin and then to Brighton, and I saw a railway for the first time." It is possible that he now made his first acquaintance with the sea, the element which was to afford him so much occupation and delight throughout life.

Not long after this Alexander Saunderson, as we have seen, determined to shut up his home and live abroad. For many years Nice was his headquarters, and here he settled in the Maison Cauvin, Rue Massena, about the year 1846. A Mr. White accompanied the party as tutor to the boys, but he only remained six months. To him succeeded a Jesuit priest. One cannot but feel some surprise upon learning that the education of the boys was in such hands as these, so little does the association fit the religious character which distinguished their subsequent careers. The father made

[1] Mrs. Saunderson's mother was Lady Anne Butler, daughter of the second Earl of Carrick. She died in 1831.

it a solemn obligation upon the tutor that he should attempt no influence upon his pupils' spiritual condition ; but he, conceiving his duty to his church to override all other claims, speedily violated his promise, and so delivered himself up defenceless. It has been related by a friend of the family, who called one day at Nice, that upon entering the drawing-room he beheld a scene familiar in later days to those who went to the theatre to see *The Private Secretary*. The three brothers occupied the sofa, armed with cushions,[1] the tutor was crouching underneath, and no sooner did he attempt to escape than he was belaboured about the head and driven back to cover.

This false position and lack of authority led to a change. Another Jesuit took his place and presumably adhered to the stipulated conditions, for he remained a long while, making way eventually for an Irishman. Very many years later, Edward Saunderson, driving with his wife and daughter near Beaulieu, recognised his old tutor, Abbé Gras, and revived with great mutual satisfaction the recollection of their remote friendship.

One might be forgiven for supposing that the circumstances which had driven Alexander Saunderson into exile, aggravated as they were by bad health, were not such as to inspire a joyous domestic atmosphere ; also that the man who had sent for his child of less than two years old to scold him "in an old grey cloak" was not likely to be entirely sympathetic or indulgent towards the antics of such lively boys. The fact remains that he was the most amiable and indulgent of parents and by nature an easy-going man. The mother was not one of those

---

[1] According to another version, dictionaries, intended for other purposes, were put to this use.

EDWARD SAUNDERSON.

NICE, 1855; ÆT. 18.

women whose sons can do no wrong; but, whatever her private sorrows and disappointments may have been, she was entirely devoted to Edward.

On the other hand we may safely conjecture that the exuberance of youth required some spacious outlet. It is a tradition that upon one occasion a craving for adventure prompted one of the young gentlemen to tweak the nose of an unoffending Frenchman in public. When he was asked to account for this outrage, he could offer no better explanation than an innate desire to create a sensation. Upon another occasion they induced a garden boy to present himself as a human target for the exercise of their practice in marksmanship; but the rattle of the pebbles (with which their weapon was loaded) about his ribs drew forth such yells that no further progress was made. Turning their attention to horsemanship, they came next upon a local painter, an excessive dandy, who was fond of displaying himself on horseback. It was the habit of the young Irishmen, when the condition of the roads was favourable, to gallop past him in such a manner as to bespatter him liberally with mud. This led to further scenes of objurgation and protest.

Edward was not incapable of presenting himself as the *enfant terrible* of the party. Once when the family were staying at Lausanne a visit of ceremony was paid by a clergyman, Sir Nicholas ———, accompanied by his wife and daughter. The conversation, which no doubt had hitherto been dignified and appropriate, was suddenly interrupted by Edward's interjection:

"Sir Nicholas, it is a very good thing that you have got no son."

"And why so?" asked the reverend baronet, evidently annoyed.

"Because he would be called young Nick, and

you would be Old Nick." It is not known whether good neighbourly relations were established after this.

Better occupation was found for these turbulent spirits when one villa in their occupation was attacked by local brigands. The assault was successfully repulsed by the father and sons armed with guns. Either the assailants were not very brave, or the Saundersons were manifestly dangerous to disturb, for it appears that there was no ammunition at hand.

Edward's passion for yachting was already alive. When living at the Maison Jaume he was allowed to engage a ship's carpenter to assist in building a small boat; but the project was interrupted. It was here that Colonel Alexander Saunderson died in 1857.

It is upon the whole, then, a matter for congratulation that, in spite of these lively and adventurous habits, there was no serious interruption of the family life. Whether the control exercised from above was lenient, or the self-control exercised below was reasonable, it remains that the boys were not packed off to school; and that if their education was neither extensive nor profound, at all events they acquired a lasting proficiency in the use of the French language, than which there are few more valuable assets in a young man's provision for life. Moreover, to this freedom from the influence of the public school and the university, which forces most young men into a social and intellectual groove, we may reasonably attribute much of the freshness and originality which distinguished Saunderson to the end.

CHAPTER II

1857—1865

THE family returned to England, and settled at Torquay, moving later to Brighton, the Isle of Wight, and finally to Kingstown.

Saunderson was to come of age at twenty-five (1862); until then the property remained in the hands of trustees. For the present the house was occupied by an old French servant who had lived with the late colonel, and who is described as spending all his time in fishing on the lake.

At Torquay Saunderson had his first yacht built, from designs of his own. She was a boat of eighteen tons, named the *Chimera*, and he constantly cruised in her. Later he had another of thirty-five tons built by Ratsey, of Cowes, and in her he sailed some races, with occasional success, up to the year 1862. This was the *Phasma*. In due time he settled at Castle Saunderson with his mother and his sister Rose, his elder sister having in the meantime married. Here he proceeded to enjoy life with great zest.

Undoubtedly the trait in his character which most forcibly impressed itself upon his acquaintance, was his intensely religious sensibility. The influence which this exercised over his life will be made apparent in subsequent chapters, but one or two instances may be given here to explain his attitude of mind.

To one friend he took occasion to say that he never

could see why a man should not speak about the relations existing between himself and his God in the same kind of language he would use when talking about a boat or a horse. To him the spiritual communion was very close and very real. He once said that he never got up to make a speech without asking God to guide him—a confession confirmed by letters which will appear. Again, he ascribed the cheerfulness and good talk at his table to the fact that before dinner he used to pray for grace and wisdom to guide the conversation.

When he began to preach on Sundays at Castle Saunderson one of his neighbours suggested that it was better to leave this to the clergyman. "Suppose," answered Saunderson, "that I had discovered a sure remedy for the potato disease ; would you not help me to make it known to your tenants ? I have found a remedy for a much worse disease than that, the disease of sin. Don't you think it is my duty to tell people about that ?"

Another friend, formerly an officer in the Navy, relates that when he first saw Saunderson his impression was that he would make a splendid captain of a man-of-war, and that it would be very pleasant to serve under him. Experience was to bring him under Saunderson's influence and affect all the sequel of his life. He was in a neighbouring house one Sunday morning when a message arrived, asking him to come to Castle Saunderson. He went ; heard Saunderson preach ; and thenceforth found his outlook on existence changed and illuminated. The preacher admitted that he had prayed that this sick and afflicted spirit might be sent to him and that to himself might be given power to administer healing and consolation.

Other instances could be given of men who attribute to Saunderson's unostentatious influence the altered tenor of their lives.

But if this was the ruling impulse, he was indeed a "muscular Christian." Although he was not essentially robust in constitution he was physically strong in limbs and muscles. Amongst his various odd accomplishments he could hold out a big chair at arm's length ; he could sign his name on a wall with a 56-lb. weight attached to his little finger ;[1] he could stand with his back against the end of an open door, and then, placing his hands on the top of it, turn a back somersault, come down astride, and sit there as comfortably as if he were in a saddle. When he was in the saddle his feats were no less remarkable. He could pick an object off the ground at full gallop. Once when he was in Palestine[2] he secured the profound veneration of some natives for whose benefit he performed this trick. They then described a wonderful thing which they had seen done by an Arab on horseback. To their great confusion Saunderson immediately attempted the exploit with complete success.

He was a bold rider and very fond of hunting. He hunted constantly in Co. Meath, and at one time occupied Kilcairne Lodge, Navan. One who remembers him there, in the early sixties, tells of a celebrated horse called The Terror, which nobody but Saunderson could ride. Throughout life his favourite designation for anything or anybody abnormal was "a perfect terror," which in some senses implied superlative excellence : perhaps this was in memory of his Meath days. "I was particularly struck," adds the same writer, "with noticing that he always kept a Bible

[1] His friends need not be reminded of the vigour of his hand-grip.
[2] He could claim to have preached a sermon in the Holy Land.

at his bedside, and read a portion of it every morning before getting up."

His brothers Somerset and Llewellyn were both in the 11th Hussars and were then quartered in Dublin. All three were devoted friends; Edward spent a good deal of his time with the regiment, and sometimes hunted from Dublin, keeping his horses at Island Bridge. The trio were not without notoriety, and were generally known as " Rats " No. 1, No. 2, and No. 3. One night after mess they amused themselves by seeing who could kick highest up the wall; with the result that they broke the glass of several valuable prints. They were all men of character, and were constantly doing sensational things, as in the old days at Nice. They were much together at Castle Saunderson also during the years that followed. Another friend says of them : " They were always doing something dangerous, either riding untrained horses at big fences, or those high-wheeled bicycles down steep hills ; sailing dangerous boats, or jumping over backs of chairs ; always brave and gay."

Apparently Edward was quite capable of " taking care of himself" in trying circumstances. Once in a country house he met a distinguished Englishman who had to sustain an exalted reputation for wit. He presumably thought that the lively young Irishman was attracting too much attention, and set out to demolish him. Saunderson was unabashed, and retaliated by asking a number of questions about his tormentor's father.

" Why ?" he was asked. " You never knew my father."

" No," he answered cheerfully ; " but I should have liked to gaze on the procreator of such a remarkable man as you."

In these early days he was also capable of practical joking.   Soon after he went to live at Castle Saunderson he asked some relations, who had never been in Ireland, to come and stay with him.   He explained that all the stories they had heard about Irishmen were quite true, and that pigs were kept in every house.   He met the ladies at the station and drove them to the house at full gallop.   There he had allotted stations to two officers from Belturbet under the billiard-table, each with a hamper; in one of them an old and very large sow, in the other a litter of young pigs.   At the proper moment these were released and a very satisfactory result was secured.   The visitors were a good deal astonished, but Saunderson reminded them that they had been warned against the peculiarities of Irish life.

He once informed the present writer that in his younger days he had contrived to upset an outside car in the streets of Dublin in order to wake up a rather dull companion.

On another occasion, one of the brothers, during family prayers, had crawled about behind the kneeling congregation and twitched the shoes from the feet of the female servants.

In 1864 Saunderson went to Denmark with Mr. George Longley, a son of the Archbishop of Canterbury, to see something of the campaign then in progress arising out of the Schleswig-Holstein dispute with Prussia and her allies.   Again he began to keep a journal, and again he broke down at the outset.   This is much to be regretted, because on this expedition he undoubtedly had some adventures worth relating.

His return from Denmark marked a critical epoch in Saunderson's life.   He was to go and stay with Mr. Forbes at Callander, in Stirlingshire.   They were intimate friends. Mr. Forbes had for some time occupied Palmerstown, in Co. Kildare, and Saunderson had frequently been there for hunting.

On the present occasion his approach was heralded by his servant, who brought the luggage, but had lost his master. Saunderson pursued his journey alone and not quite successfully; for, going to sleep in the train, he was carried far beyond his destination. When this erratic traveller eventually arrived, he found amongst other people in the house a former acquaintance, the Hon. Helena de Moleyns, youngest daughter of the third Lord Ventry. His vagaries upon the road had not led him from his allotted goal: they speedily became engaged, and the supreme felicity of a happy marriage was assured to him.

There is no evidence to show that he had as yet been thinking seriously of politics; but he entertained a great admiration for Lord Palmerston. Whatever parliamentary ambition he may have possessed was fostered by Lord Carlisle,[1] the Viceroy, who took much interest in him. Lord Carlisle had met him at Crom Castle (Lord Erne's) and had shown special delight in Saunderson's singing. He was particularly susceptible to the charm which his young friend imparted to certain Italian songs, and it is on record that he would sit in wrapt attention whilst tears stole down his cheeks and his impudent *aides-de-camp* made fun of him behind his back. At all events Saunderson decided to stand for the county, as we shall see. But he must be married first; and on June 22, 1865, the wedding was duly solemnised. His conduct on this agitating occasion is not a bad indication of his freedom from fussiness and excessive

---

[1] Seventh Earl, K.G., Lord-Lieutenant 1855-58 and 1859-1864, died December 5, 1864.

Mr Forbes had ... ... in Co. Kildare, ...derson ... there for hunting.

... ... on his approach was heralded ... who brought the luggage, ... had lost ... ...derson pursued his journey alone ... ...ssfully; for going to sleep in the ... ...rried far beyond his destination. ... the traveller eventually arrived, he ... ...her people in the house a former ... Hon. Helena de Moleyns, youngest ... third Lord Ventry. His vagaries ... not led him from his allotted goal: ... became engaged, and the su... ... marriage was assured to him.

... ...dence to show that he had as yet ... ...g seriously of politics; but he entertained ... ...mation for Lord Palmerston. Whatever ...mentary ambition he may have possessed was ... ...ed by Lord Carlisle,[1] the Viceroy, who took ... interest in him. Lord Carlisle had met him ... ...Casue (Lord Erne's) and had shown special ... ...Saunderson's singing. He was particularly ... ...ptible to the charm which his young friend im... ...ed to certain Italian songs, and it is on record ... he would sit in wrapt attention whilst tears stole ... his cheeks and his impudent *aides-de-camp* ... fun of him behind his back. At all events ...underson decided to stand for the county, as we ...ail see. But he must be married first; and ... June ..., 1865, the wedding was duly solemnised. ... ...ct on this agitating occasion is not a ba... ... ...en of his freedom from fussiness and excessi...

---

[1] ... ... K.G., Lord-Lieutenant 1855-58 and 1859-1864, die... De... ..., 1864

The Hon. Helen E. de Moleyns
(Mrs Saunderson)
1864.

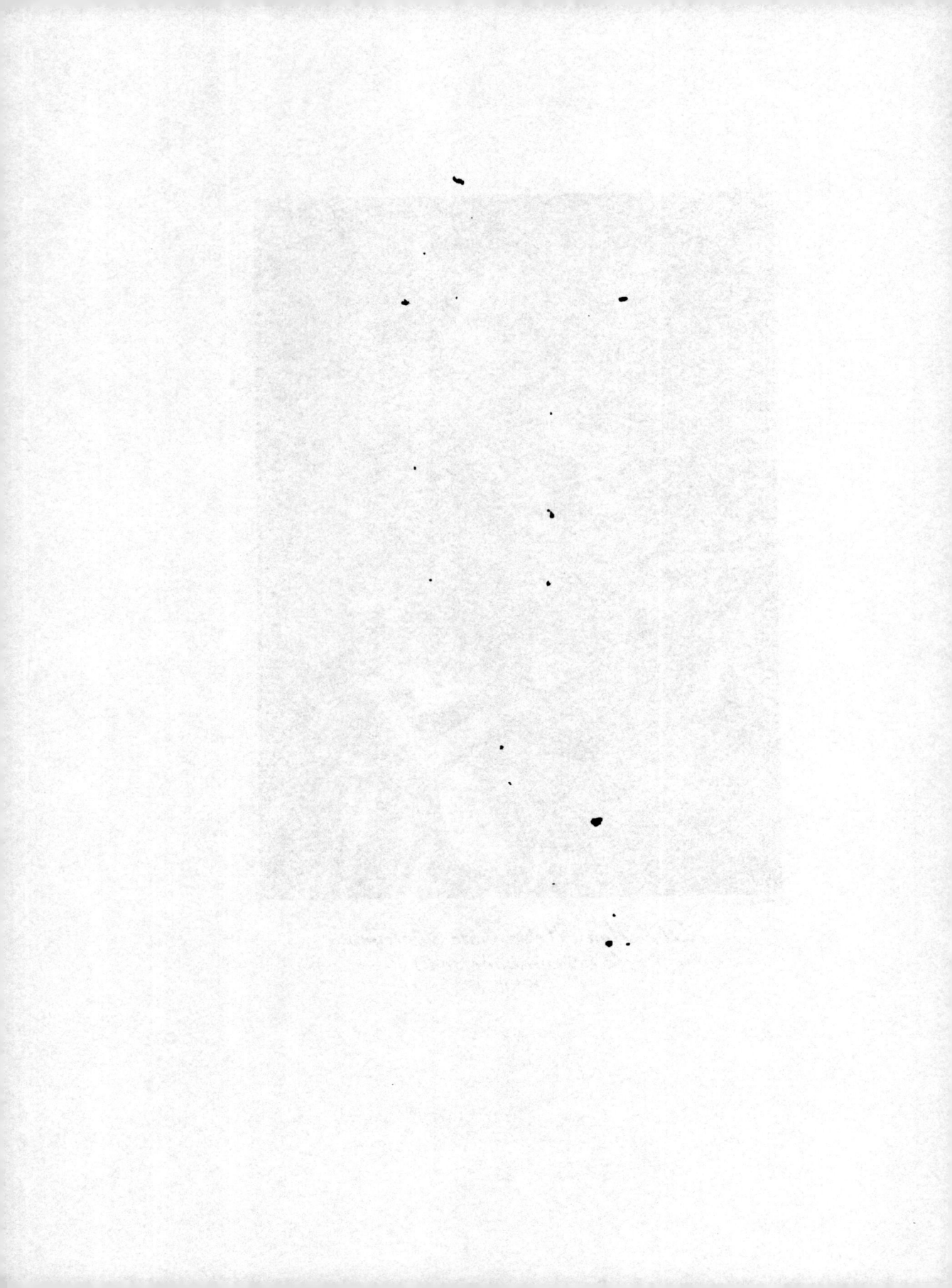

care for appearances. He spent the morning in composing his election address; after which he played
billiards until it was time to go to church. The
ceremony took place at three, and the honeymoon
was to be spent in Wales. On the point of leaving
Kingstown he found he had no money, so he handed
his bride over to the care of Lord Bangor, whilst
he went to his club to get some. But the day's
adventures were not yet concluded. On the pier at
Holyhead he had occasion to resent the roughness
of some man carrying a package; him he immediately
engaged in combat and succeeded in knocking down.[1]
The honeymoon was curtailed by a message announcing
that, to make his election sure, he should go home at
once. The wife, with proper spirit, voted for public
duty, so that his entry into politics and the married
state coincided.

As soon as the election was over Saunderson and
his wife paid a long visit to Lord and Lady Ventry
in Co. Kerry. Here he shot innumerable snipe, and
built a boat for his father-in-law for use in Dingle
Bay. He also amused himself by constructing an
enormous kite, which he attached to a rowing-boat.
The natives, who were not observant enough to detect
the cause of motion, were inclined to credit him with
supernatural powers.

His mother and sister meanwhile continued to live
at Castle Saunderson, and a situation which is not
usually considered easy was found in this instance
smooth and felicitous. But the climate did not suit
the elder lady very well, and after a couple of years
she returned to the more congenial atmosphere of
Monkstown.

Saunderson throughout his life was deeply attached

[1] He had learnt boxing from a well-known professional.

to his home and constantly resided there. But it was perhaps on account of his foreign boyhood that he lacked the instinct for minute supervision which is natural to many owners of property. He had not grown up there, and it was not surprising that when he came into possession he should be inclined to take many things for granted, to spare himself the drudgery of detail, and enjoy his own in his own way. He was clearly conscious of certain disadvantages inherent in his education, and by way of supplementing its imperfections he had made a creditable attempt, when he came back to England, to improve matters by a diligent study of Greek, besides working with assiduity at his singing and drawing.

But hitherto his happiest hours had doubtless been spent in the open air. New responsibilities may have modified his habits to some extent. For one thing he gave up riding steeplechases. He had been as ready for this form of sport as any other, and had more than once ridden at Punchestown, falling on one occasion, with rather serious consequences, at the last fence. Shortly before his marriage he had won a point-to-point race on a mare called Polly Perkins in Co. Meath. As a married man he forswore this practice. One passion, however, never failed him to the hour of his death—the designing, building, and sailing of boats ; and for nearly fifty years he found in this an absorbing occupation.

It will be well to explain briefly the history and character of the Lough Erne Yacht Club. It was founded in 1837, and can therefore claim to be amongst the oldest yachting institutions.[1] The original membership was supplied by the families living on the

---

[1] The Cork Yacht Club is the oldest yachting club in existence (1720).—R.Y.S. 1812.

lake; Lord Erne and his sons; Saunderson's father
and uncles, and Mr. Gartside Tipping, of Rossferry,
were the most active of these. At first they had
no formal racing : this was reserved for the regattas
held on the lower lake, beyond Enniskillen; but in
course of time the club became more independent and
enterprising. There are now a series of race-days
throughout the late summer, during which numerous
cups, presented by those immediately interested, or
by visitors to the lake, are sailed for. The proceedings
are strictly ordered by the rules of racing, and are
duly recorded in the pages of *The Field*. Frequent
allusions to all this will be met with.

To describe the progress and development of yacht
construction would require a long and technical dissertation. A few of Saunderson's own achievements
must suffice. One of his first successes was in 1863,
when he designed and built a boat called the *Imp*, to
sail against Lord Erne's *Gossamer*, built by Marshall,
of Dublin, and Mr. Tipping's *Spray*. Both of these he
defeated. Lord Erne got a new boat from Fyfe, of
Fairlie; Saunderson replied with a home-made *Sprite*,
and a rivalry began between the two houses which
still exists. In 1865 the lower lake regattas were
revived after an interval of some years, and the
competition became severe. New boats came in
swift succession. In 1867 Saunderson built his first
Witch. Much of his time was occupied afterward in
altering and improving her, and she was remarkably
successful.

Not content with building for himself, he supplied
his neighbours with boats : one he built in 1871 for
Dean Massy Beresford at St. Hubert's, where his son,
Mr. George Massy Beresford, now maintains the
liveliest interest in yachting ; another for Lord Lanes-

borough, at Lanesborough Lodge; as well as boats for Lord Bangor and others upon other lakes. In 1884, owing to drainage works, it became necessary to introduce a smaller type of boat, and this gave him new problems to work out. In this year also he built

" You are the greatest beggar that sour came to these parts — And I'm told. it."

A NATIVE.

himself a steam-launch. He was not quite ingenious enough to make his own engines, but he insisted on putting in with his own hands those which he bought. Racing on the lower lake in old days appears to have been rough work. There was no hotel; visitors had to live on board, and take care of themselves. Moreover, there was much local patriotism: the native spirit was eagerly excited, and was not incapable of taking shape in an assault on those who were deemed intruders. On one occasion Saunderson had gone ashore for some purpose; a very ugly and angry man at once proceeded to try and drive him away with threats. Saunderson had the presence of mind to make a portrait of him promptly, rather accentuating his ugliness; and with so much adroitness did he represent this as a compliment, that hostilities at once gave way to professions of devoted friendship.

But if these expeditions were more in the nature of business, sailing at home must have been uninterrupted pleasure. There were regular frequenters of Castle Saunderson, of whom some brought their own boats, and others sailed with Saunderson. Of his own qualities as a yachtsman we may judge from these opinions of old friends. "There never was anybody on the lake," writes Colonel the Hon. Henry Crichton, "who could build or sail a boat better than Edward Saunderson; but he always had a very restless crew, and was a little restless himself. The only way I could beat him was by keeping very quiet, and so occasionally I stole away from him." Mr. H. Gartside Tipping writes: "He always sailed fair, and gave credit to an opponent when fairly beaten. Edward Saunderson was certainly the soul of the boat-sailing on the lake; it would never have been kept up so well or been so interesting but for his vigorous enthusiasm."

The lake poet (Colonel the Hon. Charles Crichton) corroborated his brother's judgment in these lines:

There was a young man owned the *Witch*
For a buckle he always did itch

If you passed him he smiled
Though exceedingly riled,
And his canvas he changed every stitch.

Saunderson could, however, control his impatience. Once during a race, it blew so hard that his mast carried away. Until this moment he had been all eagerness and anxiety; with sudden calm he exclaimed, "Now, boys, we'll lunch."

Much must be said hereafter about the life on Lough Erne. These observations are intended to convey some idea of what Saunderson will be found describing as a "remarkable location." The Lake, as it is called, represents a community which, so far as the present writer's experience goes, is not quite like anything to be found elsewhere. It has a character of its own, not easily defined. Those who know it not must be made acquainted with it, so far as is possible, through the medium of the following chapters.

We now find Saunderson, at the age of twenty-eight, a married man and a member of Parliament. One thing only these pages cannot minutely reveal, namely, his personal appearance. A contemporary anecdote may therefore be inserted here, although the justice of its application is not willingly admitted. One day in Belfast somebody, who was interested in Saunderson, was seeking to make his acquaintance. Having satisfied himself with a steady gaze he exclaimed, " You're the bhoy; but let me tell you you're far from good-looking."

NOTE

The rule adopted in 1885 for the new type of boat was: Length, 18 feet W.L.; sail area, 250 square feet; draught limited to 2 feet without the centre board. Modifications were afterwards introduced. The dimensions of Saunderson's last boat, the *Witch*, were: Length, 18·3 W.L.; sail area 650 square feet; displacement, 2·75 tons; draught, 4 feet. His account of this boat will be found in due course; but he did not live to do the work upon her which he desired.

About 1893 Lord Lanesborough and Mr. Massy Beresford got new two-raters of Watson's designs, and Lord Crichton one from Payne of Southampton. Saunderson designed and built his *Afrit* to meet these, and generally divided the honours with Lord Crichton. He afterwards built a *Cabrit* and *Sprite*: the latter was very successful. More rivals appeared, the rules being now :—Length and sail area, 2 rating; minimum displacement, 2¼ tons; draught maximum without c. bd., 4 feet; minimum, 3 feet 6 in. The *Sprite* had rather more displacement and less sail-area than the new-comers; and although she held her own in strong weather, she was out-classed in light weather. He then turned his attention to the *Witch* (1904-5). His first *Witch* and his last *Sprite* remain the test and evidence of his originality and skill as a designer. The Lough Erne boats attracted the attention of all yachting experts, and occasionally created a sensation; as in the case of Lieut. Gartside Tipping's *Mischief*, which at Kingstown in 1887 succeeded in defeating the *Doris*, designed by Mr. G. L. Watson and hitherto considered invincible. Saunderson sailed this race with the owner. Amongst Saunderson's other productions was a little half-rater, *Imshi*. This he would play with in the narrow waters opposite Castle Saunderson, making her waltz round and round on her centre without moving outside her circle. Beyond skill of this description he was proficient in the more serious art of navigation. The six miles of water between Castle Saunderson and Crom run through some difficult and intricate channels. In old days he would sail his *Witch* (of 20 tons) all the way single-handed—a considerable feat of strength and adroitness. Subsequently he always took charge of his steam launch, and could bring her through these tortuous passages at night by his knowledge of the stars and familiar marks in the landscape.

CHAPTER III

1865—1868

PARLIAMENT was dissolved on July 6, 1865. The Hon. James Maxwell, afterwards 9th Lord Farnham, who had sat for Co. Cavan as a Conservative, retired, and Saunderson, albeit a Liberal, took his place. The other sitting member was the Hon. Hugh Annesley,[1] a Conservative, and the two were returned unopposed.

A brief summary of the situation is necessary. Lord Palmerston was Prime Minister. Frequent acts of political audacity, and a consistent spirit of what was later to be known as Jingoism, had made him a national favourite and hero; so much so as to secure him a renewal of office. In point of seniority and service, Lord John Russell alone could be his rival, but Lord John had left the House of Commons with an earldom in 1861. Of his other colleagues, Mr. Gladstone had already asserted a pre-eminence; but whereas Lord Palmerston's attitude was easy and his regard for rigid rules was in the spirit of Gallio, Mr. Gladstone was in the full blast of energy and stress. A dozen years before he had been steadily drifting towards Tory waters. The recent biographies of Sidney Herbert[2] and of Sir James Graham[3] afford additional evidence of the conviction entertained by Peelite friends that this

[1] Earl of Annesley. [2] By Lord Stanmore.
[3] By Mr. C. S. Parker.

24

must surely be his ultimate haven. Then came Lord Derby's unsympathetic attitude towards the national aspirations of Italian democracy, and a sudden turn of the tide.

In 1865 it was for his more Conservative adherents to watch his course with misgiving and dismay. On March 28 Mr. Dillwyn, the Radical member for Swansea, had moved a resolution declaring that the position of the Irish Church Establishment was unsatisfactory and called for the attention of Her Majesty's Government. The Chancellor of the Exchequer had declared himself unable to accept the motion, but he practically admitted the truth of the principle laid down. This led to momentous consequences. By many it was regarded as a long stride towards a pronounced Liberalism; by his constituents at Oxford—and this was more important —it was considered a sign of unfitness to remain their representative. In answer to inquiries and remonstrances from them, Mr. Gladstone adopted the tone that the disestablishment of the Irish Church was "apparently out of all bearing on the practical politics of the day," and that should it ever enter that region, he could not expect to be called upon to deal with it. The electors of the University were not so easily satisfied; possibly they had a larger measure of prophetic instinct; at any rate Mr. Gladstone lost his seat. Seeing that he had written privately on February 13: "I am not loyal to it [the Irish Church] as an establishment,"[1] their suspicions cannot be condemned as unjust. He had been elected simultaneously in South Lancashire, and thither he hastened, declaring at Manchester, "At last I am come among you, and I am come among you un-

[1] "Life of Gladstone," by John Morley, ii. 141.

muzzled." Edward Saunderson's entry into politics synchronized, then, with the unmuzzling of Mr. Gladstone.

Those who knew the Colonel only as an Ulster leader, fighting Home Rule in 1886 and 1893, might well find it difficult to recognise him in the young Liberal member who supported the party of Lord Palmerston. On the other hand, it has been alleged that Lord Palmerston looked upon him as a promising recruit in the House of Commons. This is an imagination. The general election, as we have seen, occurred in July; Parliament did not meet until the ensuing February, and on October 18, Lord Palmerston died.

Lord Russell became Prime Minister, and Mr. Gladstone succeeded to the leadership of the House of Commons. We need only dwell upon such matters as directly concern Ireland. Irish affairs had by no means failed to occupy the attention of Parliament. There had been an Irish debate upon the Queen's speech at the opening of the previous session, in the course of which Mr. Roebuck had remarked that the tone of the Irish members was a "mendicant whine for money"; whilst Lord Palmerston had uttered the memorable sentence, "As to tenant right I may be allowed to say that I think it is equivalent to landlords' wrong."

Fenianism, moreover, had been much under observation. The *Annual Register*, in reviewing the events of the twelve months, records that "the conspiracy which was this year brought to light, but which was happily checked before it arrived at any outbreak was larger in extent, more daring in its objects, and in some respects more formidable in its nature than any similar movement of late years."[1] Summarising

[1] *Annual Register*, 1865, p. 173.

the nature of this agitation it explains that it is a confederation of all Irishmen and their friends in America "to labour for the liberation of Ireland from the yoke of England, and for the establishment of a free and independent government on the Irish soil." [1]

But the days of Home Rule were not yet. Butt had stood at the general election as a Liberal and had lost his seat. He had been a versatile politician. [2] After contesting Mayo unsuccessfully as a Protectionist in 1850, he was elected at Harwich in 1852, and took his seat as a Conservative. In 1857 he stood for Youghal as a Liberal Conservative, and defeated his Conservative opponent on an old-fashioned poll, by 126 against 54 votes. In 1865 he stood again, as a Liberal this time, and was defeated by a Liberal Conservative, the totals being respectively 129 and 30.

It may be convenient here to anticipate events. In 1867 came the trial of the Fenians connected with the Manchester murder. Butt was counsel for the accused and forthwith adopted their principles of Irish government. Defeated at Monaghan in July 1871, he was elected at Limerick two months later, and, reappearing in Parliament, became the father of that Home Rule which was to be the object of Saunderson's relentless hostility in later years.

With Butt individually Saunderson was not destined to come into conflict: he was superseded and died

[1] *Annual Register*, 1865, p. 183.

[2] From 1836 to 1841 Butt was Professor of Political Economy at Dublin University. I find an agenda paper for the " Proceedings of the Grand Orange Lodge of Ireland," for November 1838. Amongst the county officers present appears the name of "Isaac Butt, LL.D., member of Committee." One resolution is to the effect that "the Protestants of Ireland do not enjoy free exercise of their pure and holy religion." It is seconded by "Professor Butt," and against this Colonel Saunderson makes the indignant comment: "Isaac Butt, Q.C., the Home Rule Chief was then a member of the G. O. L. I. !!! "

in 1879, when Saunderson was out of politics. The man who was to supplant him, and with whom Saunderson was to come into very violent conflict, was in July 1865 a Cambridge undergraduate with no present taste for political life. The pistol-shot, fired at the Manchester police-van, which was to convert Butt to Home Rule, was also responsible for the first stirrings of patriotic aspiration and political passion in the breast of Parnell.[1] The facts may be briefly recalled. Two Fenian leaders had been arrested in Manchester: on the way to prison three of their allies attacked the van, liberated the prisoners, and shot the police-sergeant in charge. Four men were arrested, put on trial, and convicted; one was reprieved, the others underwent the penalty of murder. It was hotly disputed who had fired. It was urged, possibly with justice, that the shot was only intended to blow off the door-lock. However that may be, Sergeant Brett was killed, three men were hanged, and the demand for Home Rule gained two historic adherents. This struggle has not yet resulted in success; but so persistent and, at times, so violent has it been, so deep an impression has it traced upon Irish life and English politics, that this solitary shot deserves commemoration not much less emphatic, albeit much less eloquent, than that which Thackeray accorded to another shot fired by "a young Virginian officer in a savage forest in Pennsylvania," which was destined to affect in perpetuity the destinies of two continents.

This anticipation of events has been made to localize the position of the "Irish question" when Saunderson arrived at Westminster. He was to spend the most strenuous years of his life in meeting

[1] "Life of Charles Stewart Parnell," by R. Barry O'Brien, i. 51.

it with an emphatic answer; but that was to be twenty years later, after much water had run under the bridge, and many landmarks had been washed away.

Parliament was opened by the Queen in person on February 6, 1866. The Government could boast an ample majority. The strength of parties was returned as 367 Liberals and 290 Conservatives, a gain of forty-eight votes to the former.[1] Saunderson writes to his wife from the House of Commons on February 5:[2] "I had a splendid passage over. The ship rolled a good deal, but it did me a great deal of good. I have just been sworn in in the most approved manner. To-morrow is the great day . . I will write you an account of it."

This promise he scarcely fulfils; but what he says is enough to prove that the unseemly scrimmage which occurred on a similar occasion a few years ago,[3] was not a sign of the marked degeneracy of parliamentary manners. "The Commons entering the House of Lords," he writes on February 6, "was the most extraordinary sight. Fancy 300 men rushing frantically after the Speaker. They caught hold of his gown and nearly tore it off. I managed to stand beside him at the bar, so I saw everything to perfection. I shall tell you all about it to-morrow, please goodness. I must go into the House now to get a seat."

He had evidently no intention of settling down into the rôle of a silent and subservient member. In fact, his character was not that which inspires the party

[1] *Annual Register*, 1865. Add one for Mr. Speaker: there were 658 members of the 1832–67 House of Commons.

[2] In all cases it will be understood that, unless otherwise stated, his letters are addressed to Mrs. Saunderson.

[3] In 1901, when King Edward VII. opened his first Parliament. The crush was so severe that one member had some ribs broken and another dislocated his wrist.

hack. He was never without opinions or the readiness
to state them. He had no scruples, as we shall see,
about voting against his leader when his sympathies
were with the Opposition, and he was generally associated with those who were inclined to gather round Mr.
Lowe in the Cave of Adullam. During the progress
of the Queen's speech he writes (February 8) : " I do
not know whether I shall favour the House with my
ideas about Fenianism to-night, but possibly I might
be induced to say a few words." Either opportunity
or inclination failed, and he made no speech. He
proceeded to take a house in Beaufort Gardens. " It
is as clean as a new pin," he writes. " I am so glad
that the house is such a nice one ; I think you will
be delighted with it."

One of the first proceedings of the Government
was to introduce a Bill for the suspension of the
Habeas Corpus Act in Ireland ; [1] but Saunderson
took no part in the debates. On April 8 he writes :

" I know how sorry you will be to know by my
telegram that I am prevented going until Saturday
morning, but the Fenian affair comes off on Thursday
(to-morrow), so I could not leave, as I don't think I
should be doing my duty if I did not stay. . . . I
expect a great row in the House to-morrow about
Ireland and the Irish. The O'Donoghue starts it, so
you may guess when the Irish Brigade is let loose
what a row will take place."

In whatever form he expected the " Fenian affair "
to come on and cause a " row," he was disappointed.
The O'Donoghue had recently been pleading for some
men arrested under the new Act, but on this occasion
he made no further movement.

The great legislative feature of the session took

[1] Passed both Houses February 17, 1866.

shape on March 12, when Mr. Gladstone rose to introduce his Reform Bill. Saunderson writes on March 13: "Gladstone made a wonderful speech considering the weakness of the Bill he had to advocate. Horsman kept the House in roars of laughter for two hours. I presented three petitions to-day—for Tenant Right, Demolition of the Irish Church, and from Presbyterians." He gives no clue to his sentiments concerning these subjects, although they may be easily guessed. His first comment is significant of the critical attitude he was to adopt.

Mr. Gladstone's speech which compelled his admiration was that which ended in a peroration often quoted :

"For the attachment of the people to the throne, the institutions, and the laws under which they live is, after all, more than gold and silver, more than fleets and armies, at once the strength, the glory, and the safety of the land."

Mr. Horsman's attack was likely to exhilarate those who viewed the measure with disfavour :

"There was nothing in my right honourable friend's speech," said he, "that we can dignify by the title of principle. It was nothing but a reproduction of the old, stale, worn-out, discredited device of the first downward movement in the direction of government by numbers."

Next day Mr. Bright described this outburst as the signal for retreat to "what may be called his political cave of Adullam."

On April 12 Mr. Gladstone moved the second reading. Lord Grosvenor submitted a hostile amendment. On the seventh evening (26th) Mr. Lowe delivered his deadly attack. On the 27th Mr. Gladstone, labouring under the prescience of defeat, achieved what by common consent was his most noble flight of oratory.

" You cannot fight against the future," he concluded, in words which cannot be too often quoted. " Time is on our side. The great social forces which move on in their might and majesty, and which the tumult of our debates does not for a moment impede or disturb—those great social forces are against you; they are marshalled on our side; and the banner which we now carry, though perhaps at this moment it may droop over our sinking heads, yet it soon again will float in the eye of heaven, and it will be borne by the firm hands of the united people of the three kingdoms, perhaps not to an easy, but to a certain and to a not-far-distant victory."

One would be glad to know what Saunderson thought of this. One imagines the passion, the fire, the defiance, of the advocate at bay; yet eye-witnesses tell us that the sentences were uttered slowly in an exhausted tone, made more impressive by the extreme pallor of the speaker's countenance, and emphasized only by the solemn uplifting of a hand as the culminating syllables fell in whispers upon straining ears. The Government majority was five: 318 to 313; and the result was hailed as equivalent to defeat. On June 18 the Government were defeated in Committee on Lord Dunkellin's amendment and immediately resigned. Saunderson, who had shown his independence by voting with Lord Grosvenor on the second reading, chose on this occasion to support his doomed leader, and voted against Lord Dunkellin.

Meanwhile one of the interminable series of Irish Land Bills had been introduced, and on the second reading Saunderson made his début in debate on May 17. No doubt, he said, if the laws in England were the same as in Ireland, there would be no room for those who represented Ireland to claim any exceptional legislation. But this objection vanished when it was considered that the condition of the two countries had in the course of centuries become entirely different, and that the beneficial legislation that had made England what it was did not extend to Ireland. It was in consequence of the exceptional legislation which had taken place to the advantage of England that this Bill had become necessary. He did not believe that this Bill, if passed, would have any effect in removing the disaffection which existed in Ireland, and he denied that the tenant farmers of Ireland had anything to do with this disaffection. Very few of them were concerned in 1798, in 1848, or in the Fenian conspiracy of 1866. It was his intense and undeniable belief that if their beloved sovereign should require the assistance of her Irish subjects, she would find amongst the Irish tenant farmers as many loyal and willing hands and hearts as might be necessary.[1]

The Liberal loyalist showed himself herein the father of the Unionist stalwart whose avowed readiness to train all "loyal and winning hands" to resist Home Rule by force of arms was to rouse the indignation of the Nationalists and their new allies twenty years later.

Lord Derby's Government took office in July, but Saunderson gave them no trouble beyond asking a question about the substitution of steel barrels for iron barrels in Enfield rifles. Parliament was prorogued on August 10 and on the 15th we find him writing from Falkirk:

"We had a very good day on the 13th, killing 45 brace. Yesterday we killed 29 brace, and we have been shooting very well indeed. . . . I shall be terribly glad to see you and mother again. . . . Kiss my mother every day for me. . . . I find the walking has done me a wonderful deal of good."

[1] The Bill was eventually dropped.

3

On February 1, 1867, Saunderson tried his hand once more at keeping a diary. Again his exordium is all that can be desired in its spirit of altruism: "Keeping a journal is one of the greatest sacrifices of the present for the sake of the future that I know of. It is a bore of the first water. . . . when tired and sleepy to sit down and write. . . . But, like all present sacrifices, how great is the after-reward!"

He proceeds with further reflections of a rather romantic character; but the result is disappointing, After so promising a preface it is no great "after-reward" to find the brief and solitary entry:

"VENICE, *February* 6.—The first thing that creates a vivid impression on arriving at Venice is the utter silence and tremendous smells. A town without noise or drains is hard to imagine and impossible to describe. . . . Venice exceeds my expectations: one forgets the exhalations on seeing St. Mark's and the Palace of the Doges. Nothing can be more delightful than gondoling."

If, however, we are to know nothing more of this expedition, some notes which he made on his return in April have a double interest. For a few days he is a first-hand reporter of political events which have passed into history.

But before dealing with these it is proper to dwell upon a matter of personal interest. It has been said that Saunderson was essentially a religious man. To the end of his life this was manifest; those who have heard him preach in the little church in the park at Castle Saunderson, or have heard him talk when conversation happened to turn upon religious subjects, can bear ample witness to the firmness of his convictions, and to a simplicity of

faith such as any Christian might envy and admire.
But in later years, much as he had God in his heart,
His name was not necessarily for ever on his lips.
It will be gathered from his correspondence in the
years following 1866 that he lived in a state of spiritual
exaltation, and was much influenced by a passionate
enthusiasm which one could hardly expect to remain
permanently at high pressure. It is significant then
to find this early description of a visit to Islington to
hear Spurgeon preach.

"*Sunday, April 7.*—I think the Hall was one of
the most remarkable scenes I have ever witnessed :
there were at least 20,000 people present, and when
the preacher appeared a dead silence reigned over the
vast assembly. The centre was occupied by sitters
and on both sides of a gangway where, there being
no seats, there were standers, so that the sea of faces
in the middle of the building was cut in two by two
lines of black coats. Then the galleries were filled,
not a spare space, nothing but faces, coats, and bonnets
everywhere. In the bottom of the Hall there was a
platform for the preacher, but behind that again faces,
bonnets, and coats. At last Spurgeon appeared. He
is a fat, very big-chested man, with a bull conformation
of neck ; in fact a vulgar fat little man with a big head,
anything but the ideal of an orator. I had great
doubts that any human being could possibly fill even
half the vast Hall, and as we were some way off, I had
my doubts about hearing him distinctly. Spurgeon
suddenly raised his hand and a voice sounded through
the vast space and rose over the heads of the dense
multitude, 'Let us pray.' Such a voice I certainly
never heard before, so tremendously powerful, so
sweet and so distinct. It filled the whole space
without an effort.

"Then followed a hymn, 'Come to the ark.' Without
hearing Spurgeon speak these words it is impossible
to conceive of what the human voice is capable. Each
verse commenced with these words, and they rang
through the building like the sound of a silver
trumpet.

"The sermon I liked very much; it was on the healing of the sick man at the Pool of Bethesda. Do not wait by the Pool of Bethesda, but come to Christ without delay. It was a splendid sermon."

It seemed wise to make this interpolation because herein, it may be, lay the seeds of a growth which was to be lastingly entwined with his subsequent career. He was ready to respond to such an inspiration.

On March 18 Disraeli had introduced his Reform Bill; on the 25th he moved the second reading and wound up the debate on the following night. Saunderson writes :

"*27th.*—I heard a speech last night to be ever remembered. Dizzy got up and spoke for about two hours. It was the most wonderful piece of acting and the most extraordinary exhibition of talent I have ever heard. He pitched into everybody, he abandoned all his principles,[1] and all through he delighted and amused the House."

Otherwise the member for Cavan does not appear to have been deriving enjoyment from the discharge of his duties. "London is already beginning to exercise its influence on me. I hate it," he writes on March 29. In another letter he laments that "Reform still drags on its weary length, . . . nothing done. . . . A Bill was introduced the other night to shorten the time of labour of women. Great laughter !" And again : "You may depend I shall start from this abominable place as soon as I can." And on April 5 : "I am forced to stay about this Reform affair. . . . I constantly dream that I am with you." On the same day he proceeds to relate the story of the "affair."

[1] "The Government will do anything to stay in," he had written two days previously.

" LONDON, *March* 5, 1867.—Get up and experience my usual feeling of horror at finding myself in London. I do not believe there is a man in the world who dislikes London more than I do.

"There is to be a meeting to-day at Gladstone's the result of which I can foresee. Gladstone will find that his party will not follow him should he desire to oust the Government. They have not forgiven him his attempt to force Reform down their throats last session, so that now he will have to swallow the bitter pill. There is nothing which goes down so badly with the House of Commons as attempting to force the adoption of any course which they dislike. And I observe there is an extraordinary feeling of rancour in the minds of a portion of the Liberal party against Gladstone for his want of temper last year, and his refusing to give up any of his opinions to satisfy the almost universal desire of the Liberal party.

. . . . . .

"I have been to the meeting. Gladstone commenced a very quiet speech to the effect that the Government was to receive the support of the Liberal party in carrying through a Reform, but (I knew there would be a but) at the same time to receive a certain amount of gentle pressure to force their adoption of a measure which should satisfy the country and the Liberal party.

"The consequence was that the following 'Instruction' was decided on :

"'That it be an instruction to the Committee that they have power to alter the law of rating and to provide that in every parliamentary borough the occupier of tenements below a given rateable value be relieved from the liability to personal rating, with a view to fix a line for the borough franchise at and above which all occupiers shall be entered on the rate-book, and shall have equal facilities for the enjoyment of such franchise as a residential occupation franchise.'[1]

"Will the Tories consent to swallow this pill? I rather think they will, if not, good-bye to Reform for another year.

[1] This " Instruction " was entrusted to Mr. Coleridge, afterwards Lord Chief Justice.

" *Monday, April* 8.—I went down to the House with the full expectation of a row. On my arrival I found the Liberal party in a ferment ; the Radicals had joined the Conservatives, so that on their sending a deputation to Gladstone the ' Instruction ' blew up. Not only the Radicals, but also the Cave of Adullam joined together, so that Gladstone had no chance whatever. So here ends the famous ' Instruction,' and the Government triumph as usual. One ounce of real common sense is of more value than a pound of genius. Gladstone does not possess the amount of common sense requisite to understand the real feelings of the House. From the first I understood the ' Instruction ' as having for its object not only to establish a principle but also to upset the Government ; so I think it was judged by the Liberals, and they split up in consequence.   I do not think the Liberal party was ever in a position of greater weakness. Gladstone is unquestionably very sore at the idea of the Conservatives being able to carry a Bill of Reform which he with his majority was unable to accomplish. No wonder ! "

The conspirators who brought about this change of policy had hurriedly assembled, to the number of forty or fifty, in the Tea-room of the House of Commons ; and in their subsequent combined action they were generally dubbed the " Tea-room Party."[1]

There was no small element of humour in the progress of this Reform Bill. On February 11 and 16 Disraeli had given conflicting notices of the intention of the Government, without succeeding in escaping hostile criticism.[2] It seems that he was fully prepared with alternative measures. After a critical meeting of the Cabinet on the 25th, preference was given to one of these so much on the spur of the moment that it became known as the " Ten-minutes Bill." It was equally ill received.   Then the Chancellor

[1] " Life of Gladstone," ii. 232, etc.
[2] " Memoirs of an Ex-Minister," Lord Malmesbury, iii. 239.

of the Exchequer hardened his heart, and, with Lord
Derby's consent, nailed his colours to the mast of the
larger vessel of Reform; whereupon three ministers
resigned, including the late Lord Salisbury.[1] Next
day Disraeli announced his intention of setting to work
in earnest on March 18. Then came the Tea-room
episode, and ten days later Mr. Gladstone announced
his intention of retiring from the leadership of his
party. So much spirit had he shown in his opposition
to the Government proposals that he had already
drawn from Disraeli a confession of gladness that there
was such "a good broad piece of furniture" as the
table of the House between them. But, as Lord
Houghton said in July, he seemed "quite awed with
the diabolical cleverness of Dizzy." In fact, in the
language of the prize-ring, he had "had enough."

In Committee Disraeli kept the fun alive. When
Mr. Beresford-Hope protested against the "Asian
mystery," the Chancellor of the Exchequer, promptly
fixing on his critic's Dutch extraction, replied that
"When he talks about an Asian mystery I will tell
him that there are Batavian graces in all that he says,
which I notice with satisfaction, and which charm
me." And so the Bill was passed to the accompaniment of historic phrases about "dishing the Whigs,"
taking a "leap in the dark," and culminating in Mr.
Lowe's decision, "We must now educate our new
masters."

On May 5, 1867, Saunderson had written from
Dublin, where he was assisting at a Church meeting.
He had brought forward a resolution, but did not
feel sanguine: "After I have been beaten, as of
course I expect, I shall go home . . . there is no
use remaining to be sat upon by the priests." On

[1] "History of Our Own Times," by Justin McCarthy, iv. 102-5.

May 23 there was a debate in Parliament upon the proposal to renew the suspension of the Habeas Corpus Act in Ireland. "There is to be a row to-night," he writes. "I don't know yet whether I shall say a few words or not." Next day he reports, "I could not screw myself up to address the House, so I remained in dignified silence." This will be strange reading to those who remember the Colonel as the most fluent and imperturbable of parliamentary speakers; so imperturbable indeed that he once said, "The House of Commons is the easiest audience in the world to address. Don't pay any attention to them: treat them as if they weren't there."

He was not happy in London. A little later he writes a homesick letter:

"I am rapidly getting my old disease back again—*mal de Londres*. I am missing you terribly. . . . I am still in this horrible place, far from you. . . . Best love to mother."

But in August he is at home with his beloved boats:

"I went out sailing, and, wonderful to relate, I succeeded in reversing the former experiment, and beat the *Witch* in the *Sprite* not only once, but several times. I am going to make an alteration which I think will make her sail better.
"*September* 2.—The boats look wonderful . . . as clean as new paint."

These boats, forerunners of other *Witches* and *Sprites*, he had designed and built himself, as we have already learnt. So far, then, it would appear that a sense of duty rather than personal inclination drew him from the privacy, which he loved, to politics, which he criticised with severity, and London, which he hated.

The correspondence of the year 1868 opens on the

same note. On February 21, "I long to be with you once more." On March 10 Mr. Maguire moved for a committee to inquire into the state of Ireland.

"We had a debate," writes Saunderson, "but remarkable for the length of the speeches more than their contents. Mayo spoke for three and a half hours. Poor fellow, he had been seedy all day, and after speaking for an hour he got as pale as a sheet and became quite fuddled. However, they brought him some brandy and it did him good."

Lord Mayo, as Chief Secretary, had replied on behalf of the Government.

Next day we find his thoughts turned to those subjects to which reference was lately made:

"I pray every day that you and I may devote ourselves to the service of Christ, for certainly it is the only ambition that ever pays. . . . I don't know whether I shall be able to speak on the Irish question: there are so many who are going to speechify. However, I have prepared a few things, so perhaps I may orate. It takes my pluck away not having you with me.

"*February* 14.—I want to address the House very much . . . it entirely depends on catching the Speaker's eye. The Government are in a shaky state.

"15*th*.—I should so like to be with you all, but business first and pleasure afterwards.

"16*th*.—I wish you had been with me to-day listening to Spurgeon. Please God, we will go together some day. How is the darling old mother? . . . I shall try and speak to-morrow, but as there are so many who want to do the same, it is very uncertain.

"17*th*.—I did not succeed in letting off my speech: there were too many who wanted to jaw. About twenty men got up when a speaker sat down. Gladstone has at last stated his intention of putting down the Establishment: they are going to move a resolution about it. Of course I am bound to support it.

"19*th*.—I think I shall be able to go over on Saturday. . . . If Gladstone's resolution comes on for discussion I cannot go away for a moment."

It will be observed that it was the Establishment that he must support; not the resolution. Mr. Gladstone, having got rid of all his scruples of 1865, moved accordingly on March 30, and beat the Government by 331 to 270. Saunderson voted in the minority.

Nobody who has sat in the House of Commons will deny his sympathy to the writer of these letters. Nothing can be more exasperating than to sit hour by hour, day after day, in nervous expectation of delivering a prepared speech, to be left unspoken after all. This is one of the trials of parliamentary life which are so difficult to impress upon the uninitiated who persist in regarding the House of Commons as a carnival of exciting interest.

Saunderson continued silent throughout the session, which closed on July 21, 1868. Parliament was dissolved in the autumn, and the newly enfranchised voters displayed their ingratitude by rejecting the authors of the Reform Act. Disraeli, who had succeeded Lord Derby as Prime Minister, resigned without waiting to meet Parliament, and Mr. Gladstone became Prime Minister.

Colonel Annesley and Saunderson were again returned unopposed in Co. Cavan.

CHAPTER IV

1869—1874

THE years 1869 and 1870 were of critical interest for Saunderson: the Irish Church was disestablished in the one, and the Land Bill rendered memorable the other.

At the outset he was absorbed in spiritual meditations, as his journal will show:

"*January*, 1869.—I passed the month quietly at home. My Sunday school, I find, is getting fuller, and I trust that God will bless it, not only to the scholars but also to the very indifferent teacher.

"February also passed at home. What a pleasant word is home! and how we ought to pray our Lord to prevent us making anything here our home!

"I started from home Saturday the 27th and slept that night with the mother at Bloomsbury. No one is more changed than the mother. All the hardness of her nature is softened, and of those she did not at one time appear to like, she now speaks kindly. What has done this? Nothing human. It has been effected by the Spirit of the Lord Jesus, which alone can really alter the heart of man. (To the eye of man many things can alter our disposition and feelings, but *really*, that is to say, in God's eyes, that alteration can alone be effected by his Holy Spirit.) It is the *new birth*, the new creation called out of the darkness and chaos of the human heart by the almighty power of Christ."

This memorandum has been allowed to stand because it illustrates an aspect of Saunderson's character. His letters have revealed a constant flow of affection towards his mother. It has been intimated that her temperament was not marked by a comprehensive tenderness and indulgence. Events had, however, so fashioned themselves as to soften the asperity of her judgments, and these remarks point to a happier spirit pervading her later life. She died in 1870. Saunderson, although he had no taste for regular desk work, preserved throughout his life a habit of composing little essays, presumably for his own guidance. Under the influence of this deep affliction he wrote many pages of reflection, from which we learn that in her his religious fervour had found entire sympathy and encouragement. As an earnest Christian and as a loving son he had been bound to her by strong and lasting ties; and it must be observed that he who had been chosen by the father to be his heir was likewise the object of the mother's special and passionate devotion. Nor would it be right to neglect in passing to remark that his brothers never permitted this bestowal of the property to diminish for one moment the cordiality and loving-kindness of their mutual relations.

On March 1, 1869, Mr. Gladstone introduced his Irish Church Bill. The journal goes on:

" Went down early to the House in order to get a place. I got my old seat, four below the gangway, on the second bench next The O'Donoghue, and heard Gladstone make his great speech on the Church. It was the most lucid and the clearest speech I ever heard him make. He is generally too verbose, but during three and a half hours I do not think he used a word too much. There can be no doubt about the fate of the Church in Ireland, and I for one do not look to the future with any dread as far as our faith is concerned. The destruction of the Church cannot affect it, as it is founded on God's eternal truth. The devil and the world, of which he is king, thought they had a great triumph when they crucified Christ, but it turned out to be only stamping on the tremendous sword that was for ever to pierce their heel. And so the destruction of the Church may simply be unfettering the bird that shall bear the truth and sow it broadcast in the land.

"The second reading is postponed to Thursday fortnight; so I am here kicking my heels about doing nothing—an occupation I by no means like."

On March 19 he writes:

"Did you read Dizzy's speech [against the second reading]? It was very amusing, but he had a hard card to play. I suppose he played it as well or better than any one else would have done. The division will take place somewhere about Friday. There will be a majority of 105 or 110 in favour of the Bill."

Disraeli had argued that if it were right to despoil a Church, it would be difficult to refuse to despoil an individual:

"There are gentlemen who have not estates . . . what would be the natural course which [they] would take? . . . Their argument would be this: we find ourselves in an anomalous position (loud laughter); our breeding is not inferior to that of our habitual companions . . . we meet in the same hunting-field; we drink the same claret (laughter); we stand opposite to one another in the same dance; and our feelings are hurt because some of our companions have . . . £10,000 a year, broad acres and extensive woods (laughter). We know the spirit of the age in which we live. (Roars of laughter and loud cheers.) We know that selfishness is not for a moment to be tolerated. . . ."

"So the poor Church is tottering to its fall," Saunderson wrote on the 22nd; and next day—

"Gathorne Hardy is to wind up on the Conservative side, but I don't know what he can say that is new. Roundel Palmer made a wonderfully deep and clever speech, and from a man who refused to be made

Lord Chancellor[1] on account of his opinion that disendowing was unjust, it had the more weight. I wanted to speak, but cannot get a chance. It is arranged by the Whips, and as I do not agree with the Government, I have no chance. Perhaps it is all for the best."

The House divided that evening; the majority for the Bill was 118, but Saunderson voted in the other lobby. On April 23 he was able to give utterance to some of his opinions when the Bill was in Committee; the following is a report of his speech:

" Mr. Saunderson said when this Act passed and he was asked to what religious persuasion he belonged, he should be placed in a considerable difficulty, and he should have to say that he belonged to the dis-established Irishmen (laughter). The first thing the Church body would have to decide would be what religion they intended to adopt. He thanked the right honourable gentleman at the head of the Government for not tying their hands, but leaving them at liberty to adopt what form of doctrine they thought most desirable and suitable. Suppose the Church body assembled in Dublin, there might be disunion among them. It might adopt the Thirty-nine Articles, but might adopt a smaller number. He wished to know whether the Church body as contemplated by this Bill would have any power of interfering or enforcing discipline in parishes of Ireland. Or if a certain number of parishes adopted the principles of the Church body, would the others still continue to belong to the Protestant Church of Ireland? The Protestants of Ireland felt that if the Church body was to meet in Dublin and to have no power at all, it would be simply a farce."

The third reading was carried in the House of Commons on May 31, by 361 to 247, a majority of 114. Saunderson gave a final hostile vote, and apparently departed for Ireland in disgust. In July

[1] " Memorials " (Lord Selborne), i. 112.

THE "WITCH" AND THE "SPRITE," 1869.

he writes from a neighbour's house in Co. Cavan :—
"The boy in the yard has had a threatening letter in case he does not give up his place, and [his host] another threatening him with extermination unless he dismisses him." This elliptical sentence suggests that the country was not wholly undisturbed; but Saunderson's spirits remained unruffled.

In August he is busy with his yachts :

"We had a delightful sail this evening (August 28). The *Witch* went very well. . . . We had a very long time of it, as we stuck on shore. I was greatly afraid I had ruined the *Witch*; however we got off, with superhuman cunning. We arrived at a quarter to nine and had our dinner at half-past ten."

Again his sense of humour is indulged :

"D—— took [Lord] C—— for a footman, and abused him in strong terms; C—— let him go on and then turned round, to D——'s horror. D——[1] changes his servants every week."

On the 13th he had written :

"We started for the Cup this morning . . . unfortunately we got a terrible bad start. . . . At last we began to move, and, to the astonishment of every one, myself included, we weathered and fore-reached the lot at the Gull. Away we all went: *Witch* 1st, *Breeze* 2nd, *Sprite* 3rd, *Zephyr* 4th. The *Witch* went like a witch, and we came in a winner with three minutes to spare. So you see the *Witch* has proved herself a clipper.

"*September* 1.—So you see your old man and his beautiful *Witch* won by four minutes. There is great confusion in the Crom[2] camp; they were afraid of the *Sprite*, but did not care the least for the *Witch*. We made such a bad start . . . that I thought it was all up; but the *Witch* all of a sudden began to move, and from that moment to the end of the race never ceased to fly."

[1] Mr. D—— was a neighbour, whose whim it was to keep an hotel.
[2] Crom Castle (Earl of Erne's).

Besides the frequent races on the upper lake, which may be called the home waters, it has always been the practice to take the yachts to sail in the lower lake nearer to Enniskillen, for some days in August. These reports were written whilst Saunderson was away on one of these expeditions. It is characteristic of his versatile temperament that the last letter should abruptly turn to this comment : " It is so delightful to be with those who love our blessed Lord. I have been reading St. John : how His disciples loved Him personally ! "

Parliament reassembled on February 8, 1870. The Speech from the Throne promised a Land Bill for Ireland. This was read a first time on the 15th, and put down for second reading on March 7th. It is hardly within the scope of this memoir to discuss in detail the measures of Land Reform which followed one another in rapid succession through the ensuing years. Irish land legislation would afford matter for a separate treatise, and these pages need not be occupied with so complicated and controversial an issue. The following letters give Saunderson's version of affairs :

" *March* 9.—The Land Bill debate goes on with a great deal of talk. I don't know whether I shall speak or not. If by speaking I can be of no use, I trust I shall not.

" *12th*.—The debate is over [1] and I am just as glad I did not speak : [2] whether I wished it or not, I did not get the chance. On the 21st I expect I shall be placed on a Committee. The Irish Land Bill on that day goes into Committee, so I am afraid I shall not see your dear old face before Easter. . . . On Tuesday night, please God, I shall begin the Romans, so you may do the same.

[1] The second reading was carried by 442 to 11. Saunderson voted with the Government.

[2] On the 11th he had written : " I shall speak to-night if occasion should arise."

THE "WITCH" ASHORE.

E. S. del.

"14*th.*—We are to have a statement from Gladstone to-night as to how he intends to make Ireland habitable.   Crichton [1] is this evening to attack the Government about the dismissal of Captain Coote."

This refers to the case of a gentleman who had been dismissed from the Shrievalty of Monaghan in consequence of his action with regard to the constitution of a jury in a murder trial.   Saunderson supported his party against the resolution, although he clearly was of opinion that something must be done to " make Ireland habitable."

Next day he has this to add :

"15*th.*—I received a letter from Uncle Som [2] yesterday, which he brought to the House, to inform me that he had received a threatening letter, and also to give me a report of an outrage committed in Cavan."

Mr. Gladstone's promised statement developed into the Bill introduced by Mr. Chichester Fortescue on the 17th.   Saunderson writes :

"I am put on a Committee. . . . I shall therefore be in the House thirteen or fourteen hours per day.   On Thursday the Bill for the Maintenance of Peace in Ireland comes on.   It will give power to try cases of a certain description without a jury.   I think this will rather astonish the " Ribbon " men, if they can be caught. . . . I walk a tremendous lot every day . . . and feel better than I ever did before in London.

"18*th.*—Last night Dowse, the Irish Solicitor-General, said in his speech that he had not much opinion of the Irish magistracy.   I am going, I hope, on Monday, to call attention to that statement, as I look upon it as an insult to the magistracy of Ireland."

Accordingly on the 21st we read :

"I have just made my speech : about half an hour long.   I have received the greatest praise from both

[1] Now Earl of Erne, K.P.
[2] Somerset Maxwell, eighth Lord Farnham, died 1884.

4

sides of the House, so I may say it was a success, which will please you, I know. I gave Dowse some hard hits, which were received with roars of laughter. He is just going to reply, and means to give me a teasing, which I do not mind.

"*22nd.*—I see my speech is well reported in *The Times*, so you will see it. . . . Although I rather pitched into the Government, Gladstone complimented me ; so did Fortescue.[1] I can't, for the life of me, help making people laugh, and you never heard such roars as when I pitched into Dowse. The last thing I did before I got on my legs was to ask God to prevent me from saying anything I ought not. The House was crammed full from top to bottom, which I was glad of, as I do not like wasting my breath on empty benches."

The speech was clearly a success. The passage which probably conduced most to the amusement of the House is reported thus :

"Just before he came over to attend to his parliamentary duties he received a threatening letter and— so curious was the development of the Irish mind— it ordered him to turn a tenant out. The writer said : 'If you don't turn him out you shall fall a victim to my balls.' However, if the writer did not shoot more correctly than he wrote, perhaps there was not much danger, after all, because he spelt balls in this style—bawls (laughter)."

He admitted, however, that great insecurity did exist in Ireland because the tenants invariably shot the landlords and the labourers sometimes shot the tenants. And he assured Mr. Dowse of the case of a farmer who was attacked by some people who compelled their victim to pay their travelling expenses.

Next day an evening paper declared that he had "displayed a humour which ought to make the Solicitor-General look to his laurels."

---

[1] Mr. Chichester Fortescue, Chief Secretary to the Lord-Lieutenant.

The Times, in a leading article, paid him further attention:

"Though in the sense of a speaker Mr. Saunderson is a young member, he delivered with great self-possession a semi-philosophical and occasionally very amusing dissertation on the relations between landlord and tenant in Ireland as bearing on the present condition of that country. He seemed to have been hit hard by a hint of Mr. Dowse that he did not hold the magistracy of Ireland in high esteem, and he retorted that it was odd, if that was the case, that the Government was about to double their powers. Otherwise he fully supported the Bill, and on the whole he was so successful, particularly from a comic point of view, that when he talked of concluding he was met by requests to go on."

His letters continue a medley of gravity and fun. He talks of a prayer-meeting to which he has been with his " Uncle Som," who preached; and proceeds to a comment on one of St. Paul's Epistles. Between these topics, however, he interpolates a riddle: " Why are chignons like Irishmen ? Because they are not generally attached to the crown."

"25*th*.—If I were conceited I should feel rather bumptious, as I have received a vast amount of compliments. Mr. Horsman got introduced to me yesterday in order to tell me that he had listened to me with great pleasure. We shall have very hard work with the Land Bill: I hope we may mould it into shape. . . . A sail on the lake would freshen me up amazingly.

"26*th*.—I got your dear violets last night. . . . I long to see you again.

"28*th*.—I heard from the mother to-day. . . . I am very sick of London. It is bad enough when you are with me, but when you are away it is abominable . . . I hope they are setting to work on the boats.

"30*th*.—I have just made a speech on the Party Procession Act. I have a bad habit, and it is this: I cannot avoid making my audience laugh."

On this occasion he remarked that Orangemen did nothing but stop indoors and beat drums to frighten Papists. His own Orange days were yet to come.

"*April* 5.—I have just made a short speech which you will see in *The Times*. I did so at Mr. Gladstone's request."

This speech is worth quoting as embodying his views and illustrating his "bad habit" of making his audience laugh.

"The Government, he said, had only three courses to pursue in order to satisfy the claim made by the Irish people for security of tenure. One course was to establish perpetuity of tenure, but he was opposed to that because it would place the Irish landlord only in the position of the recipient of a rent-charge. The next course was to establish the Ulster custom throughout Ireland—this would cause great dissatisfaction. Then there remained the course which the Government had pursued of making it an expensive amusement to evict for any other reason but non-payment of rent.

"Ireland was divided into two classes—the reasonable Irish and the unreasonable Irishmen. The reasonable Irish would receive the present measure in the spirit in which it was offered: they would accept it as an honest effort on the part of the House of Commons to do justice to Ireland in answer to reasonable demands.

"The unreasonable Irishmen, on the other hand, were men to whom Providence had not given that mental hook on which it was possible for an Englishman to hang a just inference.

"The speech of the Chancellor of the Exchequer, he declared, reminded him of what he had often seen in the hunting-field. He had frequently seen a well-bred, plucky horse with too much load on its back galloping over sticky ground, till it was brought suddenly up, and remained dismally wagging its tail to notify that it had had enough of it."

On April 20 he writes from Dublin:

"I have had a long day in the Synod.[1] . . . I seconded a proposal. . . . When [the mover] sat down I said I should reserve my remarks until the close of the debate; but as no one got up to speak, up got the Primate and put the question. Had the question been put we should have been beaten . . . so I jumped up and demanded speech. . . . Certainly God gave me utterance. I never in all my life spoke like it before, and the effect was tremendous. . . . Men I did not know came and nearly shook my hand off; —— said, 'I don't thank you, but God, for your speech.' All this came from my simply placing myself in the hands of God. My voice was in splendid order."

His letters constantly refer to the condition of his throat, which appears to have given him considerable trouble, and, at times, to have interfered with his speaking.

"*May* 8.—I paid —— a long visit yesterday and had a long talk with her about religion. I can never make her out; she is so sentimental, and you know there is no connection between the two, although the world thinks there is. It has enough of similarity to the true to satisfy and mislead, but not enough to save. . . .

"*May* 10.—I am going down to Cowes to look after my sails. . . . I daresay you have heard me mention Synan, M.P. for Limerick; he is remarkable for his stentorian voice. He makes, on an average, about ten speeches per night. Well, yesterday he was roaring *à gorge déployée* close to my ear; you could have heard him from the Castle to Cavan Gate. All of a sudden I turned away from him and called out, in a sepulchral voice, 'Speak up!' You never heard such roars of laughter; I thought Gladstone would have had a fit. . . ."

This may interest those who maintain that Mr. Gladstone lacked all sense of humour.

Saunderson spoke again on the Land Bill on the

---

[1] Since its disestablishment, the Church of Ireland has been governed by a General Synod.

19th, and then went yachting with Mr. Mulholland (afterwards Lord Dunleath) on his yacht the *Egeria* for a week. Returning to London, he writes on May 16:

"I thought of you at church. . . . I dined with Fortescue, and had a very pleasant dinner. I sat beside Sir George Grey, the late Home Secretary,[1] who is a charming old man. Gladstone and his wife were there; I conversed with her. She appears to be an intelligent woman, and very religious, as far as I could see. Lady Waldegrave[2] was full of civility, and paid me great compliments on my speaking. . . . She asked you to dinner, and wanted to know if you were coming. I told her you were a high Tory, and she asked whether that was the reason I left you in Ireland. She said she thought you could make me do anything you pleased. I am going to ask Fortescue the following question to-morrow in the House. . . ."

He was not to be muzzled with civility.

It is satisfactory to find Saunderson enjoying himself in society. In one of his letters he expresses a doubt as to whether this is compatible with leading a Christian life; but his robust temperament prevented him from giving way to mistaken and morbid asceticism, and a genuine joyousness of disposition enabled him at all times to appreciate such amenities as were customary in the society to which he belonged.

During 1871 Saunderson did not take a prominent part in politics; his mind was evidently bent upon religious matters, and his letters usually refer to visits which he has paid to his favourite preachers.

[1] Sir George Grey, 2nd Bart., grandfather of Sir Edward Grey, M.P., was still in Parliament but not in office; died 1882.

[2] Lady Waldegrave, widow of the seventh Earl (her second husband). She had married (i) Mr. Waldegrave, of Navestock, Essex; (iii) Mr. Harcourt, eldest son of the Archbishop of York; (iv) Mr. Chichester Fortescue, M.P. (created Lord Carlingford, 1874). She died 1879.

On May 19, however, he made a considerable speech
on the Protection of Life (Ireland) Bill, in the course
of which he took occasion to predict that the introduction of the ballot into Ireland would conduce to
separation ; it would play into the hands of men whose
views would be so repugnant to the majority of
Englishmen that the latter would become tired of being
ruled by Irish votes, and break the union in despair.
Of this speech he writes : " I am told it was a very
good one, about which I shall say nothing ; but at
any rate I was very well listened to. I pitched into
a Roman Catholic Bishop,[1] so I expect there will be
some wonderful things said about me. . . . However,
as you know, I don't care a pin so long as I say what
I believe to be true."

We have seen that Saunderson had received ample
encouragement to persevere in politics ; as a speaker
he had been a conspicuous success. But for the time
his ambition pointed elsewhere. He was by no means
indifferent to appreciation, but his vanity was not to
be stirred. Upon the Gospel was his attention fixed,
and during the remainder of this Parliament he concerned himself very little with debates in the House
of Commons.

In July he paid a visit to France to follow the traces
of the war.

"We met the Prussians at Amiens," he writes.
"There was a sentry with a spiked helmet, looking perfectly at home. The people . . . all walk
about in a subdued manner. . . . In Paris . . . all is
silence, like a city of the dead : no shops open ;
hardly a carriage to be seen, the horses having been
eaten. . . . Up the Champs Elysées, not much damage,
the trees all right. When we got to the Arc de
Triomphe the smashing commenced, and for a mile

[1] Bishop Nulty.

all the houses are gutted; you never saw such destruction."

Sometimes, he says, a house has been nearly cut in two, the furniture standing untouched; elsewhere there remains a sound shell, the contents being a heap of smashed-up rubbish.

Of St. Cloud he writes:

" Just think, in a town of 6,000 inhabitants there are only twelve houses left; the whole town entirely consumed and ruined. Then the palace: nothing left but bare, gaunt walls. . . . I did not feel it so much until I saw the little Prince's playground. There was the remains of the railway with which he used to play, and I thought how often the unfortunate Emperor and Empress used to walk and watch him, just as we should Baba or Eddy; and now all ruin—the railway torn up, the flowers all gone, and the trees torn and lying about in all directions; and the roughs scrambling about and calling the Emperor a pig and a *polisson*—the very people who would a year ago have licked his feet. . . .

On February 27, 1872, there was a royal procession to St. Paul's, where a Thanksgiving Service was held to celebrate the recovery of the Prince of Wales from dangerous illness. Saunderson writes:

" I was too seedy to go to St. Paul's—I went to see ——. As I was coming back, the Queen, Prince of Wales, etc., came out on to the balcony at Buckingham Palace and bowed to the multitude, which roared in return. I have got off being put on a Committee, so shall be disengaged for the Prayer-book and Synod.

" *March* 1.—I went to see Dr. Russell Reynolds. . . . Afterwards to Buckingham Palace, to cheer the Queen on her departure to Windsor. There were a great number of M.P.'s, who cheered loudly. The Queen stood up and looked much pleased. The pistol the Irish boy had was brought down to the House; there was neither powder nor ball in it, so that the

Queen did not run much danger.   He had a petition
in favour of the Fenian prisoners and also a request
that he might be shot like a true republican.   The
best thing to do with him would be to flog him and
let him go.   I am sorry he is an Irishman."

This refers to a crazy youth named O'Connor.
Although Saunderson does not say so, it is alleged
that the pistol was an antiquated flint-lock weapon.

"*April* 6.—There is to be an awful row on Monday.
Dizzy is to divide the House, and if beaten [Gladstone]
will dissolve Parliament; so I think it is extremely
probable that I shall figure before the free and independent electors of Cavan before very long."

This appears to have been what the newspapers call
a "Lobby rumour."   Nothing of the kind occurred.

"When you are away from me," he goes on, "you
can form no idea how depressed I become. . . . I am
going to-morrow with Som[1] to hear Spurgeon.   A
Mr. Saunderson died the other day, and I think
Som will get £4,000 by his death.   I hear that
I have a good chance of getting £1 10s. 6d., which
in the present state of my finances will be extremely
useful."

From Dublin he writes :

" I have been thinking very much about the soldiers
at Belturbet.   I should so like that some one should
be enabled to preach the Gospel to them. . . . Every-
one is running out of Dublin to escape or recover
from small-pox. . . . What a blessing to know that
nothing can happen to us without our great Master's
permission! ' The pestilence that walketh in darkness
shall not come near thee.'

"*June* 6.— The Government have tided over the
Alabama[2] treaty for this year, so there will be no
dissolution.

---

[1] His elder brother, Somerset Saunderson.

[2] After protracted negotiations, the arbitrators finally awarded
damages exceeding £3,000,000 to be paid by England to America in
compensation for the damage done to American mercantile shipping

"*8th.*—I went to church this morning, and heard Rainsford.[1] Although his legs are weak his mouth is not, for he preached a beautiful sermon. I went at seven to hear Roby Hill, who preached pretty well. . . . I wish you would attack the bushes round the church. I think the place from which the glad tidings are proclaimed should be cheerful to the eye.

"*June* 21.—We had a very nice meeting, at Lady Radstock's."

In one letter he speaks of a Bill which he thinks of introducing to limit the hours of employment of railway servants. However, nothing came of this; and one is inclined to surmise that it would not have grieved him deeply if there had been a dissolution, and he had been relegated to private life.

"*25th.*—My throat is better, so I may speak on Friday for five or ten minutes [on an Irish motion]. I trust that if I do, the Master will give me a word to say."

But he did not speak.

"*July* 13.—I was rather amused at the High Sheriff. He asked me whether we had any rough weather after we got through the Suez Canal before we arrived in Egypt."

In the winter he went to Egypt with his wife. "My throat has for some time given me much trouble, so that I had to give up preaching," he writes in a fragment of journal. But travel did not turn his thoughts from this deep interest; for the moment it could be said of him, "Cælum non animum mutant qui trans mare currunt."

In 1873 Saunderson took little or no part in politics.

by the s.s. *Alabama*, which had sailed from the Mersey in 1862 for service with the Confederates during the Civil War—September 14th, 1872.

[1] Afterwards a well-known preacher in New York.

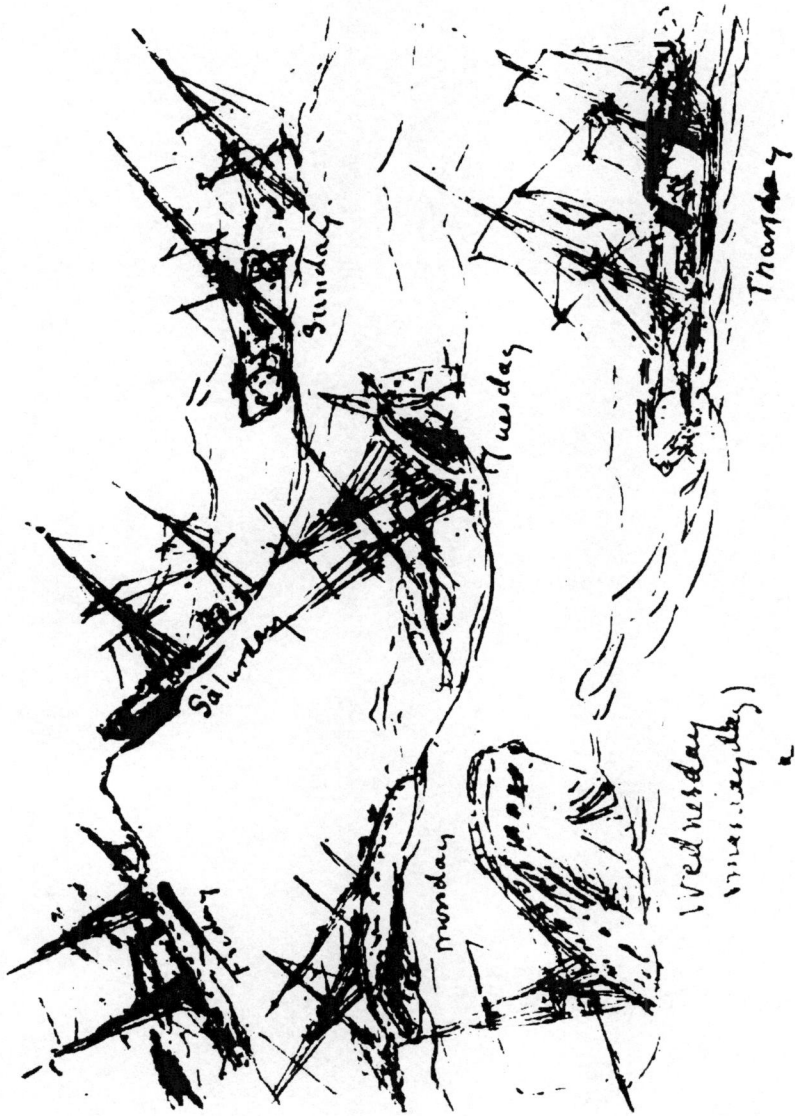

Sunday

Tuesday

Saturday

Thursday

Friday

Monday

Wednesday
(miserable day)

A WEEK AT SEA, 1873.

i.s. del.

On May 16 Mr. Miall brought on a motion in favour of disestablishment :of the Church in England and Scotland. Saunderson writes (May 17): "I should have spoken had I the opportunity; but I had not. However, I voted for the disestablishment." Presumably he thought that what was sauce for the goose was sauce for the gander: the Irish Church having gone by the board, the others might as well follow. Mr. Gladstone thought differently, and voted against the motion.

During this year Messrs. Moody and Sankey, who were making their reputation as "revivalist" preachers, arrived in Dublin, and Saunderson took a prominent part in organising their mission meetings. "Mortal man," he explained, "can have no greater honour than to be connected in any way with a work which is blessed and owned of God."

In January, 1874, Mr. Gladstone startled the world by dissolving Parliament on the eve of the new session. Saunderson had made up his mind not to seek re-election, but circumstances compelled him. The Home Rule movement had begun to roll with growing force, and two candidates were out in its support— Mr. Fay and Mr. J. G. Biggar. At the last moment Colonel Annesley decided not to stand; Saunderson was urgently pressed to come and resist the attack. He was known to be the best man available; probably the only man who could possibly succeed. Indeed he was assured that if he had remained in the field the attempt upon the seats would never have been made. It was by no means a congenial task; but he felt that it was his duty, and he accepted it.

The adverse elements, however, were irresistible. Injury to his chances was supposed to have been caused by a speech which he had delivered at the

Synod of the Church in which he had said things
calculated to alienate his Roman Catholic supporters
upon whose votes a great deal depended. Speaking
at Stradone on February 9, he declared that the
language to which objection was taken had been
addressed, not to Roman Catholics, but to his
Protestant co-religionists.

At one meeting a very ragged elector alluded to the
speech in dispute : " Shet up, Sandtherson, ye're a
bore," he called out : "me impoolses was wid ye till
ye made yer *foo-poo.*" To which another critic added,
" Sandtherson, ye bore me : ye fill me with *arnwee.*"
How these gentlemen came by their fluency in French
is not explained : it is an uncommon instance of the
Colonel being accused of dullness. He retaliated by
caricaturing them on the spot.

Probably this was not vital to the issue. The
" flowing tide " was with the Home Rulers, and
Saunderson was carried away in the stream, leaving
both seats in the possession of his opponents. So
ended the first phase of his political career. He now
retires into private life, to reappear in a very different
rôle after an interval of a dozen years. The events
of this period need not detain us long.

CHAPTER V

1874—1884

DURING the ensuing years Saunderson led the enviable life of a country gentleman who has many interests and constant occupation. It might be said of him, as it was once said of General Gordon, " His prayers or his nature saved him from selfishness and ambition." [1] His correspondence proves abundantly that he was bent on spreading the Gospel, not merely on his own spiritual welfare ; and we have seen how little personal ambition was stimulated by his success in Parliament. He was not a precise gardener, but his instinct for colour was gratified by a profusion of flowers ; his letters from many places reveal this, though not always in romantic language. For instance, he is delighted with a mass of thorn-blossoms one spring which " remind him of cream ice." Perhaps his favourite spot at home was the wild bog-garden where vegetation and foliage were always rich and bountiful.

Castle Saunderson was essentially his abiding home upon earth, even if he was persuaded that man's only true home was not of this world ; nevertheless, he was not inclined by habit or temperament to apply to estate management the fastidious care and attention which is the natural instinct of many landowners.

His yachting remained an engrossing occupation,

[1] " Charles George Gordon," by Sir W. Butler, p. 83.

and it is a pleasant duty to record that he was a good loser, even in one of his own beloved boats :

" Tipping beat me yesterday," he writes in May, 1876, "after the best race I ever sailed on the lake, by thirty seconds : only think of that. . . . I went into first place. The *Mischief* got a start which again placed her ahead of me ; and there we stuck. Sometimes I gained a little ; sometimes she did the same. So the race ended. So Tipping has at last won, more power to him."

In spite of his fine physique and his natural energy, he was never a thoroughly strong man, and he not unfrequently went abroad for the sake of his health. In May of this year (1876) he writes :

" I feel better this morning than I have done since Cannes. Perhaps I may be able to speak a little [at the Synod]. . . . A French company are going to raise the *Vanguard* [1] with wind-bags. Punch suggests that in this case they ought to fill the sunken vessel with the Dublin Synod ! "

Every year bears record of his Militia duties : [2]

" I went on parade and had to walk, as my mare was an hour late ; which improved my temper. . . . Yesterday the shooting came off ; Sommy [3] won two prizes, I being second twice. . . . I have to be at the Poor-house to-day at twelve and then go home, where Charlie Crichton meets me and takes me with him to sleep at Crom."

---

[1] H.M.S. *Vanguard* had been sunk by H.M.S. *Iron Duke* in a collision off the coast of Wicklow in September, 1875.

[2] Saunderson, as a young man, had joined a Volunteer Corps in London. He entered the Cavan Militia (4th Battalion Royal Irish Fusiliers), as a Captain in June, 1862. He became Major in January, 1875 ; Hon. Lieutenant-Colonel in June, 1886 ; and he commanded the Battalion from December, 1891, until his retirement in November, 1893. His record states that "he is acquainted with French and Italian."

[3] Somerset Maxwell, his cousin.

CASTLE SAUNDERSON.

And again:

" Our battle went off very well. I worked half the regiment and beat the enemy easily."

This may refer to an occasion of which the Colonel once told the present writer with great glee. He pointed to a large hollow on a hill-side, and related how he had placed his main body there to ambush the enemy, whom he successfully drew by displaying a detached party of skirmishers on the sky-line beyond.

The general election of 1880 found Saunderson in no humour to return to Parliament. He writes from Dublin, March 25:

" —— says that had I stood for Cavan I should probably have got in, as the people were anxious that I should try again. I am not such a fool."

Perhaps the state of Ireland had not yet appeared to him sufficiently grave to demand his services in the fight; but the time was at hand.

Early in 1881 he writes:

" At Amiens Street I found a large body of police going down by train to a sale to protect the Defence Association. . . . The primroses and bells are in great beauty, but alas! the laurels have suffered terribly from the frost."

Throughout the summer he was racing on the lake:

" We sailed a hard race, and won like men by 3 m. from the *Mischief*.
" *September* 6.—I must say I owe a great deal to Thompson, who managed everything for me, so that I had nothing to do but to mind my steering. . . . There was a strong whole mainsail breeze, just what the *Fish* wanted; and yet we managed, after being at one time behind, to work our way to the front. Everything went like clockwork; we had our spinnaker up long before any of the others, and went

a tremendous pace. . . . After the race every one came, of course, to admire the *Witch*. Had we lost no one would have looked at her."

On October 12 he writes from Dublin, where he was assisting at a large Church gathering :

"I am going to speak to-night at the overflow, and I feel persuaded the Lord will give me the right word to the right person. . . . I think I shall speak on the Passover. It never struck me before to-day,

A BUCKLE.

on looking at the subject, that although the Israelites brought their flocks and herds with them, they were not allowed to eat them. . . ."

Early next morning, in close vicinity, Mr. Parnell was arrested. Events were hurrying forward, and Saunderson was soon to be back on the political platform.

In May, 1882, he started from Ireland to join Mrs. Saunderson at Folkestone and to go yachting; the following is a graphic description of an incident of this expedition :

"*Reonagh*,¹ Dartmouth, *June* 1.—We started yesterday

¹ He had designed this boat of 18 tons for Mr. Cole, who lived at Exmouth.

THE "WITCH" AT CASTLE SAUNDERSON BOATHOUSE, 1876.

morning with a light east wind for the Isle of Wight. We were becalmed for three hours in a heavy swell, which, I said, looked as if it had wind behind it. A light breeze sprang up, and we made good way until we arrived at Portland Bill; then the wind increased, so I at once took in the balloon foresail and housed topmast. We were in the act of doing so when the gale was upon us, and from calm water we found ourselves in a high steep sea. Next I shifted jibs, which was a troublesome matter; however, we got it done and hammered away, when suddenly she pitched her bows into a wall of water. We heard a crash, and away went the bowsprit short at the stem; so here was a nice pickle. However, after half an hour's hard work in the midst of the roar of the wind and showers of spray, the wreck was secured, and I found myself about seven miles outside Portland with only a foresail and three-reefed main-sail. I ran her in to try and get shelter behind the Bill, but found none, as the wind was coming from the S.E. and the gale increasing in force. I then decided to run for Dartmouth before the gale, forty-five miles; so up helm and away we went, tearing before the gale and sea. The boat went like a sea-bird, never shipping a drop, although the waves, as they curled up high above the stern and broke like thunder, looked as if they would engulph her. However, up she rose, and never took in anything but spray. . . ."

It is to be noticed that his letters never reveal any anxiety about the state of Ireland; it would appear that his private interests engrossed him so completely that he was callous concerning the desperate condition into which the country was drifting. But this was not so; the fire had kindled, and at length it broke out. At the annual Orange demonstration on July 12, 1882,[1] he appeared on the platform at Ballykilbeg. His speech is noteworthy as the starting-point of his new political career.

---

[1] Anniversary of the battle of the Boyne.

" He had become an Orangeman," he said, " because the state of the country for the past two years had been simply unbearable.   The very foundations of society were shaken and about to crumble almost in the dust, and, he said to himself, was there any organisation in Ireland capable of dealing with this condition of anarchy and rebellion ?   There was only one answer—that there was an organisation not afraid to face and cope with it, and that was the Orange organisation ; and he determined, by God's help, not to allow one day unnecessarily to elapse before he joined that body."

We may pause to observe that hitherto his only reference to Orangeism had been made when he told the House of Commons that Orangemen sat at home and beat drums to frighten away Papists.   He proceeds :

" The Land League, founded in the country by way of affording the tenants protection, felt that they could not accomplish the object they had in view without the Orangemen.   When Parnell, Biggar, and their crew went into Parliament and said they represented Ireland, they well knew they never spoke a word in the name of the Irish Orangemen.   Their great object was to gain over the Orange body.   How did they attempt it ?   They came over to Ulster and told the Orangemen that their sole object was to secure for the tenant farmers fair play and no favour ; . . . [but] they knew what they said in Connaught and Cork : it was ' Ireland for the Irish,' and ' out with the English garrison.'   Who were the English garrison ?   They were the Protestants of the North. They tried to seduce the Orangemen, but, thank God, they had not succeeded in doing so."

He next explained that he had voted for the Land Bill of 1870 because he thought that the tenant farmer required a fair measure of protection, but " he believed that the landlord had as good a right to his property as the tenant had to his," and he would have no compromise with the methods and aims of the Land

League. Then he formulated a proposal of which we shall presently hear again.

"The main reason," he declared, "why he had attended that meeting was that he had long felt that the Orange Society required a far better organisation than it at present possessed, if they really intended to cope with the dangers by which they were surrounded. His opinion was that the Orange Society should be made a disciplined body. In Cavan the Orangemen as a rule were armed, but they did not know how to use their arms, and they should be taught to do so. The first thing to do was to adopt a uniform, because without a uniform they could not manifest to the world at large that they were ready to take the field in case they were wanted. He admitted at once that there were difficulties in the way, because at all hazards they must strictly keep within the law. . . . As to the colours of the uniform, the principal colours of the Orange institution were orange, blue, purple, and black, and if these were mixed together it would be found that they formed grey. Now, grey was the colour of Irish frieze, and they could not get a more appropriate serviceable uniform than that. . . . If England, in a moment of infatuation, determined to establish Home Rule . . . they would take up arms and ask the reason why. . . . He had only sketched out what he hoped would be carried to a successful issue."

This may appear to be random gasconade; but it was nothing of the kind. It was a deliberate and reasoned proposition. It will be remembered that Parnell had been released from Kilmainham on May 2. According to his biographer, the terms of the "Treaty" were that the Government were to introduce a satisfactory Arrears Bill, and Parnell was to "slow down" the agitation.[1] Whether the Cabinet had acted wisely or unwisely matters not: the people of Ireland recognised in the liberation of their leader a

---

[1] "Charles Stewart Parnell," by Barry O'Brien, i. 350.

confession of defeat on the part of the British Government. Lord Cowper resigned; Lord Spencer became Lord-Lieutenant, and upon the day of his entry into office Lord Frederick Cavendish and Mr. Burke were murdered in Phœnix Park.[1] " In 1882 Ireland seemed to be literally a society on the eve of dissolution,"[2] said an Irishman of consummate experience in after years to Mr. Morley.

We may safely believe that Parnell was dismayed at this atrocity, and that the offer of immediate retirement which he made to Mr. Gladstone was sincere: but the wind had been sown and the whirlwind was being reaped. It is not a matter for surprise that men in such a crisis should take views which in tranquil times seem extravagant; and although a few years later, when Saunderson continued his appeal for a disciplined resort to arms, he was rebuked in one paper as a " mouthing idiot," it is certain that he spoke in sober earnest. On the evening of the same day (July 12, 1882) he writes from Castle Ward:[3]

" I have just returned from Ballykilbeg, and have every reason to be satisfied with the result. I was listened to with great attention and, I think, placed my scheme before the audience in a clear form . . . I have . . . to see the editor of the paper at Downpatrick to arrange about shoving the project forward."

It would appear that the first consequence of this effort was to produce a threatening letter. He writes:

"—— tells me that my admirers have sent me a love-letter, which you opened. I fully expect to get many of them. The threats to the females of my family I look upon as absurd; I conceive you run no risk whatever. As to myself, I don't mind what they say

[1] May 6.   [2] "Life of Gladstone," by John Morley, iii. 70.
[3] Lord Bangor's.

or write ; I shall go ahead without swerving an inch.
Don't alarm yourself."

Castle Saunderson is connected with the lake by
a long stretch of river. Down this Saunderson sailed
or steamed in his launch almost daily year after year,
and it would not have been difficult for one of the
"physical force" party to take a leisurely shot at
him here from behind cover. I have heard it said that
in the worst times the Colonel did approach certain
spots, favourable to such a project, with a watchful
eye and a readiness for action ; but I never heard
that his precautions were put to the test.[1]

Nor did he " swerve an inch." In October he writes
from Dublin : " I have been hard at work since I came
up. Last night I addressed a meeting of Orangemen
and succeeded in carrying my ideas."

So he increased in ardour. The following year is
marked by a closer connection with Orangeism,
mitigated by Militia service, much yachting, and
some gardening : " I send you a rumbustical flower
It looks as if it was manufactured."

On December 7, 1883, he writes from Rossmore
Park : "The meeting went off first-rate, and was a real
success, you will be glad to hear." But it was to have
a sequel of a less gratifying nature. His host, Lord
Rossmore, was dismissed from the Commission of the
Peace for his share in the day's proceedings. This
is Saunderson's version of the story: An Orange
demonstration was to be held at Roslea. He, with
Lord Crichton, who was to preside, marched to the
rendezvous at the head of the Fermanagh contingent.

---

[1] It is nevertheless a fact that police protection was thrust upon
him during the worst times. Five men were stationed on the premises
and shadowed him in his own grounds. When he drove with Mrs.
Saunderson in her phaeton, they followed on a car.

Not far from the village they were presented with an official letter, requesting them to make a detour, so as to avoid a League meeting which was being held on their line of march. This they did. Presently Lord Rossmore arrived with the Monaghan division. A sub-inspector of police requested him also to change his route. The Monaghan men were weary and impatient: Lord Rossmore was entirely ignorant of Lord Crichton's motive in diverging. He inquired whether the sub-inspector was authorised to stop him, and was told that he was not. He then proceeded. Arrived at the League meeting, he met the magistrate who had written the letter to Lord Crichton; of him Lord Rossmore asked permission to go forward, and received it, provided he would be responsible for the good conduct of his men. Without further incident, they arrived; no breach of the peace occurred; the meeting was held; and Lord Rossmore was turned off the Bench. If, argued Saunderson, he was punished as a magistrate for attending the meeting, then the other magistrates present should suffer, Saunderson himself included. If, however, the alleged offence was defiance of authority, there was no case against him.

A few weeks later a great demonstration of Loyalists was held to protest against the action of the Government, and Saunderson made a speech which showed that his fighting spirit was thoroughly awake. He observed that this was a non-party meeting. He himself had formerly stood as a Liberal. In those days the issue between parties had been as to who should sit on the Treasury Bench; now they were united in the interests of her who sat upon the throne. After recapitulating the circumstances affecting Lord Rossmore, he delivered the first of those attacks on

MAJOR SAUNDERSON ON "PUNCH," 1883.

Mr. Gladstone which were to be his constant occupation in the coming years.' He quoted from Mr. Gladstone's speech at Leeds two years before, in which he had made his famous denunciation of the Land League. He complained that nothing had been done to suppress that League immediately. Tardy action had indeed been taken, with good results ; but Mr. Parnell and " my graceful and eminent successor in County Cavan," had replaced it with the National League ;[1] and with these gentlemen Mr. Gladstone had recently shown a disposition to treat. Finally the Prime Minister had complained that " the class of law and order in Ireland did not come out and give to the Government of the day their moral support." Here was Saunderson's opening. He called upon his hearers to make it manifest that " every Protestant deserving the name is as ready to fight to-day as his ancestors were two hundred years ago. . . . That we are prepared with one voice, and at all hazards, to show that we will not have these men to reign over us."

This oration led to an interview, in which the unrepentant speaker made his meaning sufficiently clear :

" The duty of offering armed resistance to the authority of Mr. Parnell and his followers would devolve in the first instance on the Orange organisation, which occupies in regard to the Irish Loyalists very much the position the Army does to the civilians in England. As the Orange Institution has been organised with the view to confronting just such a crisis as that by which we are now confronted, we could concentrate 50,000 men on any given point in Ulster with the very shortest possible notice. We have no doubt whatever that if we were permitted to settle the Irish question of Home Rule, without English interference, Mr. Parnell would find it very problematical whether he would be the Home Ruler."

[1] In 1882.

He was increasing not only in ardour, but in public favour. A few days later he writes from Dublin : "I spoke last night at a grand banquet given by the Conservative Club to Rossmore. I was not down in the list of speakers, but there were such shouts for my name that I had to give a jaw." Of another meeting, from which he was kept away by a cold, he writes : "I hear that when my name was mentioned there was great cheering."

His growing interest in politics induced him to go to London, when Parliament reassembled in 1884. On February 10 he writes :

"Did you read Parnell's speech ? He referred in fierce terms to me and quoted speeches I had made. I daresay Messrs. Biggar & Co. will compliment me on Monday. I hope to get in to hear the debate to-morrow, but am by no means sure. The crush to see Bradlaugh will be terrific."

The case of Lord Rossmore figured prominently in the proceedings upon the Address. Parnell had attacked Saunderson on the ground of the speech which has been quoted ; and if he succeeded in getting into the gallery on the 11th he must have heard a further denunciation of himself by Mr. Sexton.

With Bradlaugh[1] Saunderson had no concern ; but if he was indeed present that day he witnessed a scene that suggests one of Sir W. S. Gilbert's travesties rather than the proceedings of the House of Commons. Bradlaugh boldly advanced upon the table and swore himself in with a Bible which he had brought for the purpose. The Speaker called him to order in vain.

[1] Mr. Bradlaugh had been elected with Mr. Labouchere for Northampton. He claimed to "affirm" instead of taking the oath, on the ground of his personal opinions. Parliament refused : he then insisted on taking the oath. Parliament again demurred. His constituents upheld him and in the end Parliament altered its regulations.

The House then proceeded in deep perplexity to consider the situation, ostentatiously ignoring the presence of the intruder, who had stationed himself at the Bar, from which coign of vantage he occasionally threw in a contribution to the discussion.   Sir Stafford Northcote argued that the oath was invalid because the Speaker had not been in the chair, but standing up

MR. BRADLAUGH.

and calling Bradlaugh to order.   Subsequently, on a division being taken, Bradlaugh complicated matters by voting in his own favour.   It was then urged that he could not vote because in the eyes of Parliament he was not there, and that he could not be named because he was not sitting.   However, he was there and he did vote, and most undignified was the condition to which he reduced the House.   Mr. O'Donnell insisted that any surrender by the Government would amount to " utterly collusive action for the purpose of foisting an atheistical political supporter on the conscience and honour of this House." Nor did Mr. Labouchere, who fought for his colleague's claim, throw oil on the troubled waters.

It is unnecessary to dwell further upon the episode. Bradlaugh won in the end. Suffice it to say that no man ever entered Parliament the object of more violent prejudice, and that in the short interval before his death this had been to a great extent obliterated by his public conduct, and the manifestation of his personal character.

Saunderson now put himself into communication with active politicians. " I have just been with Arnold-Forster," he writes. " He will, as I expected, be of the very greatest use to me."[1] Mr. Arnold-Forster had spent the evil years 1880-82 in Ireland, at the Chief Secretary's Lodge, or visiting the disturbed districts. He had collected much material for a campaign directed against the Land League. In 1881 he published a small book entitled, " The Truth about the Land League," which came into great request. " He has also given me a later edition of the pamphlet," adds Saunderson.

On March 1st, 1884, he writes :

" I have been asked to stand for Armagh Co. If I should find that the electors are very decidedly of opinion that I should suit them, perhaps I might feel bound to accede to their request. I should rather stand for Fermanagh ; however, we shall see. It appears there is to be a meeting of the gentry of the Co. at which the question is to be opened ; so I shall probably hear more about it before long."

[1] Mr. Arnold-Forster was the adopted son of Mr. W. E. Forster and had acted as his private secretary when Chief Secretary for Ireland.

This admits a predilection in favour of his own neighbourhood: Cavan had gone over to the Home Rulers; but Fermanagh, next door, was still represented by Lord Crichton.[1]

In Ireland he was occupied with many projects:

"I shall cross over as soon as I possibly can, but the pamphlet[2] will keep me a day or two longer. . . . The daffys are in great blow. . . . The cattle-sheds are nearly finished . . . I am hard at work on my pamphlet: two men and self grinding away." And again, "The pamphlet gives me great trouble."

A few days later from Dublin:

"We had a great meeting at the Synod to-day. I brought forward a proposal to establish an order of mission preachers. I only decided to do so yesterday, and had to tinker up a speech. I carried my point without one dissentient voice. . . . I had a very difficult part to play, as I had to attack the preaching in our Church without giving offence.

"You will see in to-day's paper that I am to come forward for the representation of Tyrone. Rather good, isn't it? What about going abroad? I can't get over until May 5th: this I suppose will be too late?

"May 4.—It will take me all to-morrow to get my work finally finished! I hear from Fa[3] that they are going to Spain. This prevents my going, as I have

[1] He succeeded as Earl of Erne in 1885.
[2] This pamphlet was entitled "Two Irelands: Loyalty *versus* Treason." Part I. is an outline of Irish history from 1878 to 1883. Part II., entitled "The Attempted Invasion of Ulster," is an apology for the action taken by the Loyalists of Ulster in resisting the propagandist efforts of the National League in the north of Ireland. Part III. is a copious array of references to speeches and writings by which he proposes to convict the Nationalist party of complicity with lawlessness and disorder under every possible heading.

The title is borrowed from a speech of Sir George Trevelyan's at the time of his Chief Secretaryship, when he spoke of the two Irelands of order and of crime; this is duly quoted on the cover. It is a compilation of over eighty pages, the result of much diligence and research, and undoubtedly a valuable compendium of the case to be presented.

[3] Mrs. Saunderson's niece.

to be home on the 1st of June to make arrangements for starting next day for the Curragh."

Meanwhile he is much distressed by the gradual sinking of Lord Farnham, the "Uncle Som" of frequent reference, to whom he was devotedly attached. His letters reveal a most affectionate tenderness, fortified by the Christian faith which they had cultivated together.

"Had a hard day's drill," he writes later from the Curragh. "We are roasting with heat. . . . I am glad Lord Spencer was not insulted in Belfast. . . . I had only one shindy with Punch to-day: a guard presented arms, and Punch performed the most awful capers, to the astonishment and delight of lookers-on."

In July of this year (1884) the House of Lords threw out the Government Franchise Bill, on the plea that they must first know something of the intentions of the Government with regard to redistribution. In December Parliament reassembled; there was a conference between the two parties, and eventually both measures became law. Meanwhile, in accordance with tradition in all matters concerning reform, public indignation was at once paraded, and ministers went on tour. Saunderson, though nominally a Whig and a member of Brooks's, was showing determined hostility to all the policy and performances of the Liberals, and he proceeded to take up the cudgels in defence of the Peers. Having made a spirited onslaught upon the Bill at Monaghan in September, he prepared to take part in a demonstration at the Rotunda in Dublin, on October 21. "The meeting will be a tremendous affair," he writes on the 18th; "5,000 tickets have been issued. . . . Plunket [1] is to commence; I am to follow; Gibson [2] follows me."

---

[1] Lord Rathmore.   [2] Lord Ashbourne.

His speech begins with a slashing denunciation of
the action of the Government at home and in Egypt,
in Afghanistan and in South Africa. Proceeding to
recent events, he delivers some sentiments upon the
House of Lords, not irrelevant to subsequent develop-
ments. " The House of Lords . . . acted in a way it
should if it had any respect for itself or for the name
of an independent legislative assembly : they threw
it out." Now, instead of leaving agitation to the men
who desired emancipation, ministers of the Crown
had become stump orators :

" Mr. Gladstone went to the North . . . spouting third-
class speeches out of first-class carriages. . . . Mr.
Bright went down to Birmingham, accompanied by
Lord Hartington. . . . You may have heard that at
missionary meetings it has sometimes been the habit
of the missionary to bring a specimen of the class he
has been the means of reforming, . . . and he says :
' Look at that man. That man was once an irreclaim-
able and naked savage.' And so Mr. Bright . . .
concluded by saying, speaking of the majority of the
Peers, that they are an unpatriotic oligarchy. I should
think that Mr. Bright might have remembered the
unhappy oligarch who was roosting on the same
stump with himself. . . . Let me observe that a very
marked distinction exists between the English and the
Irish question of the franchise. In England, in Wales,
and in Scotland, who is afraid to extend the franchise ?
. . . There is no doubt that the voters in the countries
whom you propose to enfranchise will be just as true
to England and the Constitution as those who now
enjoy [it]. But is it so in Ireland ? Is it not true . . .
that these men in their speeches and in the journal
which represents them have invariably declared that
they aim, not at an alteration of the law, but the
separation of this country from England ?"

He makes the usual appeal to arms as the ultimate
resource, and ends with a stirring peroration :

" Deep down in the roots of the English character

I know there is a love of law, a love of liberty, and above all a love of that great Constitution under which our monarchy has gone round all the world; and appealing to that . . . asking no more than is our due, we believe that England, . . . unless she has utterly forgotten all the traditions of the past, will not be deaf to the appeal that we have made."

It is not surprising, after this, to read (December 4):

"They did me the honour to elect me Deputy Grand Master for Ireland. There were three vacancies, and I was elected at the head of the list. . . . All I said has been amply verified by the Redistribution Bill,[1] by which we are handed over to the tender mercies of Parnell & Co."

The latter sentence refers to a speech which he had recently made at the University, and which, he says, "enlivened them up, for I thought they were dull."

[1] Introduced December 1, 1884.

CHAPTER VI

1884—1885

SAUNDERSON was now in the deep waters of politics; his enthusiasm rose with the rising tide. Not content with addressing Irish audiences, he associated himself with his compatriots in London who were intent on opposing Parnellism in general, and in particular the extension of the franchise, which promised increased strength to the Parnellite vote.

Under the arrangement made between the two sides in Parliament, the Franchise Bill had been passed before the adjournment on December 6, 1884. The Redistribution Bill had been read a second time on December 4, and now awaited its remaining stages.

The Houses were to reassemble on February 19, 1885. On February 17 Saunderson writes from Brooks's :

"I have just come back from the preliminary meeting to decide on the programme for our interview with Northcote, the Marquis of Hamilton[1] in the chair. Crichton is to introduce the meeting . . . and as I am looked on as the professional orator, I am to come last, so as to sum up the views of the Irish Loyalists and to ginger up Northcote. This is by no means pleasant, though complimentary to my renown as a wind-bag.

"*February* 18.—The deputation was an imposing affair. . . . I wound up in a short sweet and smart speech, which was well received, but I expect all our

---

[1] Duke of Abercorn, K.G.

efforts are of no avail, as Salisbury & Co. have thrown us over. I put it very straight to Sir Stafford, and showed him that tinkering the Redistribution Bill in England and at the same time giving Parnell eighty-five seats in Ireland was as fatal in all probability to the cause of Conservatism in England as it was likely to be to us loyalists in Ireland. Crichton . . . made a very good speech. I don't go to Germany until Friday, as I want to see about Somerset being put down for a regiment,[1] and I have a bad cold."

On the 21st he adds :

" You remember I told you that I was commissioned to . . . give it pretty hot to Northcote. I did so with a vengeance. The deputation was delighted, but I don't think Sir Stafford was. Yesterday we had a meeting, and I was instrumental in causing the foundation of what I have always wanted accomplished, viz.: an independent constitutional party in the House of Commons entirely free to act for the good of Irish loyalty unfettered by party ties. The result will be that in future the Conservative leaders will no longer find an unswerving support, as they have been accustomed to do in the past. Our party will give its support to the Government that does most for the interests of Ireland."

Herein he adopts the policy always pursued by Parnell, with whom indeed he may be compared in some respects, as may be observed later. Meanwhile it may be asked, what were Saunderson's political principles? He was denouncing the Government roundly, yet he belonged to Brooks's, whilst Brooks's was still untroubled by the Home Rule split. He had been elected in 1868, and he remained a member until 1890. In 1886 he joined the Carlton, so that for four years he had a foot in each camp. Speaking at Hopetown in September, 1887, he declared that " he belonged to that old and very respectable and historical

---

[1] His eldest son served for some years in the Rifle Brigade.

class of politicians known as the Whigs.   He was not conscious that he had changed his politics one jot or one iota, and yet he now found himself a follower of Lord Salisbury." At Portsmouth, again, as late as August, 1891, he informed his audience that, "like Mr. Ashley, he was a sound Liberal." Mr. Evelyn Ashley was of course an avowed Liberal Unionist: but Saunderson had by this time practically, if not admittedly, proclaimed himself a Conservative by joining the Carlton. In 1885 he was an anti-Home Ruler first and everything else afterwards : possibly that remained his attitude until the end.[1]

Meanwhile Sir Stafford Northcote, who had grown accustomed to such followers as the members of the Fourth Party, probably found his withers unwrung by this "gingering" from a new quarter. Under his leadership in the House of Commons the Opposition had accepted the agreement concerning the Redistribution Bill, and so it passed into law, notwithstanding the Ulster protest. Efforts were made during the committee stage by Lord Crichton and others to vest more voting power in the boroughs, but the Parnellites knew their game and played it with a will. The Irish Unionists were left to complain that they had been thrown over, and Parnell secured his following of eighty-five.

[1] In one of his last speeches (Portadown, January 12, 1906) he said "he did not come as a Tory, for he never was a Tory; nor as a Conservative, because he never was one ; nor as a Liberal, because the word had no meaning for him.   He came there as a Unionist."

Indeed it may be observed that Butt rendered inevitable the extinction of the Liberal Party in Ireland.   Until he gave life to the Home Rule movement, Irish elections had been generally contested on the recognised lines of Conservative and Liberal antagonism, the Liberals being usually credited with the Roman Catholic vote.   Since then all party divisions have gradually been obliterated by the broad issue of Home Rule; and politicians have seldom troubled to distinguish any qualifying shades in the Unionist confession of faith.

Saunderson, for the moment, had nothing to do in London. He returned to Ireland, and went to fish for salmon. His failure on one occasion he confesses in an illustrated letter. But he found time to make some speeches, until a sudden attack of illness sent him to bed.

During the summer of 1885 political history was being made briskly, and the passages concerning Ireland were by no means the least memorable. On June 8 Mr. Gladstone's Government was brought to an end by a defeat upon the Budget. Lord Salisbury became Prime Minister, and Lord Randolph Churchill began his short spell of triumph. His apprenticeship had been irregular. Capricious and indolent during the earlier years, he had since 1880 been an indefatigable member of Parliament. Reckless and relentless in all his actions, he had become the most conspicuous of the notorious group of so-called Tories who combined with incessant persecution of Mr. Gladstone a tolerably persistent pin-pricking of their own leader. Slavish obedience to party principles and discipline was no part of their programme, and from these trammels Lord Randolph kept himself emancipated to the end. It is remarkable that, in spite of an exaggerated apprehension of his precocious youth,[1] and a most justifiable representation of his levity, the public showed no reluctance to take him now at his own valuation as a commanding statesman. He became Secretary of State for India and a controlling force in the deliberations of the Cabinet.

Much has been said about the overtures which were exchanged between the Conservative leaders and Parnell during the summer of this year. Lord Car-

---

[1] He was already thirty-six. His son was little less notorious before he was thirty.

narvon's conduct was, to say the least of it, injudicious. A Lord-Lieutenant cannot divest himself of his official character by arranging an interview with a Nationalist leader in a dismantled house in Grosvenor Square;[1] and even if it be conceded that two men, responsible for conducting opposing policies and interests, may be brought together, without previous acquaintance, to discuss abstract propositions, the one who holds office and authority must not complain if his amiable intentions lay him open to misrepresentation.

Not to be behindhand, Lord Randolph had already received Parnell in his house. His son claims for him that this implied no bargain or compact;[2] that the visit was paid before Lord Randolph took office, and that he acted as a private individual, not responsible for the future action of his party.[3] A year later he was able to assure Lord Justice Fitzgibbon that no compact had been made or attempted.[4]

It is true that between Churchill and Parnell there existed a House-of-Commons acquaintance, and it is generally understood that the stern Irishman, for some reason, excepted the other from the comprehensive hatred and mistrust with which he regarded all Englishmen. But it is futile to pretend that Parnell repaired to Connaught Place for an idle gossip with an old friend. He never wasted his time nor acted without a definite motive ; and students of history may fairly conclude that he went there to confer not only with a future minister, but with the man in whom he foresaw the dominating spirit of any Conservative Government which circumstances might bring into existence.

[1] "Charles Stewart Parnell," by Barry O'Brien, ii. 51.
[2] "Lord Randolph Churchill," by Winston Churchill, i. 393, *seq.*
[3] "The chances of Lord Randolph joining a Conservative Administration were undetermined." *Ibid.*
[4] *Ibid.*

It would be unreasonable to regard these overtures as unscrupulous. The coalition of Fox and North in 1783 has generally been condemned as involving a flagrant violation of principle in the interest of faction ; but the history of the nineteenth century consists of a series of modifications whereby the opponents of yesterday have become the allies of to-morrow, and there need be no disgrace in the attempt of Tory ministers to discover a middle way by which Ireland might be governed without, on the one hand, yielding to Nationalist demands, and without, upon the other, relying altogether on rigorous Coercion Acts. At all events, these charges are not to be hurled about by members of a party responsible for granting the conciliatory legislation of 1869, 1870, and 1881, who negotiated the Kilmainham Treaty, and eventually embraced the vital and cardinal doctrine of Home Rule. But even if these transactions must be censured as unseemly temporising, Saunderson's record is secure. He was not, and had no occasion to be, concerned in them ; and it may safely be assumed that if he had been called upon to assist, he would at once have applied another dose of " ginger."

Meanwhile he was engaged in the choice of a constituency. On July 31, 1885, he addressed the electors of North Armagh at Portadown, where the following resolution was adopted :

" That we, the farmers and Orangemen of North Armagh, offer Major Saunderson the constituency of North Armagh, and pledge ourselves to place him at the head of the poll ; but as other constituencies are anxious for him to represent them, we will leave the matter in his own hands for the present."

Concerning this meeting he writes :

" I had a truly great reception at Portadown ; I felt

quite touched by the enthusiasm of the people. . . .
My Antrim friends met me and had it out with the
Armagh people. I sat by while the fight went on, as
neither would consent to give me up. I must say I
should prefer North Armagh, as it is entirely Orange."

Objections to his candidature had been raised on the
ground that he was an Orangeman of too recent
enlistment; also that he was a landlord. But these
were not of serious importance; a greater difficulty
existed in the fact that the seat had been ear-marked
for Mr. Monroe, the Solicitor-General, who may be
described as the official candidate. We have seen
that Saunderson was not apt to be spell-bound by
official influence, and having decided to stand for
North Armagh he was by no means inclined to withdraw. Moreover the Orange spirit was aroused. One
prominent individual wrote: "I am very doubtful
whether your withdrawing would not do more harm
than good. . . . They swore that if you were withdrawn they would vote for the Liberal. . . . They
never will consent to it." Another wrote: "We think
that North Armagh has had an undoubted right to
be represented by an Orangeman."

His opponents did not fail to recall his description
of Orangemen, when he was in Parliament, as men
who sat indoors and beat drums to scare away Papists.
Saunderson unblushingly claimed this as evidence
that he had always upheld Orangemen as law-abiding
and peaceful citizens. He was fighting to win, but
not without impediments. "My throat has not got
over roaring at Ballymena," he writes on August 11.
A little later: "This is my present attitude (picture):
there will be nothing left of me before long." And
again: "I never closed my eyes all last night, and felt
so bad this morning that I sent for the doctor."

However, he did not avoid some rough work: " We had a most successful meeting last night . . . the excited multitude got hold of the brake in which we were and dragged us off, to our imminent peril."

Of another meeting :

" My men cheered frantically ; Monroe's men booed liked mad. . . . At it I went, and in an incredibly short time I had the audience quite in hand. . . . After the meeting a deputation of Mr. Monroe's men came to the hotel and asked if I would receive them.   I answered that I would with pleasure if they did not object to smoking. . . . I answered that I was in the hands of the Orangemen, to go or retire as they pleased."

To this letter he adds :

" To-night I speak at the Red Cow, in our tent.   I daresay people may hold me up as using religion for political purposes, but the Gospel is stronger than men, and if I could but win a soul it would be indeed a triumph."

Elsewhere he says :

" Many of them support me owing to my connection with the Evangelisation Society, which has done good work among them."

In the midst of his agitating labours he was not forgetful of his religious zeal.   I find a letter carefully preserved in which one who was very dear to him writes : " I am not one of those who think that a child of God should not meddle in politics ; but . . . can [such a one] expect to succeed as a politician ? "

The upshot was that Mr. Monroe retired, and Saunderson was left face to face with Mr. Shillington, the Liberal Candidate, who had secured the Nationalist vote.   The result of the polling was a majority of 1,819 for Saunderson.

These honours were not won without the usual
vexations of parliamentary life.   A former tenant,
whose conduct appears to have led to disputes and
the consequent loss of his holding, wrote to threaten
that if he was not immediately compensated he would
publish damaging statements in the constituency.
One ardent supporter who had written almost daily,
sometimes twice daily throughout the autumn, begins
as soon as the election is over to urge the member
to "come and see us now and then and not keep too
long away. . . . The Orangemen can do nothing if
the gentry sleep: meetings should be got up at
once. . . . I have told them that we expect you at
our annual soirée."   Meanwhile Saunderson had
found his way into the House of Commons and was
to assume a position of much importance for himself
and no little interest to the public.   At the end of the
year he writes: "Home Rule is now in the immediate
future staring us in the face."   He was resolved to
lose no time in entering the lists and engaging in the
conflict.[1]

[1] One paragraph in his Election Address is worth recording; it
might be doing duty now : "Although I should oppose any attempt
to tax imported food, I should be disposed to advocate a tax on
imported manufactured goods, as I believe this course would have
the effect of fostering our manufactures and reviving our trade.   I
should also strongly favour special arrangements being entered into
with our colonies of a reciprocal character, which would have the
effect of greatly enlarging the field for our commercial operations and
would bind all parts of the empire together, not only with the tie of
loyalty to the Crown, but also with the bond of common trade
interests."

CHAPTER VII

1885—1886

PARLIAMENT had been dissolved on November 18, 1885. The result of the elections showed that the newly enfranchised voters were not ungrateful to the authors of the latest measure of reform: the Liberals were rewarded with a majority. The strength of parties stood relatively thus: Liberals 333, Conservatives 251, Parnellites 86:[1] so that with a majority of 82 over Conservatives they were in a minority of four against Conservatives and Parnellites combined.

But now the contingent alliance between Conservatives and Parnellites, of which we have already heard, was to be eclipsed by a more daring and momentous move from the other side. On December 17 it was stated in the Press that Mr. Gladstone was contemplating a scheme for establishing a Parliament in Dublin. Mr. Parnell was quite prepared to close with the highest bidder, and the destination of the Irish vote became a foregone conclusion. Parliament met on January 12, 1886; on the 26th the Government were defeated on an agricultural amendment to the Address which Mr. Collings had moved, and Mr. Gladstone found the way clear before him.

The genesis and growth of Mr. Gladstone's conversion to Home Rule have been fully recounted by Mr. Morley. The rumours published on December 17

---

[1] "Life of Gladstone," by John Morley, iii. 250.

were not intended, as was once supposed, to test the drift of the wind : they came from a rash but laudable desire on the part of Mr. Gladstone's son to prevent a public impression that the Liberal leaders were already considering and quarrelling over a new Irish policy. Journalists prefer creating a sensation to allaying one, and out of Mr. Herbert Gladstone's two negative statements a positive assertion was produced.

Mr. Gladstone's opinion was that in consequence of the demand proclaimed by the electors of Ireland, concession must in some form or another be granted in their favour ; that it was the business of Government to produce a plan—not his ; that if Lord Salisbury were to develop his Irish sympathies—or, to be exact, those of his colleagues—then as Liberal leader he ought not to withhold his assistance " with reserve of necessary freedom."[1] Writing to Lord Hartington on January 18, 1886, he confessed that his first motive in becoming a candidate again at the general election had been " a hope that I might be able to contribute towards some pacific settlement of the Irish question." He had made overtures to Mr. Balfour in this sense when they met in a country house.[2] Without disputing the sincerity of these professions one may be permitted to doubt whether Mr. Gladstone was by habit or nature capable of meekly helping his opponents to carry through a constitutional revolution. But his powers of self-suppression were not to be so severely tried. Sir William Harcourt, with less gravity, proposed to watch the Tory party " stewing in their Parnellite juice "[3] ; but the Tory Government had already found their new regime little suited to the public appetite. A policy

[1] " Life of Gladstone," by John Morley, iii. 259.   [2] *Ibid.*
[3] Lowestoft, December 1885.

of resolute Government was adopted; Lord Carnarvon resigned; and before Mr. Smith, the new Chief Secretary, could set to work, Mr. Gladstone gave the signal, and the Government fell. He had been unwilling to wound until he knew their intentions with regard to Ireland; as soon as he discovered that these were entirely opposed to his views, he was not afraid to strike, and the English peasant was made the stalking horse for his Irish brother.

Mr. Gladstone's position was at least intelligible. The Irish Liberal had finally vanished: not one had been returned. There were the Unionists, mustering less than a score.[1] The remainder of the Irish representatives formed a solid body of Home Rulers led by Mr. Parnell. Mr. Gladstone could no longer disregard the overwhelming preponderance of feeling in favour of Home Rule, and he boldly decided to yield. The defections from his party were of first-rate importance, but the majority remained loyal. It would no doubt have been easier and wiser for these gentlemen, if they were prepared to accept their leader's policy, to have adopted his reasoning with it; but it became the fashion to profess Home Rule proclivities anterior to Mr. Gladstone's own. And there was some need to account for so sudden and general a change of front; for it may be observed that if the same charge be retorted on the party which in later times associated itself unexpectedly with the cause of Tariff Reform, the cases differ in this: although the movement which began in 1903 caused, in its turn, defection of first-rate importance, yet it was no new thing. Under various names it had been proclaimed by members of

[1], Sixteen Conservatives were returned in Ulster, of whom twelve were Orangemen.

the party in election addresses and at annual conferences for years past. Home Rule, on the other
hand, had never been blessed by individuals, nor
publicly held even as a pious opinion. It was accepted by the Liberal party because, in Mr. Gladstone's
judgment, it had become a matter of justice and
necessity.

For once Ireland seemed to be in luck. She had
secured an army; she was not without a man competent to lead; she had captured the one Englishman
with whom it could conceivably lie to persuade the
electors of England. Two defects in this equipment
should be noted. Mr. Parnell was a man of rare
power, an assured leader; but he was destined more
than any other man to bring the cause into disrepute.
His followers were resolute, and, at first, homo-
geneous; but they never carried irresistible weight.
So long-experienced a judge as Lord St. Aldwyn has
declared that the followers of Mr. Parnell were never
to be compared in point of ability with those who
sat round Isaac Butt. Incidentally it may be noted
that another, whom circumstances compel to be almost
as practised an observer as the Speaker himself, has
remarked that amongst eighty men, who are supposed
to represent the true Irish spirit, there has been a
conspicuous and constant absence of humour.

Amongst other forces militating against the achievement of Nationalist aspiration none was to be found
more ardent and persistent than the subject of this
memoir.

Saunderson was at first lured by an echo from the
general election. A defeated Nationalist candidate
brought him a story of political corruption on the
part of Parnell which was to ensure to the Irish
leader six months' imprisonment and inability to sit

in the House of Commons for seven years. This revelation was accompanied by the brandishing of a revolver and many threats of vengeance. " If the case goes on, it may have the effect of toppling Parnell off his plank. I feel confident we shall ultimately succeed in doing so." It is to be hoped that this confidence was placed in other methods: of the more sinister process we hear no more.

Saunderson was not at once given a formal status as leader of the party, but he appears to have assumed the position, unchallenged. Of an early meeting he writes: " I moved that Ballykilbeg[1] do take the chair in order to show that I had no personal motive in the matter." Of another:

" I intend proposing Arthur Hill,[2] if he is present, and if not, some one else as our chairman for the day. My object is to show that there is no intention on my part to usurp an authority which in the end will belong by unquestioned right to the best and wisest, whoever he may prove to be."

A little later he speaks of himself as " virtual leader of the party."[3]

However, he meant to take the substance, even if he neglected the form. He writes anxiously of the need of removing jealousies and securing harmony. "——— did not attend our meeting though he was in the

---

[1] Mr. William Johnson, of Ballykilbeg, M.P. for South Belfast.

[2] Lord Arthur Hill, M.P. for West Down.

[3] At a meeting of Grand Orange Lodge of Ireland, held in December, 1885, a resolution was passed empowering the Grand Secretary (Mr. Macartney, M.P.) to summon a meeting of all the Conservative members for Ulster at the opening of Parliament. This meeting was held on January 21, 1886, and Saunderson was voted into the chair. He was not an Orangeman of long standing; but he was a landlord, he had parliamentary experience, and he was an admired speaker. It was not until 1887 that the organisation was extended so as to include, besides the few Liberal Unionist members from Ireland, the Irish Unionists representing English constituencies.

House, so I shall . . . administer a dose of ginger to that gentleman if he does not fall into line." Some Irish Unionists, sitting for English constituencies, had designed a scheme for organising an Irish party which was to include all English sympathisers. " I pointed out that this was impossible. . . . Great rage has been the result. . . . I feel that the Ulster men must stick together ; otherwise we shall be lost in the vortex. Macartney [1] and Waring [2] are my chief allies."

On January 19 he took a prominent part at the Foreign Office, where Lord Salisbury received a number of deputations from Ireland urging the Prime Minister to accompany any acts for improving the condition of Ireland with an act that " will render it impossible for any organisation to start up and be a curse to our country under any *alias* or under any form resembling in any way the National League." Two days later he spoke for the first time in the House of Commons in the debate on the Address :

"I did not intend to speak," he writes, " so I made no preparations. I was in the smoking-room . . . when in rushed Macartney to say that Parnell was up. When I came in Parnell was orating about landlords and said nothing about Home Rule, so it was thought best that I should answer him, as leader of the party. So up I got on the spur of the moment. . . . I rather think I gave them toko. I made the House roar and the heathens rage. . . . I was much congratulated, and I think I have secured the ear of the House."

It was a spirited effort. He attempted no reasoned argument against Home Rule. He ranged at will through the catalogue of charges which he had to bring against the Irish party; he touched airily on the case of interference in an election by Mr. Parnell,

[1] M.P. for South Antrim, now Deputy Master of the Royal Mint.
[2] M.P. for North Down.

which has already been recorded, and which Mr.
Parnell promptly disavowed; he brought up two of
his opponents with appeals to order, but escaped with
a gentle warning from the Speaker; he undoubtedly
pleased his friends and angered his antagonists.

"I am still receiving congratulations from both
sides of the House," he writes next day. "The fact
is the House delights in laughing, and I made them
roar . . . when I said that the Parnellites resembled
rows of political bagpipes with hats on which squeak
only when squeezed by the member for Cork."

One London paper observed that "the Loyalists
of Ireland have at last found a capable exponent of
their views in Major Saunderson, M.P., who is certainly
the best speaker on that side that has been heard for
many years." Another journal, after pointing out
how ineffectual had been all previous efforts of Ulster
Unionists, went on to say, "Now things are entirely
changed. . . . A succession of such speeches as Major
Saunderson's will soon put a very different aspect on
affairs."

Nor was he disposed to confine his energies to what
is called "the floor of the house." He avows a determination "to deal directly with Government."

Thus he writes from the Carlton Club:

"I have just had a talk with Randolph Churchill.
From what he says, the Government are going to
act in a straightforward way, so we may expect the
National League to be put down before long. I had
a long talk with Ashbourne[1] and told him plump
that unless this course were absolutely adopted we
should be forced to oppose the Irish policy of the
Government. His answer was, 'Don't be in a hurry,
my dear fellow: there are two Cabinet Councils before
next Thursday. . . .' Randolph went and lay down,
so I took the occasion to draw him asleep (picture)."

[1] Lord Chancellor of Ireland.

A little later :

" I have just had a long interview with Sir M. Hicks Beach,[1] and pointed out to him clearly the course I should feel bound to adopt in case the Government did not give us some definite assurance that they intended to act with vigour and promptitude."

Randolph Churchill asleep in the Carlton Jan 17 1886

"RANDOLPH WENT AND LAY DOWN."

Apparently this appeal was not in vain, and the intention to resort to resolute government was confided ; for he adds :

" The Press are bothering me for information. I am in possession of [some] . . . which would astonish the world."[2]

[1] Chancellor of the Exchequer and Leader of the House of Commons.
[2] On the day of their defeat the Conservative Government announced their intention of suppressing the National League.

But he was not impatient to give a *quid pro quo*. Three days later he writes :

" Just back from a critical division : the Conservative party was nearly smashed. In the middle of the debate Hicks-Beach sent for me, so I went and found him and Randolph Churchill in a state of trepidation. He asked me to get my friends to continue the debate so that it might be adjourned. I told him . . . it would never do to make asses of ourselves even to save the Government. . . . We won by twenty-eight."

Yet he remained in favour, for he writes next day :

" Randolph Churchill came to me to-day and placed himself at my disposal for a meeting in Ulster whenever I thought it necessary to hold one."

Then comes a candid confession, written after the fall of Lord Salisbury's Government : [1]

" It seems queer to me to become suddenly a political personage, hob-nobbing with Cabinet Ministers. I don't feel in the least elated, but take it as it comes. I have no doubt that it was owing to the determined stand I made with Hicks-Beach that the Government decided to proclaim the League."

There is much in all this which throws light upon Saunderson's character. The tone is masterful ; he assumes leadership as his right. In the final sentence he even claims to have controlled the policy of the Government. Such an attitude of mind deserves examination.

It is fair to contend that no man inspired by so thorough and sincere a spirit of Christian faith can have been wholly lacking in the principle of humility. Ambitious, in the selfish sense of the word, he was not : we have seen how little his success in 1870 stirred his personal aspirations. Vain he was not,

---

[1] January 26, 1886, *v. s.*, p. 88.

because he never appeared to care what other people thought of him. A single instance comes to mind: he once said of a member of the Government, " He does not like a bone of my body "—an unfounded allegation, to be sure, and a very rare, if not unique confession that he noticed or imagined coldness or neglect. He was not conceited in a commonplace way; to appreciate his character one must understand his entire self-confidence.

Physically courageous, he was never afraid of riding over a stiff country, or of risking his neck in turning somersaults over chairs in a smoking-room ; morally intrepid he was equally ready to signalise his reappearance in the House of Commons by replying impromptu to Parnell or to assert his independence with Cabinet Ministers.[1]

He sincerely believed that in every act he was guided and upheld by Divine assistance ; and whatever his hand found to do, he did it with the conviction of right and power. He liked, as we have seen, to hear his speeches praised, but without morbid craving for admiration. He was satisfied that they were good. So certain was he of the strength and justice of his cause that he scarcely doubted his own connection with the decisions arrived at by the Cabinet.[2]

" For years past," he once said in a speech at Lurgan, " I have felt that we wanted in the House of Commons men who would be able to state the cause of the Loyalists of Ireland in clear, plain, unmistakable language ; and although I did not believe that I was possessed of any exceptional talents, yet I did believe and felt convinced that Providence had given me the power to state a plain case before any assembly in the world fearlessly."

[1] *Vide supra*, p. 94, etc.   [2] *Vide supra*, p. 96.

And at Belfast : .

" I determined that if ever I should have the honour of finding myself in the House of Commons I should, without any hesitation, get up in my place and confront Mr. Gladstone."

On subsequent occasions he repeated that he had been induced to go back to Parliament by the lack of debating power apparent amongst the Irish Loyalists, and by his conviction that he could supply the deficiency.

A word must be added concerning the character of his speeches, although this must be more fully dealt with hereafter. In Parliament, still more upon the platform, whatever he said is reported with punctuations of "laughter," "loud laughter," or "roars of laughter." It must be confessed that in cold print the provocation is not always manifest, and a fastidious critic might sometimes deny a high standard of wit or humour; but here comes in the personal element. To illustrate this application the following instance will suffice : One morning on Lough Erne a guest at Castle Saunderson related how the Colonel had told an extraordinarily funny story, which he proceeded to repeat. Nobody smiled. " Now that I tell it," he confessed, " it doesn't sound a bit amusing ; but you get the Colonel to tell it." This was done : the story was narrated almost in the same words, and every one who heard it shouted with laughter.

Consummate assurance, then, and a lively and forcible eloquence were two of the new leader's most valuable assets. He believed himself to be the right man in the right place, and it was not his nature to affect a diffidence which he did not feel.

On February 1, 1886, Mr. Gladstone became Prime Minister. On April 8 he introduced his Irish measures.[1]   On June 8 the Home Rule Bill was thrown out by a majority of thirty in a full House, and the Government went to the country on a clear issue. They had to contend with insuperable disadvantages. Lord Hartington carried his great influence into opposition, and with it went the lofty character of Lord Selborne, the historic traditions of Lord Derby, the acute intellect of Sir Henry James.   From the Radical wing there passed away a powerful democratic element fortified by the growing authority of Mr. Chamberlain.   Nor were these wrecking secessions the limit of their difficulties.   A friendly biographer records that—

"a remorseless criticism in Parliament detected in both measures an abundance of faults which could not be denied even by those who believed their general principles to be sound.   Mr. Gladstone's best friends urged him either to accept such modifications as should disarm his critics, or to withdraw his Bills and substitute for them a Resolution affirming the principles of Irish autonomy."[2]

The British public are fond of strong emotions in single doses: for the moment their attention was concentrated to the pitch of enthusiasm on the question of Home Rule.   Saunderson's party of sixteen, if not "lost in the vortex," were surrounded by it: he had added his full share to the flood of oratory both in and out of Parliament.   On February 22 Lord Randolph Churchill fulfilled his promise to speak in Ulster.   "A most splendid success," writes Saunderson from Belfast.   "Nothing could beat it.   Lovely weather; the whole town on foot."

[1] The Home Rule Bill was accompanied by a proposal for buying out Irish landlords.
[2] "William Ewart Gladstone," by G. W. E. Russell, p. 256.

On February 19 he had spoken in the House of Commons on the abstract merits of Home Rule, declaring that the first intimation of Mr. Gladstone's intentions had had the effect of sending down the shares of the Bank of Ireland 45 per cent. The true motive of the Nationalist party was—" to demoralise the people by teaching them to make the property of their neighbours the object of their covetous desire" under the pretence of securing justice and benefit " for all honest men. (Parnellite cries of 'Shame.') That did not apply to honourable members below the gangway. (Much laughter)." It is hardly necessary to add that his speeches in Parliament from this time forward present a uniform series of scenes of interruption and protest. So on May 26, after observing that Sir Thomas Esmonde, a baronet and a landlord, had been condemned as unfit to be a member of the party " until he proved to demonstration that a relative of his was hung in 1798," he went on to declare that the House was being influenced by "eighty-five members subsidised by America." Mr. O'Brien jumped up and accused him of stating what he knew to be false. Lord Randolph Churchill, from the front Opposition bench, insisted on an apology for this accusation, and a spirited altercation followed. The Speaker rebuked Mr. O'Brien, but was obliged to add that the remarks of the honourable and gallant member were of a very irritating nature.

One critic at this time wrote : " The hon. and gallant member never argues or debates. His speeches are a succession of jokes or quotations, and his extracts are so happily selected that they have all the charm of original humour." Part of this Saunderson would not have denied. More than once he told his audience that he had been accused of depending entirely upon notes.   He carried many notes, he confessed, but they were not his own ideas; they were " elegant extracts " from speeches made by his opponents, which were the best justification of his own case.

It was at this time that a story went about to the effect that a Nationalist member had said to Saunderson that they really admired him, and that if he would join their party they would give him a high place.   " Yes," said Saunderson, " with a nine-foot drop underneath."   Some years later another Home Ruler expressed surprise at Saunderson's pre-judice: separate government would afford many chances of a distinguished career, and he was sure to come to the top of the tree.   " Yes: hauled up with a rope round my neck."

At St. James's Hall and elsewhere, he continued to proclaim that Irish Loyalists were ready and determined to resist the infliction of₁ a Nationalist Government by force of arms.   Presently Mr. Parnell taxed him with having said that the contest would be decided " by the bullet and not by the ballot," upon which Saunderson adroitly retorted that the Orangemen had been given to understand that if they did not submit to the new condition of things, they would be shot down.   Another allusion to the busy time coming for gunmakers he had to explain as a proposition that any community must have re-course to arms if they are left to the mercy of tyranny and lawlessness.   But his appeal to arms had been specific, and amongst his papers are price-lists sent by foreign firms, desirous of furnishing the Orange army with rifles.

" Toby M.P." interviewed the terrible Major: inci-dentally he reports him as saying, " Bedad, then I'm as hungry as Jonah before he swallowed the whale ";

which is undesignedly apposite, because Saunderson's favourite quotation from Dickens was Mrs. Gamp's apostrophe to "the Ankworks package"—"I wish it was in Jonadge's belly, I do!" which he used to declare was the drollest conception that ever entered into the mind of man.

Punch, of course, invents this saying as a typical Irish perversion. Did Saunderson make "bulls"? It is on record that during a debate about Eastern Roumelia, he declared "she was man enough to ——" and finished the interrupted sentence by admitting, "Sir, I can't help showing my nationality." He once wrote to the editor of a paper thus :

"Sir, I am made to say by a waggish reporter in a recent speech, that Mr. Dillon fired barbed arrows at Colonel Caddel in order that some of the mud might stick. What I said was that Mr. Dillon fired barbed arrows at a man who was not there to defend himself" (which by the way is not a bad specimen as it stands), "on the principle that if plenty of mud is thrown, some of it may stick. This is not nearly so funny as the words placed in my mouth, but the fact is I do not like adopting a bull from another herd into my own. I believe most Irish speakers in due time are pretty sure to own a certain number of these oratorical animals, and I have, I imagine, a fair share of them ; but this one is not mine. . . . I am not in the least ashamed of the bulls I have to own, but I will not have this one, as I do not want to mix the breed."

In April came a notable token of popularity. "The children will be greatly amused," he writes, "to hear that I am being put into Madame Tussaud's waxworks." His work was disturbed by the death of a sister. He pays a short visit to Boulogne, at Easter, where he dines with Lord Ashbourne, and meets Lord Halsbury and Sir Michael Hicks-Beach, again "hobnobbing with Cabinet Ministers" of the past and future.   Early in May he is back in Dublin for a mass meeting in the Rotunda.

In June he was plunged deep in the stream of elections.   His own seat was safe : a Nationalist opposed him, and was defeated by nearly 3,000 votes; but the contest was no empty formality.   " Those beastly Parnellites are determined to put me to the trouble of a contest," he writes; " of course the expense is a bore, but otherwise I am glad."

One afternoon his supporters proceeded to drag him round Portadown in a " huge brake," until they came upon a meeting of his opponents.   This is what followed :

" A line of police separated us from them, so all our people could do was to vent their rage in yells of an awful description.   Some, however, found out a way of turning the police, and gained a point of vantage whence they could shell the rebel meeting with stones. This they did.   The police charged, but our people drove them back with great slaughter.   Military were telegraphed for to Armagh. . . . I am nearly dead with work : I am just off to hold five meetings running . . . on Thursday, 8.   I expect I shall be altogether pumped out."

It is the usual practice to find an opponent for a man in Saunderson's position, in order to pin him down and prevent him from assisting his neighbours. To this extent he was kept at home, but his influence was not to be exclusively restricted.

Outside his own constituency, his energy was principally devoted to Belfast.   The member for one of the divisions was said to be anxious to retire, and Saunderson desired to replace him by nominating his cousin and close friend, Somerset Maxwell (afterwards tenth Lord Farnham).[1]   Pressure was, however, brought

---

[1] Nephew of " Uncle Som "; *vide supra.*

to bear upon the sitting member to remain, and an appeal on his behalf was said to have been addressed direct to the Prime Minister, who caused a message to be conveyed deprecating disunion. Saunderson, however, brought out his man, and exciting days followed. " There is to be a presentation of a requisition to Sommy on Monday in the Shankhill Road, the scene of the riot. It will probably be a warm affair." He was not mistaken. There had been frequent tumults in Belfast, and on a recent occasion the police had exchanged shots with the mob. Saunderson and his friend, after being chaired at their meeting, were stoned on their return. " When we came through the Papist district stones began to be thrown, one by one they whizzed past my ear." He was satisfied that his action tended to add strength to his parliamentary force, but he decided to refer the matter for advice to Lord Randolph Churchill, from whom he received the following letter :

"CARLTON CLUB, *June* 28, 1886.

" MY DEAR SAUNDERSON,
"I have most carefully considered the subject of your letter. I quite admit that I noticed with concern the parliamentary inefficiency of the Ulster party, and I quite share and sympathise with your desire to lose no opportunity of remedying that defect. At the same time, improvements may be attained at far too high a price, and any action which could by any possibility imperil a Unionist seat and produce the smallest appearance of disunion among the Unionists would be fatal. The issue is too great to be trifled with nor should ulterior considerations of future parliamentary action be at all taken into account now. A disaster in Belfast would be terrific, and would be a sorry reward to English politicians who at some risk of misconstruction have identified themselves with Ulster. I therefore on the whole implore you to restrain Somerset Maxwell for the moment, and not

to allow yourself to be led into action the consequences of which you might most bitterly regret.

" Yours ever,

" RANDOLPH S. C."

Saunderson was not obstinate : he advised his friend to withdraw. Whatever may have been his private vexation, he must have found comfort in the situation at large. As a result of the general election there were returned 280 members pledged to Home Rule, 390 pledged to resist it, giving an ample majority of 110.

Lord Salisbury resumed office, and the second phase of the controversy began.

CHAPTER VIII

1886—1887

EARLY in August Saunderson was in France and went to see his second son:

"I arrived at Versailles and had then to walk miles to Bouffement. On arriving there I found that the abbé and Eddy were breakfasting at Mons. Something or other 2¾ miles further on, so on I tramped in a blazing sun. There I found my gentlemen just finished *déjeuner*. . . . Walking back, we met the Marquise de —— to whom he (the abbé) introduced me, saying at the same time, 'I hope you will give us dinner to-night,' so you may imagine my feelings. However, he is lord of all he surveys, and the marquise invited me at once, and told the abbé to call at the château and order dinner, which he did to some purpose, for it turned out a very good one. . . . I rather think she found me captivating, as she approaches the age at which my charms never fail to attract: she is over 60."

After this he betook himself to yacht-racing at home, until the meeting of Parliament on August 19. The distribution of parties was novel: the Liberal Unionist members elected to remain amongst their old friends on the Opposition side of the House, thus presenting the embarrassing necessity for gentlemen in friendly communion to rise and dissent emphatically from another upon the topic of first importance. Lord Randolph Churchill was Chancellor of the Exchequer and leader of the House; the Irish Office was represented by Sir Michael Hicks-Beach, and to

Irish affairs attention was speedily directed. At the
outset the Nationalists and Opposition made great
play with the appointment of Sir Redvers Buller
as Under-Secretary at the Castle. Lord Randolph
Churchill had announced that the General had been
invested with such powers as would enable him to
bring the reign of terror to an end. In the intervals
between protests against this unconstitutional proceeding, there were angry denunciations of the official
support given to the arbitrary treatment of the tenants
on Lord Clanricarde's estate, where evictions were
being effected to an accompaniment of bayonets and
boiling water.

Upon the Address Mr. Parnell moved an amendment ; Mr. Gladstone and Lord Hartington defended
the action of their respective parties, and on August 25
the Ulster leader has to announce his contribution :

"I have made a speech. I had no idea, when I went
down to the House, that I was in for such a shindy. . . .
When it was heard that I was to come on, the House
filled up, the Home Rule benches crowded, and I had
not got far before I had the nest of hornets in full
buzz. I have been much complimented, so I suppose
it was a success. The 'throttle-valve of crime' is likely
to become, I hope, an historic phrase."

No wonder there was a "shindy." He began by
attacking Mr. Harris for a recent speech. Mr. Harris,
entering the House, requested the speaker to repeat
a passage to which, he understood, special reference
had been made. The report proceeds :

"Major[1] Saunderson : With the greatest possible
pleasure. [The hon. and gallant member again read
the extract.]
"Mr. Harris : Will the hon. and gallant gentleman
read what I said before the quotation ?

[1] He had recently become Colonel : *v.s.*, p. 62, note.

"Major Saunderson : This is the only part of the speech that is worth repeating. (Loud laughter.)"

Mr. Harris then made a personal explanation which only made matters worse. Thus :

"Major Saunderson : The hon. member has not denied the accuracy of the quotation. As far as I can understand, he now informs the House of an interesting fact of which I was not aware before—namely, that he belongs to the Ribbon organisation. (Much laughter.)
"Mr. Dillon : I rise to order. I wish to know whether any member of this House is entitled to accuse another member of belonging to the Ribbon organisation. . . .
"Mr. Harris : I repudiate it as being a most infamous falsehood. (Loud cries of ' Order.')
"Major Saunderson : The hon. member himself speaks of having been to Ribbon lodges.
"Mr. Biggar : I rise to order. The hon. and gallant gentleman stated——
"Major Saunderson : I never made a charge. . . . If I stated, and I am not ashamed to state, that I occasionally visit Orange lodges, the inference would naturally be that I was an Orangeman."

Having got through this storm he went on to observe that "all trades, occupations, and professions in Ireland were unfortunately in a more or less depressed condition except one, and that was the occupation of professional politicians" : yet he declared "the tenants had less cause for complaint than others, inasmuch as prices had advanced in recent years . . . butter from 65s. to 95s. (' No,' and cries of ' Where ?') At Cork, which was celebrated for two marketable commodities—butter and Home Rule Amendments." Then, turning to the member for Cork, he reminded the House that Mr. Parnell had, in moving his amendment—

"informed them that there would be crime and outrage in Ireland in the coming winter. Honourable members

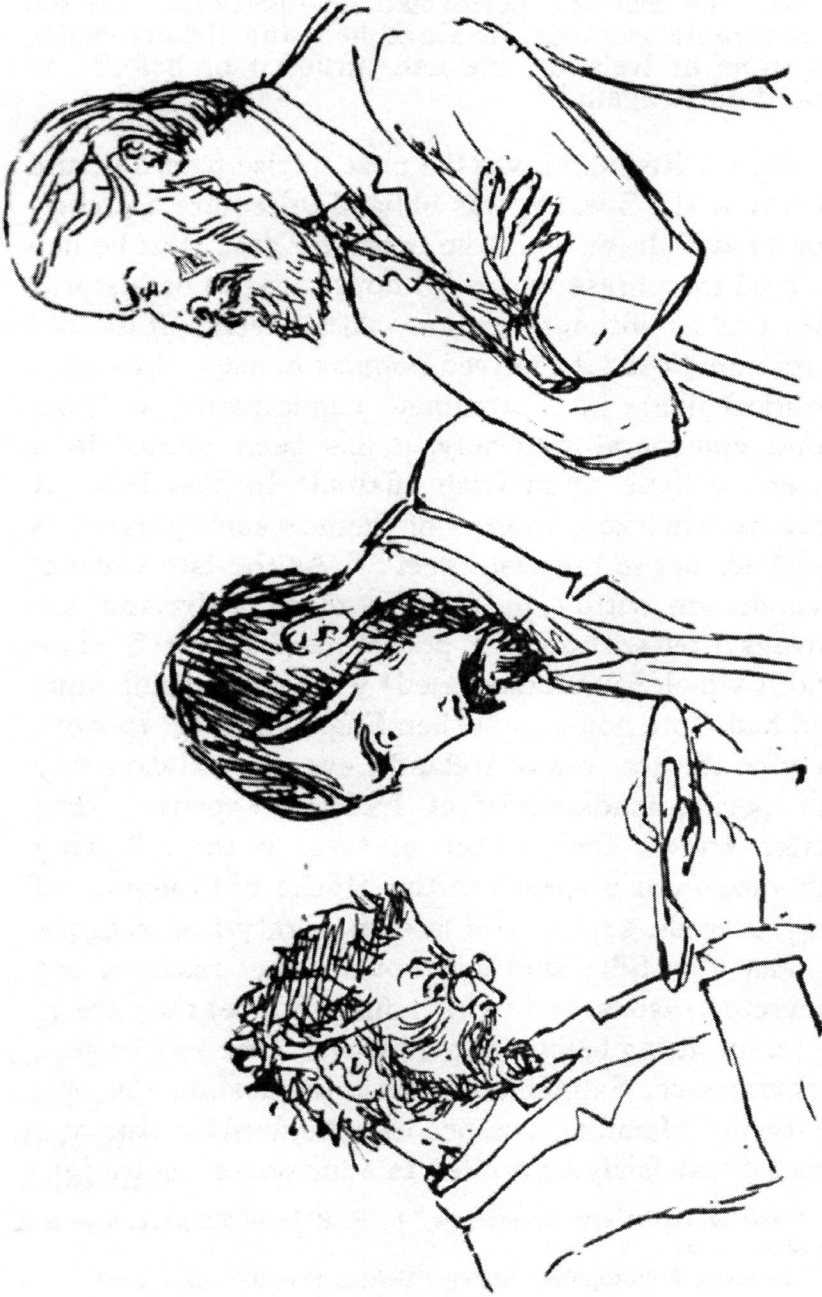

THREE "REASONS AGAINST THE BILL": MR. W. O'BRIEN, MR. DILLON, MR. PARNELL.

might sometimes have seen an engine-driver with the throttle-valve in his hand, which he could turn at will and admit the steam or shut it off. If he admitted the steam the machine performed its functions. So the honourable member for Cork held the throttle-valve of crime in Ireland. He had turned it on before : he could do so again."

Mr. W. Redmond was the next to rise to order, and this time the Speaker was obliged to require Saunderson to withdraw, which he promptly did. But he had uttered the phrase which he hoped was to be historic. Nor was he without warrant. At all events, it did not pass unnoticed : it received popular homage through a political jingle in a prominent comic paper, and, beyond ephemeral notoriety, it has been quoted in a recent volume upon Irish affairs.[1] In this book, it may be remarked, another of Saunderson's phrases is recalled, not to the best effect : " As the late Colonel Saunderson wittily put it, the tears of Ireland are always dried with an Irish pocket-handkerchief."[2] The words which Saunderson used[3] were more picturesque and had more point : " When Englishmen set to work to wipe the tear out of Ireland's eye, they always buy the pocket-handkerchief at Ireland's expense." But better known than either of these is the following sentence from a speech in the House of Commons of May preceding : " I will assign eighty-five reasons against the Bill : they are not abstract reasons, but concrete reasons, and (with a fine gesture) they are to be found sitting below the gangway." One may be sure that whenever Saunderson's wit is in question, this will be the most familiar instance. And indeed for dramatic effect it may fairly be ranked as a fortunate inspiration.

[1] " Ireland To-day and To-morrow," by E. B. Iwan Müller, p. 8.
[2] *Ibid.*, p. 123.
[3] University Philosophical Society : Dublin, Nov. 28, 1884.

To return to the throttle-valve. He had not forgotten
it nine years later, when he said in the House of
Commons :[1]

"He remembered well that some years ago . . .
he pointed out in the presence of the late Mr.
Parnell, that that gentleman had his hand on the
throttle-valve of crime. He did not know who had
their hands on it now.
"Mr. W. Redmond : You withdrew that statement
immediately afterwards by order of the Speaker.
"Colonel Saunderson : I did not withdraw it. I
never withdraw anything. (Laughter.)"

If the laugh was with the Colonel, it must be admitted that his opponent was in the right.

The reception accorded to his speech was an
additional cause of satisfaction to the Colonel. On
August 28 he writes :

"You will be glad to hear my speech has made a
very great impression. There were leading articles
in most of the papers on it both in London and in
the provinces. The answer of Sexton yesterday was
very weak. I wish you and Rosa[2] had been in the
House ; no one ever saw such a scene. We shall
have a fine debate on the Belfast riots."

The subject of the Belfast riots was introduced by
Mr. Sexton's amendment on September 1. Following
this, Mr. Labouchere moved a further amendment to
the effect that the riots were due to the language
which had been used by the Chancellor of the Exchequer in Belfast. Saunderson desired to bring out
in the debate the connection between the Irish Nationalists and American Fenians. At the first attempt he
got little way beyond observing that "successive
Governments had tried to settle the Irish question,
but the Irish question had settled successive Govern-

[1] April 5, 1895.   [2] His daughter, Mrs. Head.

ments," when the Speaker ruled him out of order, and he sat down—some hostile critics said he collapsed. It was alleged at the time that this abrupt termination was due not only to the Speaker's ruling, but further to a curt message from Lord Randolph to "shut up." Saunderson was not likely to be deterred from a course on which his mind was set by such treatment as this. It has further been insinuated that he was compelled to persevere because what he intended to say had already been telegraphed to New York. It remains that his speech of September 2 was not a success, possibly because he decided not to waste good material, and that next day he boldly moved an amendment of his own to that of Mr. Labouchere. Meanwhile some kind of negotiations had been in progress between the Government and Parnell. This insistence was therefore most inopportune and, as one paper reported, "put a complete spoke in the policy of conciliation." Saunderson's amendment was negatived without a division ; but he achieved the delivery of his speech. The following letters tell the story. It will be observed that he says nothing of his first attempt.

"*September* 1st.—Sexton made his attack on the Orangemen and rioters to-day. It was for the most part the speech he had prepared for last session, so that if he had not succeeded in getting delivered he would probably have burst. I am to speak to-morrow. . . . I am going to ask whether Parnell & Co. deny any connection with the Fenian conspiracy, and if so, why they have not contradicted a report which, if true, should consign them to penal servitude. In the morning I am to be interviewed, and what I say is to be cabled over to New York, so you may imagine how the heathen will rage.

"*2nd.*—In an hour's time, God willing, I shall be engaged in making what will undoubtedly be the most desperate speech I have ever attempted. I had my interview with the American papers . . . it has been wired across the Atlantic. . . .

" I feel confident God is with me, and that He will give me the stone of David which will bring the giant crashing to the ground.

" *4th.*—Fighting Parnell at 80° in the shade is no joke. In the opinion of the House I scored off my enemies last night. . . . I caused undoubtedly considerable confusion in (their) ranks. . . . The night before R. Churchill advised me to bring the question on in the shape of an amendment to the Address, so I determined to do so. At the last moment Churchill asked me to put it off as a personal favour to himself. This was because Parnell showed signs of relenting in his threatened obstruction. I resisted all entreaties, so my lord got into a rage. However, I can't help that : I must fight the battle as leader of the Irish Loyalists in the best way I can.

" I think my speech was considered successful. You ought to have seen Parnell's face when I asked him to disclose which platform he intended to fight on—Westminster or Chicago ? "

Saunderson made occasional excursions to speak in the country : here follows a note upon one of them.

" MELBURY, DORCHESTER,[1] *September* 5.—This is by far the most beautiful place I ever saw. . . . Coming down in the train I met a gentleman who spoke about Irish affairs. Amongst other things he said, ' I hear the leader of the Loyalist party is a tall and very fat man.' I informed him that the gentleman he referred to could not in this manner be accurately described. In the end I told him who I was. . . . He laughed some."

For the rest he remained steadfast in the House of Commons.

" *September* 8.—I want to nail Parnell on to the Chicago Convention and then to try and arouse public attention to his attitude. . . .

" *9th.*—I had a long interview to-day with Hartington at Devonshire House. I succeeded in persuading him

---

[1] Earl of Ilchester's.

to help me in clinching the effect made by my last speech in the House, so I think some of his men will take the matter up.

"10*th.*—I think on the whole affairs are going well. Randolph Churchill is still furious with me, but I don't care, as sooner or later I am bound to come to logger-heads with him, as Ulster interests will probably clash with ministerial tactics. He may cool down. He will if he is wise, as fighting with me can do him no good and may do him harm.

"I have the great majority of the Conservative party entirely with me in the course I have taken ; also, I am sure, the Unionist Liberals. I am confident that the line I am fighting is the winning line and, God willing, I shall fight it out, come what may. I have just told R. Churchill the position I was placed in, but he is still enraged, so he may cool at will.

"17*th.*—We were in the House till 4 this morning. . . We shall probably be up until 5. I feel quite fresh."

On September 20 Parnell moved the second reading of his Tenants' Relief Bill. It was rejected by 297 to 202 votes ; but Saunderson did not speak.

"*September* 20*th.*— Randolph has made it up, so we go on as before. . . . I was to have followed Morley half an hour ago, but Chaplin wanted to go on and I did not wish to stand in his way. I am to try and speak to-night. I say 'try,' because I feel so ill that I don't know how I shall get through. . . . If I am well enough I shall start to-morrow night."

On September 25 Parliament was prorogued.

The conspicuous feature of this short session was of course the new alliance. The word is chosen advisedly. There was at present neither a coalition Government nor a fusion of parties. Lord Beacons-field's assertion that England does not love coalitions was true for its day. It has already been observed that during the middle period of the nineteenth century there was a continual process of setting to partners and taking a turn with the *vis-à-vis* ; but

neither in the case of the Protectionists after 1846, nor
in that of the Peelites after 1850, was there a deep and
permanent cleavage across the dividing line of parties.
No Liberal joined the Conservative Government of 1886;
the Liberal Unionists to this day retain their separate
organisation.   Indeed a formal compact was ratified
between the Whips of the two sections of Unionism
under which all seats then held by Liberal Unionists
were ear-marked for their sphere of operation.   The
bargain has on the whole been faithfully observed and
has worked smoothly.   Now and then a constituency
has suffered from a limited range of selection ; an intrusion has occasionally caused jealousy and friction ;
sometimes the right of nomination has been voluntarily
surrendered, sometimes from necessity.   At the
present moment the safest Conservative seat in England is in the keeping of a Liberal Unionist by deed of
grace.[1]   It may be thought, and it is often urged, that
after twenty years the two parties have become so
closely identified that further discrimination is waste
of energy and money.   Members of Parliament would
be puzzled to say whether this or that colleague was
a member of the Carlton or of Brooks's.

Viewed broadly, the alliance must be pronounced
a success.   It answered its purpose for the moment
and the effect was not ephemeral.   The Opposition
naturally made the most of the delicacy of the situation, and prophesied a speedy disintegration.   What
the contracting parties in their hearts believed as to
its strength and durability no one can say.   Only
Lord Randolph Churchill revealed a cynical spirit.
On October 2 he made one of his most memorable
orations to an open-air assembly at Dartford, in which
he paid a high tribute to the loyalty of his Liberal

[1] St. George's, Hanover Square (Mr. Lyttelton).

Unionist supporters in Parliament. At the annual conference of the National Union of Conservative Associations held at Bradford in November he exulted over the Separatists who had predicted disunion, and urged his audience to reciprocate the attachment of their new friends. It was startling, then, to hear him declare in the House of Commons soon after his resignation that he had only regarded the Liberal Unionist party as a crutch, convenient for temporary use, and destined to be cast aside.[1]

The conspicuous personality of the session was Lord Randolph himself. His rapid advancement had not been watched without suspicion and perhaps jealousy. One member made a private protest on the ground that they had been at Oxford together and that he was not prepared to acknowledge in his familiar companion the qualities of a leader. Some were shocked at his audacity; others doubted his stability. But the best judges of parliamentary capacity seem to have agreed in allowing him ample abilities to justify so dazzling a pre-eminence. In a moment, most dramatically, he fell. The story has been told in all its details by his son. On December 20, 1886, he wrote his ultimatum to Lord Salisbury from Windsor Castle in a spirit, as it seems, of unaccountable levity. To Lord Salisbury's reply, he rejoined with a definite resignation which he forthwith communicated to *The Times*, in violation of all etiquette and complete indifference to its formal acceptance by his sovereign.

One point is worth noting in connection with these letters. In the first he writes:

" I am pledged up to the eyes to large reductions

[1] It is worth noting that a member of Parliament once declared that the Radicals used Lord John Russell as a walking-stick. See *Life of Lord Durham*, by S. J. Reid, ii. 82.

and cannot change my mind.   If the foreign policy of this country is conducted with skill and judgment, our present huge and increasing armaments are quite unnecessary."

Therefore he could not be a party to spending thirty-one millions on the Navy and Army.   Those days seem not far remote, yet a present Chancellor of the Exchequer may well envy one to whom such estimates appeared huge.   If Lord Randolph were alive to write such a letter now he would be denounced as a "Little Englander" of the worst type.

In his second letter he speaks of "the sacrifice of a Chancellor of the Exchequer on the altar of economy." This letter he read subsequently in the House of Commons, and upon the ground of economy alone were based the reasons then given for his resignation.

But on New Year's day 1887, he wrote a letter to the Chief Conservative Whip in which he followed a much broader line.   He has never, he says, taken his eyes off the next general election, and he foresees that the party is about to lose its hold on the country by reason of "a domestic policy which would be marked by stagnation rather than progress."

Mr. Churchill observes that "it is remarkable that this letter has never been published."[1]   I may be permitted to say that as private secretary it was my duty to copy it, under the obligation, of course, of extreme secrecy.   Not to be forgotten was my horror at reading one day on the contents sheet of *The Morning Post*[2] "Lord Randolph Churchill's letter to Mr. Akers-Douglas."   I was innocent; but the purport of his communication became known, although it was not printed *in extenso*.   It seemed "remarkable" to me then, and it surprises me still, that the discrepancy

1 "Life of Lord Randolph Churchill," ii. 265.   2 January 6, 1887.

between these two apologias elicited so little comment.

The motives of Lord Randolph in resigning and the failure of his calculations, if any such he had formed, are no part of our business here. We may be content with the explanations with which he retired.

To Saunderson, his secession was a source of regret. There was little in common to the two men in point of temperament. Saunderson's life was guided by a simplicity and singleness of purpose, and inspired by a stern and conscientious fidelity, which suggests the Covenanter and the Ironside. It would never have occurred to him to belong to a Fourth Party. He pursued one object with unswerving directness. Churchill, on the other hand, made the whole world of politics his province. His political principles were varied and diffuse; he was not afraid of political expedients; his horizon was wider, his goal more remote, his ways of approach more devious and secret than those of the Ulsterman, who cared only to dash at Home Rule and smite it down at a blow whenever it showed its head. This does not mean that he had no other opinions. His Election Address of 1885 has been quoted to show that he was an ardent Fair Trader—the Tariff Reformer of the day. It is true that he had not then arrived at any contemplation of a tax on corn: "you might as well expect cocks and hens to vote the knife to cut their own throats," he declared at Portadown; but he was a convinced opponent of Free Trade as we have it now. His letters frequently reveal a strong interest in Egyptian affairs; and he was imbued with a lofty conception of England's mission; but he carried no stock-in-trade as a party politician. It has been made abundantly clear that he cared very much for the Ulster party and very

little for the official politicians at Westminster:
"Ulster interests will probably clash with ministerial
tactics." His business was to champion a cause, not
to manœuvre for a faction. He welcomed Lord Randolph's assistance in opposing Home Rule; they
could never have been in intimate communion in the
wider schemes of political strategy.

Yet they were drawn together by some personal
affinity. Both were marked out for leadership; confidence and courage were the predominating elements
in both characters; neither heeded the fear of consequences when the purpose was determined; each
recognised and admired a masterful spirit in the other.
It was not to be expected that two such men could
work together without occasional collision when their
objects differed; but Saunderson was at once inclined
to take a favourable view of Lord Randolph's action
and the following letters were exchanged :

"CASTLE SAUNDERSON, BELTURBET, *January* 12, 1887.

"DEAR LORD RANDOLPH,
        "I have been thinking of writing to you for some
days past, but I have hesitated doing so as I feared
you might think it an intrusion on my part. I have
decided on doing so, however, and can only hope you
will take it as it is meant. I have spoken to several
audiences in Ireland and I have always mentioned
your name with the view not only of expressing my
own opinion, but also of testing the feelings of the
Loyalists in this country with respect to the action you
have recently taken and the position you occupy.

"This is what I have found to be the opinion and
the feeling of the party which does me the honour
to look on me as their leader. While deeply regretting
that you will no longer lead us in the Commons, a
position for which we believe you so eminently fitted,
we at the same time absolutely refuse to condemn
your action until you put your case before the country,
believing as we do that a man who has rendered our
cause such signal services in the past, must have some

very cogent reasons for the course he has pursued. Of one thing I can assure you, that under any circumstances we, the Loyalist party in this country, feel that we owe you a debt of gratitude for the staunch support you gave us at a critical period of our history which we can never forget or repay. The position of affairs over here I look on as extremely critical. If the Government prove firm I feel confident the League could be smashed up in a very short time ; but if a policy of drift and vacillation is pursued, which I fear is very possible, we shall go from bad to worse with alarming rapidity. Very bitter feelings are rising up amongst the northern Loyalists owing to the fact that the lawless portion of the community are allowed to have everything their own way. If it should continue to be shown that disloyalty and lawlessness mean amongst other things immunity from paying just debts, I need hardly point out how popular disloyalty and lawlessness are likely to become.

"Ever yours truly,
"EDWARD SAUNDERSON."

"2, CONNAUGHT PLACE, W., *January* 14, 1887.

"MY DEAR MAJOR[1] SAUNDERSON,

"I am very grateful to you for your kind and encouraging letter. You are perfectly right in assuming that my attachment to the Union and to the loyalists of Ulster and of Ireland has undergone no diminution. But we must strive to identify the cause of the Union in the minds of the English people with creditable government, with a practicable and honest application of Peace, Retrenchment, and Reform.

"If we fail in doing this, the Repealers will certainly be placed in power at the next general election. Although on good and solid grounds you have adhered to the Tories, I feel sure that all your sound Liberal principles influence you as strongly as ever and that you will not disagree with the views I have expressed above. Ireland is certainly in an anxious state. The one encouraging fact appears to be that there is no increase of crime or outrage.

"Yours very truly,
"RANDOLPH S. CHURCHILL."

[1] He was Colonel. *Vide supra*, p. 62, note.

Saunderson was justified in describing the state of affairs as critical. Upon the prorogation of Parliament in September, 1886, Parnell had written a manifesto to the National League of America declaring that the English Government and the Irish landlords had begun a combined movement to exterminate the Irish tenant farmer. What the landlords were to gain from so suicidal a policy was left to surmise; but a violent agitation was foreshadowed, which speedily took concrete form in the " Plan of Campaign." The Nationalists proposed to intercept all rents. Tenants were to take three pledges: 1. To abide by the decision of the majority. 2. To hold no communication with the landlord or any of his agents except in the presence of the body of the tenantry. 3. To accept no settlement for himself which was not given to every tenant on the estate. If the landlord should refuse what the tenant chose to offer, that amount was to be handed over to the local committee to be at their absolute disposal for " fighting purposes."

On November 26 Mr. Dillon put this proposal into action by receiving the rents of Lord Dillon's tenants less 25 per cent.—the discount which they had demanded and which the agent was not authorised to concede. Similar cases followed. Meetings were proclaimed, some arrests were made, yet inflammatory speeches were defiantly delivered. Strife and bitterness were rampant throughout agrarian Ireland, whilst from Belfast came the echo of the riots in the proceedings of the Commission of Inquiry which revealed a passionate antagonism between Protestants and Catholics. In December the " Plan " was declared illegal and was duly proclaimed. Proceedings for conspiracy were taken against Messrs. Dillon, O'Brien,

Redmond, and others.[1] Still the agitators prevailed, and Saunderson did not greatly exaggerate when he said that the lawless portion of the community were allowed to have everything their own way.

Whilst the Home Rulers were making play so boldly in Ireland, the Unionist cause was to pass through a crisis of another kind. Before Parliament met again, there assembled what was known as the Round Table Conference. The two wings of the Liberal party had not yet separated so distinctly as to be without hope and desire for reunion. It was therefore arranged that Sir William Harcourt, Mr. Morley and Lord Herschell, on the one side, and Mr. Chamberlain with Sir George Trevelyan on the other, should meet and inquire whether terms of agreement could be found. It was a moment of vital importance. Had the Liberal Unionists as a body been reconciled to their former allegiance, not only the issue of Home Rule, but the entire political future would have been affected. The Unionist party as we have known it during the last twenty years would have borne a very different character, bereft of some of its most valuable assets. Those who cared greatly for these things endured anxious days. But they were spared. The negotiations proved futile; Sir George Trevelyan indeed retraced his steps later on; but Mr. Chamberlain went upon his way; such waverers as there may have been resolutely turned their faces with him, and the new connection was confirmed.[2]

[1] The jury disagreed and the case was dismissed.
[2] It will be remembered that Saunderson had, from the beginning, aimed at effecting a combination in the House of Commons, unrestricted by the usual party limits, for the preservation of the Union and for "the good of Irish loyalty." See p. 80.

CHAPTER IX

1887

PARLIAMENT reassembled on January 29, 1887. There were two important changes in the composition of the Cabinet: Mr. W. H. Smith had taken the place of Lord Randolph Churchill as leader of the House, contenting himself with the comparative sinecure of first lord of the Treasury; Lord Salisbury having left this for the Foreign Office, upon the sudden death of Lord Iddesleigh.[1] The Exchequer was therefore vacant, and to this office was appointed a Liberal Unionist, Mr. Goschen.

It is a matter of common agreement, if not common knowledge, that Lord Randolph had believed that he was inevitable; that the party could not go on without him; that his personal following would ensure the acceptance of his conditions and the triumph of his purposes. He did not lack devoted adherents, but he inspired no general revolt.

The process of dropping the pilot, which afterwards, in connection with another country, was rendered famous by a cartoon in *Punch*, was here reversed: the young and masterful spirit succumbed, and the trusted pilot was left in undisputed control. One of those unstudied phrases, which often fix attention more surely than an elaborate epigram, illuminated the situation: Lord Randolph, when he cheerfully

[1] January 12, 1887. It was known that Lord Iddesleigh was to be transferred to another department.

indited his Windsor letter, "forgot Goschen"; it turned out that he was not indispensable: the Tory Democrat had slain his own career, and given birth to Conservative Whiggism.   Mr. Goschen was without a seat in Parliament.   He contested a vacancy in Liverpool and was defeated by seven votes.   The offer of a peerage failed to lure one old Tory from a safe seat; ultimately Lord Algernon Percy retired from St. George's, Hanover Square.   The letter of the compact was thereby broken, but the new Chancellor of the Exchequer was returned with a comfortable majority of 4,157.

If Lord Hartington had been prepared to enter the Unionist Cabinet at this juncture it is conceivable that the Liberal element would have had even greater pre-eminence than was subsequently the case.   Whilst approving of Mr. Goschen's action, however, he preferred to remain outside, and when he and his friends joined in 1895 it was obvious that the Conservatives were entitled by seniority and service to regard themselves as the predominant partners; so that there has not yet been a Liberal Unionist Prime Minister nor leader of the House of Commons.

With little prospect of ease Saunderson came back to Parliament.

"*January* 13.—I am in despair with the Government: they are in a hopeless condition, and are letting everything drift.

"*26th.*—I met Randolph.   He asked me, as a special favour, to let him sit in my seat,[1] which of course I was glad to do.   I propose taking the seat behind him: that will be next the corner.

"*February* 5.—I get into a horrible mess over my letters.   I sit in front of a growing pile and feel like

[1] By act of grace certain seats are recognised as belonging to a few privileged members.

an idiot. Certainly when you are not with me my better half is absent. . . . I am terribly pestered to go and speak all over the place."

During the autumn he had addressed various meetings, generally in Ireland and Scotland. At the annual meeting of the Irish Loyal and Patriotic Union on January 12, he blew a warlike blast, of which two notes may be repeated. Here he cracked a joke which is frequently recalled, but which has also been condemned as unworthy of his reputation. As long as Mr. Gladstone remained where he was, said he, the Government might rest secure; but—

"if it should unfortunately happen that he should be called to a higher and more peaceful place—(a pause)—I mean the House of Lords, and if his party should come under the leadership, as it probably would, of Mr. Chamberlain . . . it would be a more doubtful matter."

The audience were perhaps quick-witted enough to appreciate an innocent travesty; but it gave an opportunity to his critics for declaring that he had jested about Mr. Gladstone's old age and possible death, which was neither true in fact nor tenable in imputation.[1]

Further it will be observed that Saunderson was not without misgivings concerning Mr. Chamberlain. The Round Table Conference[2] had not met and parted, and the time had not yet come when his position in the Unionist party was regarded with confidence as an established fact and abiding power.

Saunderson lost no time in speaking upon the Address. On January 28 he writes:

---

[1] It has been asserted that this was an impromptu, and that he was surprised and pained to find that his words had been misinterpreted; but he deliberately set the same trap subsequently in the House of Commons. See p. 275.

[2] *Vide supra*, p. 122.

"I have just made what they are pleased to say is my best speech. The House is very good to me. Gladstone took what I said very well."

He made a great point of the fact that, out of fifty-seven murders committed during a given period, only four had been perpetrated on landlords : "so that landlords came off very well." Blood was not shed to avenge the Irish tenants, but to enforce the authority of the Land League. It was a fight, not between landlord and tenant, but between the law of the land and the law of the League. He declared himself in favour of giving the Irish tenantry a direct interest in the soil, and the best means, he thought, would be found in a generous Land Purchase Bill. He admitted that the Act of 1881 had laid the foundation-stone of the Irish question, although it had failed in operation ; which upon the whole was an intrepid admission from one who reckoned on the allegiance of all landlords, whose ideas of generosity might be personal and diverse. Finally he laid it down that—

"the separation party was a fabric raised on British Radicalism and Irish-American Fenianism, with the right honourable gentleman himself (Mr. Gladstone) the chief corner stone, and the two pieces of ornamentation were two gargoyles—one the honourable member for Northampton, and the other the honourable member for North-west Cornwall."

This sally was gleefully received. Mr. Labouchere probably enjoyed it as much as any one. The other gentleman was a different type of member, of more solemn disposition, one who took his position very seriously, although he did not persevere in a political career. He had recently been introduced to an Irish audience as a fine type of the young democracy of England whose sympathies were all with Home Rule ;

and those who remember the zest with which the Colonel held up this "fine type" for the admiration of the House, will remember his most formidable style of invective, and recall the animation in eyes and voice and gesture which delighted his audience. As he came out of the House one of the Government asked him what made him think of gargoyles. "Oh, because they are always spouting all over the place." Next day he wrote:

"*January* 30.—My speech has made a great sensation, at which you will be glad. The gargoyle joke fetched the House tremendously. The Government are delighted with me—they expected that I should give them a tearing, but I knew better. . . . Hartington said that . . . when I concluded he gave a sigh of relief."[1]

And again :

"*January* 31.—I am glad to find that my speech has made a considerable impression all over the country. If I was a conceited man I should go about with my tail up.

"The Speaker congratulated me on my brilliant speech, but Lord John Manners told a friend of mine that he thought it one of the best speeches he ever heard in the House. You ought to have seen Gladstone's face: it was a picture. He did not know which way to look. Randolph Churchill came down expressly to hear me and applauded greatly. I dined with Chaplin afterwards, and met Hartington and others. They drank my health."

On February 4 he wrote the following letter and fulfilled his promise of speaking about Egypt :

"I sit to-morrow for my picture in *Vanity Fair*. . . . What it is to be famous!

"I had a tender farewell with Randolph, who will be away for a month. Having set the political kettle boiling, he leaves it to cool. . . .

[1] One can hardly believe that the jester was being hoist with his own petard !

"I told you that I had written to Lord Salisbury about——. I have just received a very kind letter from him written by himself. . . . It is very good of him, in the midst of all his business. . . . I am thinking of speaking on the Egyptian debate to-night. As you know, I feel strongly on the subject.

Mr. Cremer had moved an amendment to the Address, urging the withdrawal of our troops and the termination of our interference. Possibly the speech of Mr. W. Redmond decided the Colonel to take part ; it was too much for his patience to sit still whilst one of his most ardent opponents was at large. Launching out with a dash at Home Rule and all Home Rulers, he laid it down that "the party to which the honourable gentleman belongs is a party whose deepest aspiration is the downfall of the empire." After which he proceeded in a calm and reasoned tone. He deprecated any desire or rash disposition to say things capable of offending foreign governments, especially at a time when "there was a smell of gunpowder in the air." Yet he declared that Bismarck had done a service to the world when he "stripped diplomacy of reserve and encouraged plain speaking." He scouted the charge of sordid and selfish motives, and upheld England's title to pursue her beneficent work on behalf of the Egyptians, whom he knew well and regarded with liking and compassion. It was a speech worth recording as a proof that Saunderson was capable of other things besides belabouring Parnellites and taunting Mr. Gladstone.

Early in the session Lord Dunraven resigned his office as Under-Secretary for the Colonies. He was careful to explain, in his statement in the House of Lords, that he had no complaint to make against the colonial policy of the Government. He took his ground principally upon the necessity for economy ;

and, as he was known to be a close friend of Lord Randolph Churchill's, this was generally regarded as an echo of the more important renunciation. But he took occasion to utter some warnings against any neglect to enforce law and order in Ireland—devolution not at present being the alternative recommended. Saunderson was ready to do all the urging that was required towards ensuring due enforcement of law and order, even if he sometimes wearied of welldoing. On February 6 Mr. Parnell moved an Irish amendment to the Address and Saunderson writes :

"*February* 5.—To-morrow the Irish debate, of which everybody is heartily sick, begins. I do not, as at present advised, propose to speak again. I have said all that is necessary, so far as I know."

Nor was he backward in "hob-nobbing with Cabinet Ministers." Some Irish county appointments had been quoted by Lord Dunraven as a sign of wavering or weakness on the part of the Government. On February 13 Saunderson writes :

"*February* 13.—I am writing to Salisbury to ask for an interview, as our party are greatly dissatisfied at some recent appointments. . . . I met the American minister Phelps, who is a charming man. Also Augustus Sala, who is very amusing."

For a few days he was absent in Lancashire. Mr. Rylands, a Liberal Unionist, had died and the seat was to be contested by a Conservative, Mr. Thursby.[1] Saunderson's comment illustrates the difficulty which here again arose in adjusting the respective claims and sensibilities of the two wings of the Unionist party. His fears were justified ; the Gladstonian candidate was returned.

"*February* 17.—We commenced work at 7 o'clock last night and I made four speeches running. . .

---

[1] The late Sir J. O. S. Thursby, Bart

Should God give us the victory here it will be a great triumph for the good cause. . . . They are bringing out a picture of me here. . . . I think even the Radicals are inclined to take to me."

"BANK HALL, BURNLEY.

" 18*th*.—Last night I made three speeches and wound up the oratorical campaign. . . . I fear Thursby will be beaten, as I expect a good number of the Liberal Unionists will abstain from voting for a Conservative candidate.   However, if we manage to win, it will be a mighty triumph.   The Burnley people appear to take to me, and are quite wild about my tail-twisting epithets.   T. P. O'Connor devoted most of his speech last night to me. . . . I feel much better to-day.   I think hard work agrees with me.

" The meeting is expected to be stormy," he had written before starting, " so they pitched on me as the most likely man for the work.

" 18*th*.—I made three speeches last night : the last was a very good one, I flatter myself.   I think it had effect.

" I have just received a letter from Lord Salisbury, appointing to-morrow at three to meet him, so I must give him a piece of my mind."

His threat of giving Lord Salisbury "a piece of his mind " may provoke a smile in any one who ever had an opportunity of knowing the august, the suave, the courteous patrician who towered above all other Unionists ; but if there was any man who could attack him without awe and hesitation it would be the intrepid Ulsterman, who was equally devoid of false pride and false modesty.   Saunderson never assumed equality where it did not exist ; he never pretended to be the intellectual peer of Lord Salisbury or Mr. Gladstone ; but he was leader of his party, and they were leaders of theirs, and therefore he was as good as they were.   Thus he said in a speech in 1891 : " Mr. Balfour and I are constantly called over the coals."   Mr. Balfour was now leader of the House of Commons, and a leader was a leader, whoever he

might be. And it is only fair to add that he was
never supercilious or arrogant towards men of smaller
calibre. He had one manner for all mankind—and
woman-kind: he cringed to none; he was insolent to
none; and he was as hearty and open with the least
distinguished of his acquaintance as he would be with
Lord Salisbury in administering "a piece of his
mind."

These notes record the progress of his labours:

" *February* 19.—I have just been with Lord Salisbury.
On the whole it was satisfactory. I am making arrangements to get English and Scotch members to . . .
urge the necessity of taking strong measures to restore
law and order in Ireland.

" *21st.*—I had a very difficult job to-day. The Conservative party met at the Foreign Office. Lord Salisbury
made the opening statement and then sat down. No
one got up. There was a dead pause. Erne said to
me 'Get up,' and up I got and made a speech. . . . I
then went for ——, whose offences culminated in the
appointment of ——. I hear the Conservative party is
pleased. . . . So far, good. . . . I hate shoving myself,
but it seems by some unaccountable means I am forced
to take a leading part: so I can't help it."

In connection with appointments it should be noted
that during the early part of the session Colonel King-
Harman, member for the Isle of Thanet, was made
Parliamentary Under-Secretary for Ireland. It was
an experimental office; its creation was adversely
criticised, and it presently lapsed. At the time some
gossips wanted to know why Saunderson had been
" passed over"; which was a foolish speculation.
Colonel King-Harman had a longer parliamentary record, and therefore a prior claim, for what that was
worth; but nothing could have been less in tune with
Saunderson's mind than such an offer. He was the
militant leader, before all things independent. To

find himself in a subordinate post, tied down to an occasional official statement, would have been a calamity deserving his favourite epithet " desperate. "[1]

He was far too eagerly intent on his own fighting work to have a thought for such an alternative as this; and he was frequently in action. It is unnecessary to quote his speeches *seriatim*: he aimed at one point, and beat upon it without ceasing. After the Irish amendment to the Address came the introduction of the Crimes Bill, with a preliminary debate on the motion for urgency, and a sequel of a prolonged second-reading stage. Later on came the troubled controversy leading up to the Parnell Commission. In all these scenes Saunderson took his part, and a lively one it often proved to be. Perhaps the liveliest was played on April 14, during the second reading of the Crimes Bill. The Colonel had declared that—

" he did not accuse the honourable member for Cork and those who sat opposite him with ever having imbrued their hands in blood, but he did accuse them of having associated with men whom they knew to be murderers."

This was throwing down the gage with a vengeance. Mr. Healy tartly observed that there was nothing for him to do but to call the honourable and gallant gentleman a liar, which accordingly he did. The Speaker requested him to withdraw, and he refused; whereupon he was named and suspended. Then the battle raged more fiercely than before. Other Home Rulers sought self-immolation by joining in the charge. Mr. Sexton, to strengthen the case, called the Colonel a cowardly liar, and refused in his turn to withdraw. The Colonel was in the heart of the storm and would probably

[1] The intentions of the Government were, in fact, communicated to him.

have preferred to keep the thunder rolling; but consideration for the Speaker, who was hard pressed, may have checked his noble rage: he consented to modify his accusation, and give it a Pickwickian significance. Mr. Sexton accepted the concession and was permitted to withdraw, without paying the penalty for his first disobedience. It is not without interest, after this, to read in a subsequent debate, after some heavy work with Mr. T. P. O'Connor and Mr. Dillon:

"Colonel Saunderson: I have no particle of animosity against any single member of the Irish party.[1]

'Mr. T. Healy: No more have we for you."

The Criminal Law (Ireland) Amendment Bill, known as the Crimes Bill, or Coercion Bill, according to the predilection of party, was the principal Government measure, and it failed not to arouse interest beyond the walls of the House of Commons. On April 11 a demonstration was held in Hyde Park to denounce it. One need not be reminded that a demonstration can be organised in London for or against anything; but it is evidence of public interest that it should have been thought worth while to assemble this multitude, estimated at 100,000 people. It was part of the programme that as the procession passed the Carlton Club they should make a hostile demonstration and the bands should play the Dead March in *Saul*. Colonel Saunderson, upon the entrance steps, endured this outburst undismayed; then, pushing his way into the middle of the crowd, he took his share in the subsequent proceedings.

The introduction of this Bill was memorable for another reason: it marked the advent of Mr. Balfour.

[1] The best comment upon Saunderson's power of engaging in conflicts of this kind without leaving bitterness behind will be found on p. 316.

Mr. Churchill, in his Life of Lord Randolph, speaking of the situation in 1886-7, dismisses Mr. Balfour as unknown.[1] That is perhaps an exaggeration. He had been looked upon as one of the Fourth Party, but he was more in it than of it.[2] He was not so much a smashing political gladiator as a dialectician, who took delight in the cunning art of fence. As Secretary for Scotland he had a recognised status, but he was not the man of the moment. Those who like to speculate on luck may consider what would have been his career if Lord Randolph and Sir Michael Hicks-Beach had not resigned. The former had gone: not many weeks later Sir Michael was compelled by an affection of the eyes to quit the Irish Office. Ireland was to be the centre of interest; whoever might become Chief Secretary would be tested to the utmost. Inside the House there was a measure of first-rate importance to carry against vindictive resistance; beyond the Channel there was turmoil to be dealt with, capable of daunting the stoutest of hearts. Mr. Balfour went to Ireland. The appointment was received with suspicion. The new Chief Secretary was believed to be a delicate man, and people questioned whether he would bring sufficient vigour and firmness to the task. So much vigour and firmness did he bring that he speedily earned the distinction of becoming the best hated of all Chief Secretaries, and his position in the front rank of politicians was instantly assured.

The two colleagues who stood in his way had disappeared; the opportunity for a flight upwards in the eyes of Parliament and the nation was his to seize, and he seized it. So "thorough" indeed was

[1] Vol. ii. 244.
[2] Compare, however, "Rambling Recollections," by Sir Henry Drummond Wolff, chap. lvii.

his policy that Colonel Saunderson was able to say in a speech a year later :

" I took up the other day . . . *United Ireland,* and I find in the leading article that it called Mr. Balfour ' Bloody Balfour' six times. It has invented many epithets for him. It has called him by the name of almost every animal in the Zoological Gardens ; and having exhausted natural history, they are now calling him ' sleuth-tiger '—an animal I never heard of before, but which may exist in some parts of Ireland I have never visited."

The prime cause of his offence may be traced to the memorable Mitchelstown episode. The police had interrupted a proclaimed meeting ; they had been attacked by the mob, and had fired, killing two and wounding others. Mr. Balfour was credited with having encouraged the Constabulary to use their rifles ; Mr. Gladstone inflamed the excitement by sending the solemn message, " Remember Mitchelstown," thus recalling a forgotten adjuration, " Remember Peterloo,"[1] and from that day Mr. Balfour was represented both in picture and print as the incarnation of merciless cruelty.

Meanwhile the tension was acute. During March *The Times* had published a series of articles entitled " Parnellism and Crime," which set out to connect the Irish members with the " physical force " party on the lines followed by Saunderson in his speech recently quoted. On April 18 was published what purported to be a facsimile of a letter from Parnell condoning the murder of Mr. Burke, if not of Lord F. Cavendish. The sequel may be narrated here. Much parliamentary time was occupied. On May 3 a *Times* article

[1] St. Peter's Fields, Manchester, August 16, 1819. A Reform meeting was attacked and dispersed by yeomanry. A few were killed and many injured.

attacking Mr. Dillon was made the subject of a
Privilege debate in the House of Commons. On the
5th Mr. Gladstone moved for a Select Committee;
this was refused, the Government proposing as an
alternative a libel action against *The Times*, to be
conducted by the Attorney-General, and another
counsel chosen by the Irish members. Nothing however was done, and the matter drifted on till next
year. In July, 1888, Mr. O'Donnell, a former member
of Parliament, brought an action for libel on his own
account, without success. Parnell insisted on a Special
Committee. The Government decided to appoint a
Commission of Judges, which they did in the face of
much protest and criticism, carrying the necessary
Bill in August. The trial was lengthy and eventful.
It transpired that much of the material, including the
famous letter, had been supplied by a broken-down
journalist named Pigott, who was known as a hack-
writer and begging-letter-writer to men of all classes
and parties in Ireland. Mr. Labouchere, scenting
mischief, got hold of the man and received from him
a confession of fraud. Immediately repenting, the
witness withdrew this, and went into the box. Here
he broke down completely; made another full confession[1]; fled the country; and shot himself in Madrid.
The Times of course withdrew this part of their
charge, expressing regret by the mouth of their
counsel. The remaining stages of the Commission
were comparatively uninteresting; but the Report
was awaited with eagerness. On the gravest counts
there was a verdict of innocent; but some of the
leading Irish members were declared to have advocated the absolute independence of Ireland; those of
them who had encouraged boycotting, were found

[1] To Mr. Labouchere and Mr. G. A. Sala.

guilty of a criminal conspiracy ; one was reported to have argued that "the shooting of land-grabbers was one of the incidents of civil war"; the Clan-na-gael was proved to have adopted the policy of dynamite ; finally it was reported that the men assailed, though not guilty of directly inciting to crime, did incite to intimidation, and that the consequence of that incitement was that crime and outrage were committed. It was a tolerably severe condemnation ; but the fiasco of Pigott had prejudiced the result, and played into the hands of the Parnellites. One Cabinet Minister observed : " It is quite good enough for me ; the public are such fools that they won't see the importance of it ; we will make it our business to point it out to them."

Parnell at the moment was entitled to some commiseration. There is no reason to doubt the sincerity of his dismay, and his offer to retire from politics, on the occasion of the Phœnix Park murders.[1] It was rather hard to have so shocking a misrepresentation of his sentiments paraded before the world at this time of day. He faced the ordeal with his usual stern indifference. He had begun by saying that never since 1879 had he signed his name as it appeared in *The Times* letter. Presently he got up in the House and said that, on reconsidering the matter, he found that he had occasionally done so. His enemies might have been pardoned had they taken this to be a retreat to get out of an untenable position ; but it was the truth, which Parnell uttered not perhaps because his respect for the House required it, but because his contempt for it made him callous.

Some partners in a London bank amused themselves one day by comparing Parnell's signature in their book

[1] *Vide supra*, p. 68.

with the forgery. None of them could see any difference, except one old clerk, expert in such matters, who was able without difficulty to point out the discrepancies.

To return to the session of 1887 : the Crimes Bill was read a third time in the House of Commons on July 24, and the Government proceeded with their Land Bill. In dealing with this measure Saunderson attended less to its economical effects than to the symptoms of Land League virus which permeated the agrarian system throughout Ireland. "It was not reduction of rent they sought," he said in the House of Commons, "but the annihilation of a class." Subsequently in Scotland he spoke of the commercial immorality that was spreading through all classes : a creditor, upon being pressed for a shop debt, wrote—

"DEAR SIR,
       "I am surprised that an intelligent man like you should imagine that I am such a damned fool as to give you the money that I want a damned sight more than you want. . . . I don't mean to give any money in these hard times."

At Leeds he told the following story :

"A man came down to the House of Commons—a farmer from the county of Cork—and on his head he wore a billycock hat . . . it had five holes in it. . . . He said to me, 'Sir, I have brought this hat the whole way from Ireland to show it to you.' He refused to join the League, and . . . because he refused . . . he was fired at five consecutive times . . . and they hit him in fifteen different places."

On the whole Saunderson was inclined to bless the Bill. It was read a third time on August 6. Speaking in Leicestershire on August 1, he said :

"The Land Bill tells the Irish tenant that under no circumstances shall he be turned out from his holding if he can show clearly to the Court that he is suffering from circumstances over which he has no control. Is there any tenant in any other country in the world who has got such a privilege as that ? With . . . [this measure] which will give such immense help and assistance to the Irish tenants, I believe the Government, if it is firm and decided, will make for itself a name in English history that will never be forgotten."

But the Bill did not become law without considerable agitation. I have decided to quote from my own journal for the purpose of sketching in outline the sequel of events. If it gives no valuable insight into affairs, at all events it reflects the prevailing impressions and current gossip of the House of Commons :

"*August* 11.—Great indignation prevails owing to the reduction of rents in Ireland. Irish Tory M.P.'s are sorely tried in their loyalty. Irish Tory landlords outside say they may as well vote for Home Rulers; they can be no worse off under an Irish Parliament.

"12*th*.—Irish Land Bill in the Lords. The Duke of Argyll made a curious speech : 'A bad Bill, but it can't be helped,' which even Lord Salisbury seemed to admit. The event was the amendment of the reduction of rent clause, Lord Cadogan [1] accepting it 'as a guide to the Commissioners.'

"13*th*.—Great distress in the House of Commons. The Opposition are furious at Cadogan's action. Smith and Balfour protested that it is only carrying out their intention ; but Chamberlain threatened opposition, and Hartington suggested postponement of the clause, which was agreed to. I hear that the Commissioners object to such wide responsibility.

"15*th*.—The L.U.'s are fidgety. It is said that if we go out and Gladstone comes in . . . [Chamberlain] will turn Home Ruler.

"16*th*.—Busy till 10 p.m. writing to M.P.'s to come up on Thursday to vote for the Lords Amendments. . . . The Government mean to stick to their guns."

At this juncture Saunderson wrote :

"*August* 17.—I am just off to speak at Ramsey, in

[1] Lord Privy Seal,

Hunts.[1] I am not so well as I was; this beastly place is telling on me.

"I have received satisfactory answers from the Government about the League and about the stand they intend making on the Land Bill. Thursday and Friday will be exciting days. I must get old —— to tinker me up. I don't like speaking to-day, but I can't help it. I wish I could put some of the stiffness in my neck into the Government's back."

The journal goes on :

"18th.—The Cabinet is sitting to discuss the proclamation of the League. All the young Tories are very eager for this . . . but some L.U.'s will go over, headed by Chamberlain. . . .[2]

"22nd.—The Government proclaimed the National League on Friday. It had little effect; the House was empty, and few Irish were present. George Wyndham, A. J. B.'s private secretary, was beside me in the gallery.

"25th.—Some Radical M.P.'s . . . have joined the National League and gone to attend a demonstration in Dublin. . . .

"27th.—Gladstone's address to the Crown to set aside the Proclamation[3] was rejected yesterday by seventy-eight votes. Chamberlain and four or five L.U.'s voted with the Opposition. . . .

"September 3.—Philip Stanhope[4] is going to speak at a proclaimed meeting in Clare. What a farce it all is!"

"Mr. W. H. Smith to Lord Wolmer.[5]

"I am most anxious to get two hundred men here by 5 p.m. on Tuesday, to put an end to the torture to which parliamentary institutions are subjected by

[1] The Hon. W. H. Fellowes, M.P., had succeeded to the peerage on the death of his father, Lord De Ramsey. The Hon. Ailwyn Fellowes was elected (afterwards President of the Board of Agriculture and Fisheries).

[2] This is allowed to stand as a specimen of the worthlessness of contemporary political estimate.

[3] Of the National League.

[4] M.P. for Wednesbury; now Lord Weardale.

[5] Earl of Selborne. Then Liberal Unionist Whip.

the Home Rule Brigade. We are bringing men from Scotland and Ireland. . . . Pray do your best and bring up your friends."

"*9th.*—Very late hours in the House of Commons. Each night this week the sitting lasted beyond four o'clock : twelve hours' work."

By dint of urgent whipping the requisite majorities were maintained, and the session was brought to an end on September 16. This extract ought to be included :

"As speakers, Gladstone is unique : after him I like best George Curzon, Col. Saunderson, and R. Churchill."

I doubt whether, when this was written, I had ever spoken to the Colonel; consequently it is the unbiassed confession of a youthful private secretary, who was fond of taking notes.

CHAPTER X

1887—1888

SAUNDERSON had rapidly become a personage. As we have seen, he never liked London, and troubled himself little about Society. Hitherto there have been few records of dinners, although this undated note shows that one discriminating hostess quickly marked him for a man of interest: "I dined last night with Mrs. Jeune.[1] There were two very nice people, the Beerbohm Trees—this is the way the name sounds."

Now his letters contain a catalogue of dinner engagements; as often as not he writes "on such a day I dine with ——" and then a picture of his host. He liked good company and good living; he never talked about his diet, and apparently never thought of it. It would be difficult to imagine him dabbling in patent feeding-stuffs. He appreciated a fine vintage and relished a good dish. Once during a heavy luncheon, some one protested against the length of the menu: "Not at all," cried the Colonel, "there is no pleasure you can give me like feeding me." He was no glutton, but he ate and drank with the same gusto as he applied to all other occupations, as this fragment, of unknown date, testifies:

"I cooked the dinner, and John liked the chops very much. We did them in the drawing-room. This

---

[1] Lady St. Helier.

morning I did a devil, which was good ; also I fried bacon, which the flames devoured. John took up a plate which he had placed before the fire to warm, and it was so hot that he threw it into the fire to cool it. The bacon was of the consistency and tasted like camptewlicon ; do you know what that is ? "

But he could order dinner too. He was hospitable by nature; he was essentially sociable; and his presence at a table was, to borrow the metaphor of

LORD DUNLEATH.

R. L. Stevenson, as though another candle had been lighted. Yet he remained to the end unconventional to some extent. He was incapable of platitudes and banalities. He enjoyed attention and liked to talk; but there was no effort and no pose; he was exuberant, spontaneous, and never bothered himself about effect. He could never have been a sycophant; he was too much at his ease in all companies and in all surroundings. He had no social ambition because he never had misgivings as to his social status. Fond as he was of yachting, he never aspired to membership of the holy of holies at Cowes. He was a frequent and welcome visitor, and Lord Ormonde permits me to say that he often urged him to become the owner of a boat of the prescribed tonnage, so that he might be eligible for election.　Perhaps to him the Lough Erne Yacht Club was dearer and more distinguished than any Squadron.　He spent much time on the *Egeria*[1] with the late Lord Dunleath: but he had numerous friends, and he enjoyed being at the headquarters of yachting.　Many of his letters are dated from the R.Y.S. *Castle*.　Thus he writes on August 8:

"R.Y.S. CASTLE, COWES.

"I came down yesterday.　To-day I went to church and then came on to the Club.　I met the Prince of Wales, who took me off and made me sit beside him, and give him an account of the political situation. . . ."

During the autumn he made a considerable tour in Scotland, repeating again and again his denunciation of Home Rule and all Home Rulers.　He liked a Scotch audience and found them sympathetic.

In September he was the guest of Lord Hopetoun[2] and combined business with pleasure, as these notes testify.

"LEADHILLS, N.B.

"*September* 1, 1887.—We have had two pretty fair days.　We killed in two days one thousand one hundred grouse.　Only think of that! . . . I killed fifty-nine grouse in one box: not bad for an old creature like me. . . ."

"HOPETOUN HOUSE, SOUTH QUEENSFERRY.

"*September* 8.—The demonstration is over and has been a great success.　Hopie spoke first, and got on very well.　Then I went on and got a very good reception. I appear to hit off the Scotch: if I find such to be the case, I might do some good work in Scotland."

Later on he spoke at Edinburgh, Stirling, Perth, Cupar, Clydebank, and Ardrossan.　The Stirling

---

[1] She won more than seventy prizes, including some seconds.
[2] Marquis of Linlithgow.　Died 1908.

speech gave rise to a heated correspondence. He had accused Mr. Gladstone of fraternising with men whom he had previously denounced as guilty of murder, treason, and robbery. Mr. Gladstone at once denied that he had ever said anything of the kind, and demanded evidence. The Colonel rejoined by quoting one speech in which the Irish members had been taxed with rapine and a desire to dismember the empire [1] (robbery and treason); and another in which the steps of the Land League had been identified with the steps of crime [2] (murder). Mr. Gladstone retorted that this was deliberate misrepresentation, and that Colonel Saunderson's language last year had placed him in nearer relation to crime than any in which Mr. Parnell had ever stood. Saunderson was unabashed. He professed ignorance of this allusion to his own stalwart avowals of resistance to a Home Rule Government, and added that a *tu quoque* was no answer to an allegation. This application of Mr. Gladstone's words had perhaps been stretched to undue lengths; but he was quite content. In one of his speeches he made a boast that " If I have a talent for anything I have a talent for being able to rub my opponents up the wrong way," and he could flatter himself that he had thrust home upon his greatest antagonist.

He was generally credited with a craving for single combat. During the session there had been paragraphs in the papers reporting his declared purpose of chastising any member who might give him personal provocation, and *Punch* printed what was assumed to be his latest form of invitation: " At

[1] " They wish to march through rapine to the disintegration and dismemberment of the empire."—Liverpool, Oct. 27, 1881.

[2] " With fatal and painful precision the steps of crime dogged the steps of the Land League."—House of Commons, Jan. 28, 1881.

home from 7 to 8 a.m. Pistols and coffee. R.S.V.P."
Saunderson was too deeply saturated with the spirit
of an Irishman to be indifferent to so inspiriting an
atmosphere of action and defiance.

That he was tinctured with the infirmities as well
as the virtues of the typical Irishman, this outspoken
missive from the organiser of a banquet may bear
witness :

"MY DEAR SAUNDERSON,
    "You are a thorough Irishman, brilliant, agree-
able, fascinating, but most damnably uncertain.
There I went and arranged a toast specially for you ;
told everybody you were going to speak, and fluttered
no end of hearts ; and here you go and throw me
over in three lines."

The condition of politics was to afford him ample
scope for his activities. When Parliament met in
February, 1888, the strife of parties was bitter ; nor
was the internal state of the allied Unionists entirely
happy. Every one expected propagation of discord
by Lord Randolph, and no little alarm was caused
when Sir M. Hicks-Beach spoke of him at Bristol
as a "bright political star," and referred to the Cabinet
as "my late colleagues" ; although he was understood
to be a member of it nominally, without office. Men
who cared for such things seriously contemplated Sir
Michael's secession, and one deeply concerned with
the affairs of the party was heard to lament, "What a
bore it will be if a good man like that goes wrong."
However, on February 14 it was known that he had
accepted the Presidency of the Board of Trade, and
one cause of anxiety was removed.

Three days previously two Irish members had been
arrested under the Act of 1887, one whilst approaching,
the other whilst leaving the House of Commons. This

caused an uproar, and one jubilant politician, in the inner circle of Opposition, exclaimed : " We shall be in before the end of the year, and most of the Liberal Unionists will be with us. Balfour has gone too far." There were symptoms of friction between the two sections of the party. One minister complained that " the Liberal Unionists seem to think they are to dictate their own terms on every subject." Later in the session a meeting was held at the Foreign Office to consider the position. Lord Salisbury alluded pointedly to the right wing and left wing of the party; and Mr. W. H. Smith spoke of being ready to retire if he had lost the confidence of his followers in the House of Commons. The Whips complained that members cared for nothing but their constituencies, their own whims, or their own interests. They would make no concessions to the exigencies of party government. They acted as though Parliament were made for man, not man for Parliament; in fact, there was manifest demoralisation.   " You have only to mention Ireland to bring them into line," said some one anxious to offer comfort. " It is more to the point to mention general election to bring them to their senses," was the savage answer. Bye-elections went against the Government. In Edinburgh Mr. Buchanan, following Sir George Trevelyan's example, went back to the Liberals, resigned his seat, and was re-elected, in spite of a fiery speech from Saunderson, who wrote : " I came just at the right time, as the Conservatives were rather hanging back, not liking to support the Radical Unionist."[1]

At a bye-election in Southwark a majority of 116 was turned into a minority of 1,194. In the strong-hold of Kent the majority at Thanet was reduced by

---

[1] Mr. Raleigh.

nearly 1,500. Other seats were lost. The Government suffered irritating defeats in the House of Commons. The victorious army had not followed up their victory by a resolute pursuit of the enemy; they had not secured the position they had won; and they seemed to be about to suffer a determined counter-attack.

Both inside and outside Parliament political issues led to personal vindictiveness. Much comment was made on the withdrawal of an invitation by a Unionist peer because his expected guest had met Mr. Parnell at dinner. A letter in *The Times* accused Mr. Balfour of having said, in private conversation, that the Irish members would suffer severely under the Act of 1887, and that Mr. Dillon, being delicate, would probably die. An eminent Unionist was heard to declare that a leading Liberal, who had lately been his guest, had admitted that he knew Parnell received money from America which he employed for the encouragement of crime, but that he meant to support him none the less. One evening a newspaper boy was heard shouting, "Good news for the Irish members: death of Colonel King-Harman."

From Ireland came nothing but lamentation. An Irish landlord applied to the Patronage Secretary for an appointment in some public office for his son. He was told that the only nominations to be had here were intended for old soldiers or retired servants. "Never mind," said he, "things are so bad in Ireland that I must take what I can get."

Inside the House of Commons the Irish were making a determined fight, and something had to be done to counteract the forces of obstruction. New procedure rules were introduced to obviate continual late sittings, and the number requisite to vote closure was reduced from two hundred to one hundred. The

latter proposal was objected to by many prophetic
gentlemen, who foresaw an expeditious passage of
Bills by future Radical Governments.   Mr. Biggar
was there to exhibit the science of obstruction, in its
fullest development, but Mr. Parnell at no time
showed much sympathy or admiration for it.   I find
a note of my own for April 20: "The Irish tried to
count out the House.   Biggar led them into the
Lobby, where they met Parnell, who drove them back
like so many pigs."

Saunderson might well feel that his work was only
half done, and that there was danger of the gained
ground slipping from under his feet.   Throughout the
winter he was indefatigable in visiting large towns in
the North, and fulfilled a long series of engagements,
in spite of continual trouble with his throat.

" HORSFORTH HALL, LEEDS.

"*November* 25, 1887.—The night before last at
Bestwood I coughed for two hours, and thought
I was done.   However, after I began at Leeds my
voice became all right, and I blathered away in great
style. . . . I have just been out to plant an oak, in
memory of my visit.   An oak stood hard by which was
planted to commemorate the crowning of William IV.
They asked me what my oak was to be called,
so I said that as the other is called the Coronation
Oak, let mine be called the Blatheration Oak, in
memory of my performance last night.   So it is to
be called."

" WHALLEY RANGE, MANCHESTER.

" 26*th*.—I had a doctor with me this morning, as my
throat has been very bad. . . ."

" STALYBRIDGE.

"*January* 15, 1888.—The meetings went off very
well.   We are treated here like princes, so to show
my gratitude I drew a water-colour sketch of the
Filibuster,[1] which they are going to frame."

[1] His steam-launch at Castle Saunderson.

When Parliament met, he lost no time in taking up his text.

"*February* 13.—I am to follow Trevelyan to-morrow. Parnell made about the weakest attack imaginable on the Government.   It will greatly strengthen their position.   I spoke to-night at Southwark, and had a great reception.   It was as good as Belfast."

On February 15 he made a very long speech, re-tracing his former arguments and accusations, and taking special delight in attacking Sir George Trevelyan who was now back amongst the Gladstonians.

"THE G.O.M. WAS TERRIBLY ANGRY."

"*February* 15.—I have made, I suppose, a good speech.   I think it has had more effect than any speech I have as yet made in the House.   The G.O.M. was terribly angry . . . he looked quite mad. Trevelyan . . . I regularly flattened out."

His task was not difficult, because the ex-Chief Secretary was of all men most hampered by former deeds and words.   *The Times*, in a leading article next day, observed that—

"Colonel Saunderson, in his witty and effective speech, briefly exposed some of the inconsistencies and absurdities of Sir George Trevelyan's position. But, in point of fact, Sir George Trevelyan can be most effectually confuted out of his own mouth."

Mr. Labouchere, who followed, laid emphasis on an important event which had occurred.

"The speech of the honourable member was important," he said, " because he spoke, not only in his individual capacity as a member of the House, but also as the head of an important body.   Yesterday the honourable gentleman was elected the sessional chairman of what he could only describe as a new Fourth Party."

Saunderson's leadership was now formally recognised.

In April he went, in an Orient Line steamer, to Gibraltar, with Mr. Somerset Maxwell, and afterwards proceeded to Tangiers.

"GOVERNMENT HOUSE, GIB.

" *April* 6, 1888.—Here we are in state, staying with the Governor, Sir A. Hardinge, whom I met at Abercorn's last year. . . . I met a tall officer in the street yesterday so like Stuart Wortley that I asked him if that was his name ; he said ' No, but Stuart Wortley is in my battalion.'   Wasn't that funny ? . . . The pleasantest thing that happened on board was an address I gave to the emigrants on the gospel, the evening before we arrived at Gib.   The whole deck was cra mmed, and they appeared to like what I said. As I left the ship they gave me a parting greeting. . . .

" THE CONVENT, GIB.

" I enclose a flower—a creeper growing on the wall.   It looks beautiful."

He further relates that on the outward voyage an Irish priest, bound for Australia, had inquired whether Colonel Saunderson was on board, adding, " He is a very good man : he is a straight, hard hitter."

In May he was busy again in the North.

" *May* 10, 1888.—I send you a Sheffield paper. . . . I spoke for one hour and five minutes. . . . The people gave me a great reception at the beginning, and terrific cheers at the end. . . . I am just off with Mr. Daglish to go down his mine, and take a walk under the German Ocean. . . .

" I have just come to the surface, and enclose a piece of coal I hooked out of the two-foot-six seam, under the German Ocean. I was delighted with the mine."

We have seen that the event of the session which most nearly concerned Saunderson and his friends was the appointment of the Parnell Commission. He would not have been human if he had not been elated at seeing his own attack reinforced by such a startling and relentless onslaught from such a quarter; but he had not sought for reinforcements in this form, and he had no connection with the Pigott manœuvre.

One of his colleagues, who was in a position to testify, writes thus :

" I am able to assert most positively that Saunderson knew nothing of the transaction with *The Times*, and was as ignorant as I was that they came through the Secretary of the Irish Loyal and Patriotic Union."

His attitude was defined in the course of a debate on August 3. He said :

" This Commission . . . must take the whole question and deal with it as a whole, and not take up part of the question only. . . . If the Commission decided that the honourable member for Cork had not signed the letters, it would not alter one iota of the objections that they had expressed over and over again to placing Ireland in the hands of those who had shown by their actions in the past what their actions in the future would probably be."

Presently Mr. Healy spoke :

" When the honourable member for North Armagh

said that what he wanted to know was not so much whether these letters were or were not forgeries, but whether the honourable member for Cork and his friends were assassins or were angels——"

Colonel Saunderson: " I never said that they were angels . . . what I did say was that it would not affect me in the least whether these letters were proved to be false or true."

Saunderson had brought a Bill into Parliament to amend the Linen Act, and there is the humour of contrast in the occasional introduction into his fighting speeches in the North of Ireland of a technical dissertation on double chains, cuts, and weavers' tickets, and his declared eagerness to press the interests of the trade upon the attention of the House of Commons. He was not forgetful of his duties as representative of a local industry.

In March Mr. Parnell had introduced a Land Bill; in April another Irish member brought in an Arrears Bill; both measures received short shrift. In May there was a long wrangle over the circumstances attending the negotiations between the Conservative party and Mr. Parnell in 1885. Lord Carnarvon made a statement in the House of Lords; Mr. Parnell retorted at the Eighty Club; and Lord Carnarvon sent a rejoinder to *The Times*. In June Mr. Morley moved a vote of censure on the Government for their administration of the Crimes Act, with the usual result of enabling them to close up their ranks and show an unbroken front. But apart from the Commission, it was not an Irish Session. The Local Government Bill, creating county councils, was the chief measure; and involving as it did a revolution which directly concerned many members, it occupied the greater share of time and attention. There was, however, no cessation of activity in Ireland, and several members were arrested and imprisoned during the summer, including Mr. Dillon. On August 13 Parliament adjourned until November.

When it resumed work the Government introduced a measure to extend the provisions of Lord Ashbourne's Act of 1885. So successful had been the working of this scheme, and so full of promise was its future, that it was alleged that the jealous Liberal leaders were prepared to offer the Government facilities for carrying through the remainder of their business if they would leave this alone. But they were not to be seduced, and the Bill passed into law.

There was comparative calm. Lord Randolph Churchill, who in April had vehemently attacked the Government for not extending their Local Government proposals to Ireland, was a perplexing and menacing element to be observed. It was generally believed that he had repented at leisure, and now bore vindictive feelings towards the colleagues whose sentiments and resources he had misjudged. If he were to seek personal recuperation in open hostility, Home Rule would have gained a redoubtable ally. But his movements and intentions were shrouded in an ostentatious attitude of aloofness. " I hope I shall live to see you back in power," said an older man who met him in the Park. " I sincerely hope your wishes won't be fulfilled," was the frigid reply.

Meanwhile Lord Salisbury proceeded serenely, occasionally enlivening the monotony of the conflict by such sage pronouncements as his description of Home Rule as "three men sitting on two others and maltreating them"; whilst the Irish members continued to be arrested. There was a sharp squall when an officer of the Royal Irish Constabulary called at the House of Commons, and, having sent in

his card to an unsuspecting member, proceeded to
serve him with a summons.   The outraged gentleman
rushed into the House and insisted on interrupting
the debate.   The case was recognised as urgent, and
the House took the unusual course of appointing a
committee of inquiry on the spot and suspending its
proceedings for an hour and a half.   By an odd
coincidence, the Chamber of Deputies in Paris adopted
a similar method of delivering themselves from an
awkward dilemma on the same day.

Saunderson took his full share of work both in
Parliament and out of it, as these characteristic
letters testify :

"*November* 15, 1888.—I spoke last night [in a North-
London constituency] and returned thanks for the
House of Commons. I suppose I spoke well in a sense,
as I brought down the house. In the course of my
remarks I said that the principal occupation of the
House was foolish talking and endless walking through
the lobbies.   In fact, we suffered from foot-and-mouth
disease.   This appeared to tickle the people.
" Webster [1] has got me a ticket for the Parnell trial
to-morrow, so I shall be there all day.
" 16*th*.—I went to hear the Parnell trial to-day.
The Star describes me as looking like a mousquetaire
of Louis XIV.'s time with a bunch of violets."

"CARLTON CLUB, 2 a.m.

" 21*st*.—I have just spoken forty minutes long.
Everybody says it is the best speech I ever made.
" 24th.—I went to a great meeting at Holborn last
night. When I got up to speak the row commenced.
About thirty people roared and groaned, evidently
sent especially for me, as they did not mind the
others : so I made no speech at all.
" I enclose a picture of Trevelyan up a tree. I have no
time to do anything but speak and get ready to speak
—a speech in the House always takes it out of me.

[1] Then Attorney-General, now Lord Alverstone. Lord Chief Justice.

" 27th.—We are debating away as usual. I have just fired a shell at Shaw-Lefevre.

" I enclose a lovely picture in *The Graphic* of me. I look like a murderer. . . . To-morrow I have to speak at Aldershot, and now they are making every effort to get me to go and speak at Edinbro' with Lord Salisbury, but I won't. I have to speak again on the third reading of the Ashbourne Bill, and I shan't take any more meetings than I have at present. . . . They appeared to be pleased with my jawing powers. . . .

" 29th.—You may see by the papers that I vexed the enemy yesterday. *The Times* says, in its leading article, that they were dumbfounded.

" 30th.—I enclose a sketch of T. Healy when in the midst of his rejoicing he suddenly heard that he had been misinformed as to the result of the Holborn Election.[1] I spoke last night on the spur of the moment, and they say I made a very good speech."

" GORHAMBURY.

" *December* 8.—I spoke last night. . . . I have to go to Maidstone, where there is an election. . . . Also on Wednesday in London and on Friday at Doncaster. . . . I am sick of jawing. My throat is all right again . . . not bad for the ninth speech running. . . . We shot 550 head to-day."

At Portadown, on November 6, he gave his views upon the Ashbourne Act :

" For many a long day his view had been that, as far as possible, the Irish tenant should be made possessor of the land he tilled. He said that, and he had pursued it steadily ever since. . . . In a large extension of the Ashbourne Act was to be found a real, a final, and a just solution of the Irish land question. As to the scheme of compulsory purchase, he was absolutely opposed to it."

He had also some remarks to make upon the state of parties. When he spoke of the Scottish Separatist members in the House of Commons and was assailed

[1] Mr. Gainsford Bruce (C) defeated Lord Compton (L).

with cries of "Oh," he ingeniously amended his phrase
to "the Scotch members who support the leader of
the Separatist party." In the course of an interview
he was credited with this prophetic utterance on a
new fusion of parties:

"I accept democracy fully and unreservedly. There
must be, sooner or later, a new party. The difficulty
is a new name. National is too like Nationalist. I
feel like calling it the Empire Party, only Imperialistic
would be rather a mouthful."

And amongst his accustomed flouts of his foes he
let fall the luminous suggestion that as Mr. O'Brien,
who had refused to put on the regulation prison
trousers, desired to be regarded as a martyr, he
ought to be painted with a halo round his legs
instead of round his head.

In strange contrast with such levities I find full
notes for his Christmas sermon of this year. The
point which he appears to have desired most to
drive home was that man made in the image of God
had failed: God made in the likeness of man should
triumph:

"This is the great plan," he says, quoting Romans
v. 19: "For as by one man's disobedience many were
made sinners, so by the obedience of one shall many
be made righteous."

In connection with these years the following notes
taken from the fly-leaf of his Bible are worth preserving:

"1887.[1]—The most eventful year of my life. We
have overthrown Gladstone and his Home Rule Bill.
"1888.—The cause still prospering."

[1] Presumably retrospect of 1886.

CHAPTER XI

1889—1890

PARLIAMENT met on February 21, 1889, and Saunderson as usual made a great pronouncement during the debate on the Address. Amongst other things he joined issue with Mr. T. P. O'Connor, who had recently declared at Maidstone that speech was not free in Ireland. This Saunderson denied; but he pointed out that language might be used with impunity at Maidstone which might have dangerous consequences in Ireland. "A homely illustration would exactly point out his meaning": to light a cigar in the smoking-room of the House of Commons was a perfectly legal act; but to light a cigar in a coal-mine, in "an atmosphere filled with inflammable particles," would be a criminal act of a heinous kind. Presently he made a direct and personal onslaught upon Mr. Gladstone. It had transpired that some evictions had recently taken place on the Hawarden estate, and the Colonel wanted to know, if Mr. Gladstone approved of the principles and practices of the Land League in Ireland, how he would like to have the system set up in Flintshire. Why did not the English Home Rulers, who had a taste for going across the Channel to support the Irish agitation, let their charity begin at home?—

"I have to ask the right honourable gentleman and his friends, would they look upon it as a right and just thing if I were to go into Flintshire and start an organisation for intimidation, murder, and outrage upon any incoming tenant who takes the widow's [Whitehead] farm ?"

Mr. Gladstone, he went on, had written to *The Times* to complain of wanton intrusion into the private domain : yet his friends had been committing this very outrage all over Ireland.   If the thing was morally wrong in England, it was wrong in Ireland.

This was a violent use of personal illustration. The circumstances attending the Hawarden evictions were explained in the Press, and there was no further attempt to make capital out of them ; but the temptation to hoist Mr. Gladstone with his own petard was too great to be resisted.   Saunderson made it his business to fire at the godfather of Home Rule whenever he could get a shot, and he was not likely to show mercy.   Not content with attacking him in his speeches and in letters to *The Times*, he never wearied of relieving his feelings in caricature : sometimes these found their way into the newspapers. During the winter Mr. Gladstone had been in Naples, concerning himself a good deal with Italian politics. He had written a letter which had made some stir in Rome, although he was disposed to repudiate the published version.   We now know from Mr. Morley's book that he found himself drawn into affairs : " I find myself hardly regarded here as a foreigner."   He had strong views upon the current foreign policy of the country, and with an allusion to the " standing menace" of Popedom, he decided not to go to Rome : " If I had to talk to the King and the minister I should be treading upon eggs."[1]   Observing this spirited attention to the destinies of Rome, Saunderson must needs

---

[1] " Life of Gladstone," iii. 413.

make an elaborate portrait of Mr. Gladstone as Pope,
and send it to Mr. Chamberlain. Mr. Chamberlain
could not be aware that Mr. Gladstone had written,
six days before : " They look upon me as having had
a real though insignificant part in the liberation," [1] or he
might have had some point to make about liberation
being interpreted by union in Italy and separation at
home ; but he remembered that Pitt's Union policy had
been denounced by an epithet of extreme vituperation,
and he sent the following lively acknowledgment.
The tone and spirit of the postscript perhaps suggest
a natural affinity which made the two men close and
congenial friends.

"Highbury Moor Green, Birmingham,
January 16, 1889.

" My dear Saunderson,
    " We shall not be in London till the open-
ing of Parliament, but then I hope that we shall see
you. Meanwhile, we have laughed over your sketch,
which I shall have framed, as a permanent record of
the G.O.M.'s last craze. If he would only denounce the
Italian Union and 'that blackguard' Victor Emmanuel,
he might be content to leave Ireland alone, and forget
the crimes of Pitt.
            " Yours very truly,
                " J. Chamberlain.

" P.S.—I have been asked to go to Cork. If I did,
in the autumn, I wonder if the southern Loyalists have
courage enough to show themselves."

It is worth noting in this connection that, in spite
of his inherent fighting instinct, Saunderson frequently went out of his way to speak smooth things
of Mr. Morley. About this time he used the curious
phrase in the course of a speech, "Of Mr. Morley I
speak with the highest respect as a republican and a
Home Ruler": which was an unaccountable abuse

[1] " *Life of Gladstone,*" p. 414.

of terms. Whence he had derived his conviction of Mr. Morley's republicanism, does not appear. Some months later this character was to be disavowed, when the Newcastle Socialists received a distinct refusal from their member to accept their views upon the abolition of the monarchy, the House of Lords, and all hereditary offices. Less questionable was the tribute which had been paid at Bradford in the previous year :

"Although I differ from Mr. Morley, I am bound to admit that he is the only man in the Separatist party who has not turned a political head-over-heels. I look upon him as the conscience-keeper of the Gladstonian party, and . . . when I read one of Mr. Morley's speeches, looking upon him as a man who honestly believes the political line he has taken up, I read it with considerable attention."

Early in the session Mr. T. P. O'Connor did a thing which showed a passing lapse of judgment and humour, and must have greatly pleased the Colonel. A gathering at Portadown had recently been inspirited with a renewed assurance that Ulster was ready and resolved to resist Home Rule by force of arms. Mr. O'Connor brought the matter before Parliament, and asked whether the Chief Secretary intended to prosecute the speaker. The only results were to exhibit Mr. Balfour's ingenuity in dealing with such emergencies, and to give a publicity to Saunderson's proud boast such as his soul loved. One frightened member inquired whether the Colonel's alleged promise to produce 80,000 armed men in a fortnight meant that they were already equipped. The Colonel had no occasion to take part in the wrangle, and enjoyed a gratuitous advertisement without having to answer any awkward questions.

The Government were entering their third year of

office.   The flush and enthusiasm of victory had paled :
the Unionist cause had not lost ground, but Home
Rule was no longer the critical issue which had once
absorbed public attention.   Those who, like Saunderson, cared greatly, found small excuse for complacency.
The Gladstonians were making great play with their
new friends.   In Ireland the Nationalist members
were as active as ever, and continued to agitate in
defiance of all repressive legislation.   It became the
fashion for English Radicals to obey the Scriptural
cry, "Come over and help us."   Several responded,
with varying rewards : some were presented with the
freedom of Dublin ; others lost their own freedom in
Irish prisons, which at all events did credit to their
consistency.   The Nationalists had discovered that all
their preconceived opinions of Lord Spencer were
mistaken, and they spared no pains in making amends.
Mr. Parnell and his old enemy sat in peace together
as the guests of the Eighty Club.   Before the year
was out the Irish leader was to be a visitor beneath
Mr. Gladstone's roof.   There was no sign of wavering on the part of those who had promised Home
Rule.

In the Unionist party there were cooling elements at
work.   The opening of Parliament (1889) synchronised
with the collapse and tragedy of Pigott.   To the superficial observer his letters constituted the foundation
of the case against the Parnellites, and the ignominious
withdrawal by *The Times* of this part of the charge
undoubtedly modified public opinion, and dealt a
blow at the Government's prestige.   Mr. Gladstone
was confident of turning them out before Easter, so
it was reported to the Whips; every seat in Scotland
would be lost at the next election, so they were informed by a magnate from the North : the party there

were losing heart. Sir William Harcourt was assuring an audience at Derby that at the time of the Round Table Conference Mr. Chamberlain was at heart a Home Ruler. And Lord Randolph Churchill was still a possible source of danger. Early in the year the gossips were busy whispering that at a Levée he had spoken to none but Liberal ex-ministers.

It is true that when Mr. Bright died in March Lord Randolph was eager to be the Government candidate at Birmingham. In 1885 he had fought his memorable contest, and left a deep impression on the constituency. Perhaps he saw an opening for arresting once-more the interest and attention of the country. But he was foiled. Again the terms of the compact were in question, and in this case the difficulty of adjustment was acute. In the end the claim of the Liberal Unionists was admitted, and Lord Randolph had to content himself with South Paddington, and soothe, so far as he cared to do so, the constituents whom he had proposed to desert. His principal effort hitherto had been in conjunction with the Liberals to oppose Lord George Hamilton's Navy Scheme on the ground of extravagance. Remembering the reasons given for his resignation, this was almost inevitable; but after the Birmingham episode, the gossips were again busy with his private relations. It became known that he had dined with Sir Charles Russell to meet Mr. Gladstone and Mr. Parnell; it was rumoured that in his intimate circle a boycott of Mr. Chamberlain had been decreed. In fact, he was no longer to be trusted in the fighting line.

Saunderson was less prominent in debate because there was a lull. Occasions did not arise for the stormy scenes of recent sessions; they were to come again in due time. Parliament was not prorogued until August 30, but he loyally remained to the end. The following extracts from his letters give occasional glimpses of his movements and affairs :

"'EGERIA,' GUERNSEY.

"*June 7*, 1889.—We have had a very pleasant time. The first day we had a good deal of swell, which came natural to me ; some of the others did not like it. . . . Guernsey is a garden : forcing-houses everywhere. The roads are in reality lawns, sunk below the level of the surrounding fields, something like Kerry boreens ; and you cannot conceive anything prettier than they look, as they wind along with the sun glinting through the leaves and making lines of sunlight across the way. I am engaged to-day in finishing off my speech, and in making a plan for a centreboard. Each morning we tub like this [picture]."

"CASTLE SAUNDERSON.

"*July* 10.—I travelled over with Mr. W. O'Brien. He was received on the platform by four very drunken corner-boys, who cheered as well as whisky would permit."

"R. ST. GEORGE'S Y.C., KINGSTOWN.

"*July* 17.—I sailed Bangor's boat to-day, but did nothing. The *Bonito* is outbuilt by two Scotch boats.

"*August* 1.—Lady Londonderry was delighted with the description I gave her from *Freeman's Journal* of Londonderry and myself : the empty-headed fop and the Court buffoon.

"12*th*.—I am located at Holly Lodge [1]—for how long I don't know. The Government have brought in a beastly Welsh Tithes Bill which blocks the way, so that we cannot get on to the estimates. . . . They are very kind to me here, and make me as comfortable as possible."

"HOLLY LODGE.

"*August* 13.—I hate to think of remaining. . . . Staying out at Holly Lodge makes a great difference. The air is bracing, and driving home at night is very refreshing.

[1] Baroness Burdett-Coutts's house at Highgate.

A Water-Colour Drawing by Colonel Saunderson.

... finally remained to ...
... from his letters give ...
... ... ents and starts:

"D ..."

... We have had a very pleasant ...
... ... Head of swell, wh ...
... some of the others did not like ...
... ... racing boats ... over ...
... ... by ... sank below the ...
... ... boat ... ... thing like ...
... conceive anything ...
... as they wind along with th ...
... ... boats and making lines ...
... I am engaged to-day in fin ...
... ... making a plan for a c ...
... ... we tub like this [picture].

"CASTLE SAUNI ..."

... ... well over with Mr. W. O'B ...
... on the platform by four very dru ...
... ... cheered as well as whisky w ...

"F. St. GEORGE'S Y.C., KINGST ..."

... spoiled Bangor's boat to-day, but ...
... The *Boat* is outbuilt by two Se ...

... ... Lady Londonderry was delig ...
... description I gave her from *Fren* ...
... of Londonderry and myself: the en ...
... top and the Court buffoon.

... I am seated at Holly Lodge¹—for how ...
I do not know. The Government have brought ...
... ... Welsh Tithes Bill which blocks the w ...
... we cannot get on to the estimates. ...
... very kind to me here, and make me as comfort ...
... ...

"HOLLY LO ..."

... 16.—I hate to think of remaining ...
... at Holly Lodge makes a great differ ...
... ... and driving home at night is ...
... ...

¹ ... ...ness Burdett-Coutts's house at Highgate.

A Water-Colour Drawing by Colonel Saunderson.

" *22nd*.—I have to see Lord Salisbury on State affairs on Friday. I am quite sure that had I not been at Holly Lodge I should have knocked up altogether. We never got to bed before three or half-past, so in the morning I am pretty well done.

" *24th*.—I had a long talk with Lord Salisbury yesterday. It was very satisfactory. . . . I have been most of the day with Long,[1] who has made a most spirited picture. He is greatly pleased with it, and intends sending it to the Academy next year."

During his usual autumn campaign he enjoyed the distinction of being elected Grand Master of the Orangemen of Scotland. It was during this recess that two facts bearing upon Home Rule became known : one, calculated rather to reconcile wavering Liberals, was that Mr. Gladstone had finally decided that the Irish members must be retained at Westminster ; the other, destined to shatter for a time the Nationalist party, was that Mr. Parnell was to be made co-respondent in a divorce case. Saunderson must have realised that both these events were to influence his policy and labours, but he was not at his highest pressure at the moment.

In August he had been concerning himself with Irish licensing legislation ; subsequently he was denouncing the proposal to establish a Roman Catholic University ; not, he protested, from motives of bigotry, but because, in his oracular words, he objected to any attempt to buy the Roman Catholic Church, not only with Protestant money, but the money of the people of Ireland, and because he believed that it would be repugnant alike to Protestants and Roman Catholics who valued freedom of education. Another of his *obiter dicta* of this period was a pronouncement [2] upon dual ownership, which appears philosophic rather

---

[1] Mr. Long, R.A., painted this portrait for Baroness Burdett-Coutts.

[2] At Lurgan, Jan. 7, 1890.

than conventional, when it is viewed in the light of recent professions :

"Mr. T. W. Russell . . . says . . . that what is called dual ownership . . . must cease. That I absolutely deny. Why? When I went into the House of Commons first, long before I ever dreamt of standing for North Armagh, I remember speech after speech being made in the House of Commons, holding up certain provinces in Ireland as specimens of prosperity, of loyalty, and of peace, and the main reason adduced for that happy condition was that this dual ownership existed there, and that they had what was called tenant right. What was meant by tenant right? Dual ownership. That always had existed in Ulster, but . . . you can never do away in Ireland or in any other country with dual ownership. It will always exist, for this reason : Let us suppose that you sweep all the present landlords away, as it is proposed to do under a Bill of compulsory purchase, and turn over property that belongs to us to the tenants, do you mean to tell me that it is possible to stereotype and fix those small properties so that they are never to become larger or smaller, and that no proprietor in future is ever to have a tenant ? . . . The moment you create new proprietors there will be men anxious to take land from them. They will offer higher prices than we landlords get; and will you tell me that one of these new landlords . . . will refuse to accept a tenant on these advantageous terms ? Certainly not, as long as every man can do what he likes with his own."

It may be said that the last sentence annuls the the preceding argument, inasmuch as Irish landlords have long been learning that they cannot do what they like with their own; but, apart from the point or value of his opinions, it is well to pause and note the gratifying fact that throughout these stormy times there was never occasion for Saunderson to defend his personal character as a landlord. Often enough he was attacked as a member of a class, and that class he was always ready to defend; but, well as it would have suited his opponents to hold him up to public odium in his private relations with his tenants, at no time were peace and harmony disturbed on the Castle Saunderson estate, and no one could find a stone to fling at him. Before the year 1889 was over he had found time to pay a visit to Naples, Sicily, and Malta with his daughter and his youngest son—one of those expeditions in which he found unfailing pleasure.

When Parliament met in February, 1890, the Parnell case was prominent. First an attempt was made to obtain a condemnation of *The Times* for publishing the forged letter and a record of apology to Parnell. This was defeated. Then came the Report of the Commission; following that, a motion by Mr. Gladstone amplifying the terms of reparation already denied. On this occasion Randolph Churchill contributed a violent attack on the Government for their conduct in appointing the Commission and their way of receiving the Report. The withers of Government were unwrung, and they contented themselves with accepting it without comment.

Enough has been said in a previous chapter concerning this Report and its purport. Saunderson's attitude is made sufficiently clear by a speech which he made in London a few days later.

"The accusations," he declared, "against a party whom Mr. Gladstone proposed to make the rulers of Ireland were of far more importance to them than an attack on any individual of it. The accusations against the party of founding an organisation with the object of establishing in Ireland a nation entirely independent of England; that this organisation was a conspiracy of a criminal character, and had for its object to drive from the country the British garrison— were all absolutely proved up to the hilt."

He had made his annual onslaught during the debate on the Address. Taking note of a novel demand that Ireland should help herself and not be humiliated by receiving alms from England, he blandly observed that he had never in his life met an Irishman who would do work at his own expense when he could find some one else to take the pecuniary burdens off his shoulders. However, it was not to be an Irish session. A Land Purchase Bill was introduced, but congestion of business caused it to be withdrawn, to reappear in the autumn. The Prorogation took place on August 18, and before the close the atmosphere had cooled to such an extent that the evening papers were able to record that the Colonel had been seen at tea with Mr. and Mrs. Gladstone one afternoon on the terrace of the House of Commons.

Out of this calm there had passed away one spirit of the storm by which Saunderson's career had been directly influenced—Mr. Biggar, who had defeated him in Cavan in 1874 and driven him to Ulster; Mr. Biggar, who had developed the science of obstruction to its ultimate expression; of whom Mr. Barry O'Brien says[1] that his great object was to do as much mischief as he could to the British Empire; Mr. Biggar was dead, and one of the most memorable figures of the Parnell epoch had vanished.

It remains to be noted that in 1890 Colonel and Mrs. Saunderson reached their silver-wedding day. Whatever trials and perplexities the years may have brought him, in domestic affairs at all events the Colonel's life had been abundantly blessed.

[1] "Charles Stewart Parnell," i. 81.

CHAPTER XII

1890—1892

IN the autumn of 1890 Saunderson paid his customary visit to Scotland. With Lord Erne he attended a great Orange demonstration in Glasgow, not on this occasion with his wonted satisfaction, as the accompanying letter shows:

"GLASGOW.

"*November 7*, 1890.—I was delighted you were not with me. . . . It was blowing great guns, and raining as I never saw it rain before. . . . One heavy sea broke over my shelter and filled my boots. . . . I was like a drowned rat. They gave us supper. . . . I ate as much as would fill two ordinary men. . . . We have had a great meeting, the largest they have yet had in Glasgow. . . . Crichton [1] was much pleased with my speech—I was not. It was a difficult audience to speak to, owing to women and babies; the latter caterwauled at the wrong time, which is trying to an orator."

During his visit of the previous year he had declared that he would depart with a promise of £40,000 (some papers said £80,000) in the event of an Ulster army being required in the field. This year his tone was less bellicose, if his principles were no less stout. He made several speeches in Ireland, but Parliament reassembled on November 25, and his campaign was consequently limited.

It is notorious that nothing excites so much interest

---

[1] Earl of Erne.

in the House of Commons as a personal affair, but
there was reason enough for elevating the O'Shea
divorce case into a matter of first-rate importance.
Not only the fate of an individual was at stake; a
party and a cause were vitally affected. Parnell had
disciplined his forces and manœuvred them with
infinite determination into a favourable position. It
is true that there had been some murmuring at his
supineness of late; he had not scrupled to yield to
distracting pre-occupations when it pleased him; but
he still maintained personal authority besides titular
command. In a moment he had divided his followers
and alienated his allies. It seemed at first as if he
were to hold his own; habit or timidity made men
reluctant to revolt, and his brigadiers professed
fidelity. Then Mr. Gladstone spoke, and his doom
was ordained. Sentiment, which regulates right and
expediency in excessive measure, was astir. The
merits of a cause were to be forgotten in the immorality of a man. If Parnell were to remain the
leader of the Home Rulers, then a vast number of
English voters would withdraw their sympathy and
support from Home Rule. But Parnell showed now
what manner of man he was. He elected to fight,
and he was beaten. The majority of his supporters
threw him over; he broke up his party; in the end
the struggle killed him, but he died fighting. His
conduct in one way was wholly illogical. At the
time of the Phœnix Park murders, of which he was
innocent, he had offered at a word from Mr. Gladstone
to retire into private life; now that offence had come
through himself, he resolutely refused to retire,
although Mr. Gladstone explicitly enjoined him to do
so. Judged coolly on public grounds, his death was
the only happy issue out of the dilemma. It is idle to

speculate on what might have happened if he had
never gone astray ; the Lords would have thrown out
Home Rule none the less, and his continued inspiration could never have provoked sufficient ardour in
the country to render their resistance perilous. When
he was dead his sins were forgiven, even if his deserts
were to some extent obscured. Had he lived a little
longer the Home Rulers would have had one more
prejudice to encounter. His downfall did much injury
to the cause for which he had lived ; his death did
but little to make the damage good, but to some
extent it relieved the strain. The sensational proceedings in Committee Room[1] No. 15 have nothing
to do with Saunderson's life except in the result.
He was the last man to regard with complacency
a Divorce-court scandal, nor did it concern him who
were the partisans when the rupture came ; but that
his opponents should be externally discredited and
internally disorganised was an obvious cause of satisfaction. Whatever was bad for them was good for
him. Parnell aggravated the trouble by making public
what had passed between himself and Mr. Gladstone
during their interview at Hawarden ; also an alleged
proposal on the part of Mr. Morley that Parnell
should become Chief Secretary for Ireland under the
next Liberal Government. The usual disclaimers
were immediately forthcoming, together with protests
against the violation of confidential communications.
Saunderson immediately wrote to *The Times* to point
out that when Parnell had made public what had
passed between Lord Carnarvon and himself, not
only was he spared reproach, but, in spite of Lord

---

[1] The Parnellite members held a series of stormy meetings in
Committee Room No. 15 of the House of Commons to consider the
question of future leadership.

Carnarvon's disclaimer, Mr. Gladstone and his friends had continued to abide by the version of Parnell.

The end of the story may be told here. The Nationalists became a party divided against itself. At Irish bye-elections Parnellites and anti-Parnellites fought one another. A test case in December resulted in the victory of Sir J. Pope Hennessy for North Kilkenny over Parnell's nominee. But Parnell plunged with unquenchable rage into the turmoil. His friends warned him that the physical effort would be fatal; perhaps he was indifferent; relentlessly he strove, and inexorable was the penalty to be paid: within a year he was dead. With him there passed away a figure worthy of a place in history. His career has been related fully, and not with undue partiality, by Mr. O'Brien. His hatred of England was perhaps a narrow-minded prejudice. His methods in scheming for Home Rule may have brought him into contact with associates whom civilised society must at once condemn; he was the incarnation of a faith which to most Englishmen was abhorrent; he was no orator; he was stern, frigid, incapable of courting popularity. More than that, amongst Roman Catholic tenants he was a Protestant landlord, a former member of the Synod of his Church, and sheriff of his county. He lacked the Celtic eagerness; he had none of the demagogue's resources; he made no pretence to wit, none to erudition; on his own confession he was ignorant of Irish history, and had no aptitude for legislative detail. In the last respects he was no match for some of his Parliamentary colleagues. Yet, with all these disadvantages, he not only reanimated the languid spirit of Home Rule; he became the leader; he marched to the threshold of victory; and both in the

House of Commons and in Ireland he was master of
his legions as absolutely as any of whom political
history bears record.[1] For the injustice done to him
by *The Times* he deserves compassion, by the irregularity of his private life he forfeits respect; but, as a
man of strength and courage, one cannot deny him
admiration. As one standing out distinct amidst his
generation he is entitled to enduring memory.

At the same time[2] died Mr. W. H. Smith, whose
character affords a striking contrast. Parnell was
a born leader, and ruled by the terror he could
inspire. Mr. Smith was a born leader only to the
extent that he quickened his followers with a personal
affection. He was as indefatigable a slave to detailed
work as Parnell was indifferent; he radiated a wide
and bright benevolence, where Parnell was cold and
dark. In two respects they were alike; neither had
the art of captivating oratory, and both eventually
died of overwork. Mr. Smith deliberately gave his
life to his country. He knew that nothing but repose
could save him; yet he persevered. His very virtues
of simplicity and frankness tended to impair his
reputation; only those who were his colleagues could
appreciate his shrewdness and capacity for affairs.
So far as political life can be peaceful, his figure
stands serene where that of Parnell is shrouded in
continual storm.

Mr. Smith's death made necessary a rearrange-
ment of the Government. Mr. Balfour was by
general agreement the proper man to lead the

[1] He was notoriously superstitious, and strangely credulous. It is
alleged that at one time he was persuaded that the Government
intended to poison him, and for a while would not eat anything in
the House of Commons. As to his movements and habits, he was
studiously secretive.

[2] October 6, 1891.

House of Commons, and so he quitted Ireland. The new Chief Secretary was Mr. W. L. Jackson,[1] but he was not to have much scope for his energies. The Parliament was moribund; thoughts were turning towards a general election, and, so far as Unionists were concerned, not turning with sanguine hopes. The following extract from a letter written by Lord Salisbury on January 15 had possibly breathed a more optimistic spirit than in truth inspired him :

" From Lord Salisbury

"*January* 15, 1891.—Our struggle is by no means over ; but we have every ground for encouragement and hope. The hollow and deceptive alliance of parties, with antagonistic principles and inconsistent aspirations, which has been menacing the integrity of the empire, could not have lasted very long. But events have broken it up somewhat earlier than our enemies counted on."

The session which had preceded these two deaths was renewed on January 21, 1891, after the Christmas adjournment. Before the prorogation on August 5, a Land Purchase Act for Ireland, in lieu of that which had been dropped in the previous year, was duly passed into law. Saunderson had begun the year with a long letter to *The Times* in which he joined issue with Mr. Price Hughes and paid attention to the Nonconformist Church bodies, whose sympathies were with Home Rule. Religious tendencies were still engaging his attention when Mr. Gladstone introduced his Bill on February 4 to remove the religious disabilities of Roman Catholics to hold the offices of Lord Chancellor of England and Lord-Lieutenant of Ireland. On this occasion Saunderson forsook his customary all-round style of hard hitting and

[1] Lord Allerton.

made a studied debating speech. Rallying Mr. Gladstone on his own opinions as set out in his "Vatican Decrees" pamphlet, he recalled the passage in which it was alleged that the converts to the Church of Rome were amongst "the highest classes of this country," and that such converts would, in the case of conflict between their Church and their Queen, owe their first obedience to the Pope.

"If the Home Rule policy of the right honourable gentleman were successful," said the Colonel, "they might see one of these interesting captured neophytes placed in the position of Lord-Lieutenant. And so, with a Roman Catholic Parliament, they would have Roman Catholic judges, Roman Catholic juries, Roman Catholic police, and a Roman Catholic Lord-Lieutenant. He would like to know what chance the Protestant minority in Ireland would have then."

The Bill was thrown out on the second reading. The Irish measure of the session was, of course, the Land Purchase Bill. It had never been Saunderson's habit to deal with intricate financial details; he preferred to watch proceedings, and, when he saw his chance, strike in with the kind of argument which he knew how to apply. As an illustration of this, one occasion will suffice. During the Committee stage Mr. Gladstone, happening to be in the House one day, was tempted to make some casual observations. Up got the Colonel, and immediately claimed that he had supported the Bill. The tone of Mr. Gladstone's rejoinder is material evidence for those who wish to know whether Saunderson really had the knack of "drawing" him, and was indeed regarded as an adversary not to be ignored:

"I am very sorry," said Mr. Gladstone, "that the honourable and gallant gentleman has dragged me into the debate by gross mis-statements. I know that the eloquence of the honourable and gallant gentleman is as ungovernable as I am afraid it is sometimes unprofitable. In the exercise of the understanding which the Almighty has given him, he has represented me as being a supporter of this Bill."

The Colonel might not unreasonably assert that Mr. Gladstone was vulnerable to his attacks when they could provoke such an outburst of petulance and personality as this. At the same time Saunderson was receiving a tribute from another opponent, a Liberal member, who had occasion to lecture his constituents upon the House of Commons.

"The Irish members," he said, "had amongst them a very brilliant set of speakers, and there was none more brilliant than Colonel Saunderson, who was a man of great humour, and always popular in the House."

A further personal view of this date is afforded in rather a ridiculous way. When the papers are hard pressed for copy, nothing is too trivial for publication. One day the Duke and Duchess of Teck, with two or three other duchesses, happened to be at tea on the terrace with Saunderson and a few more members. A good deal of nonsense was written about this party, but the following extracts are worth reproducing because they give some idea of the Colonel's appearance to the eye of the hack journalist:

"Colonel Saunderson," says one, "in a dress according to the art of Poole, talked and looked in face like a Spanish don of Mary's days."

Another gravely reports:

"One of them was Colonel Saunderson, tall, thin, with the sunken cheeks, the high cheek-bones, the cavernous eyes of the representative Cromwellian."

One uncertain element meanwhile had been removed from the House—Lord Randolph Churchill had informed his constituents that he was about to visit South Africa. It had occurred to him that the representative of so important a constituency ought to know something about the country. This perhaps was intended as a salve to the feelings which might have been wounded by his recent proposal to migrate to Central Birmingham. At all events he started off, and, in company with some of his friends interested in the trade of the country, he made a pilgrimage which became the subject of a series of letters to *The Daily Graphic*. It afforded matter for reflection that, whilst Mr. Balfour was establishing his position in the House and the country with increasing security, the fallen favourite should be accepting a salary from an illustrated paper for a description of his travels.

In Ireland the confusion of parties was complete. June brought another source of gratification to the Colonel and his friends. In the previous year the Nationalists, amongst their numerous exploits, had hit upon the notion of forming a kind of Adullamite's cave. A number of cottages, with an adjacent market-place, were erected for the reception of evicted tenants and christened "New Tipperary." The Tipperary tenants had been forbidden to pay any rent to Mr. Arthur Smith Barry,[1] because he had been assisting other landlords to resist the Plan of Campaign. New Tipperary was to be a haven of refuge for those who should be called upon in consequence to leave their holdings. But the experiment was not a success, and in June, 1891, " four streets, one mart, and one weighing machine " were advertised for public auction. The tenants were crying out bitterly against

[1] Lord Barrymore.

the hardships of their lot, and laying their sorrows to the charge of their political leaders.

Parliament was prorogued on August 5. When it met again (February 9, 1892) there was an evident sense of unreality. Members who were not going to seek re-election were indifferent; members who were, no longer cared for anything but their prospects at the poll. Mr. Balfour introduced an Irish Local Government Bill, and his introductory speech made a bad impression. His heart did not seem to be in his task, and he made the curious confession that the proposed electorate was not devised on a satisfactory basis, but that it had been adopted in the case of the School Board, and that, after all, a bad plan which had been tried was better than any other which had not. A reaction against his popularity suddenly commenced. He was assailed in the Press even by his admirers: there were critics and murmurers in the party. The Government were beaten on a motion to refer a Church Bill to a select committee; another motion which the leader opposed in the House was nevertheless adopted. A cloud was passing over the sun which had risen so steadily and with so much promise.

Saunderson supported the Local Government Bill, whilst making it a text for his invariable sermon.

" I quite admit," he said during the debate on the second reading, " that there is the same amount of difference between Ulster Loyalists as there is between the Tories in this country. They differ very often on the land question; they differ on other points. But there is one good thing, at any rate, that the honourable gentlemen opposite have involuntarily done for our country, and it is this: they have welded into one solid whole the Ulster Loyalists. Although we may differ on some grave political points, we are absolutely at one upon the great point, and that is that we should never permit honourable gentlemen opposite to rule over us.   We are quite at one in favour of this Bill."

Next day Mr. Gladstone spoke (May 24) and his speech is worth reading as one of the last specimens of the classic oratory which was formerly the glory of the House of Commons.   The Bill was read a second time, but on June 13 it was withdrawn.

As the prospect of a dissolution drew near, the menace of Home Rule resumed formidable proportions. Early in the year it was resolved that a monster demonstration of protest should be held in Belfast. Saunderson was much concerned in the initiation of the scheme, and meanwhile he began to fan the flame in Ireland.   At the end of May he uttered one of his repeated threats that he and his brother Loyalists would never render allegiance to a Home Rule Parliament.   This speech led to an amusing correspondence.   Sir William Harcourt, speaking a few days later, wanted to know on whose behalf he spoke. Saunderson wrote him a defiant letter, and sent it to *The Times*; but it must be admitted that in this venture he "caught a tartar." Sir William's answer was so full of humour and good nature that it rather damaged the effect of the Colonel's proud indignation, and yet gave no excuse for grievance or resentment.

" May 28, 1892.

"Dear Sir William Harcourt,

"In a recent speech you referred to a remark I had made in Belfast to the effect that should Home Rule be established in Ireland 'we should seek to overthrow it.' Commenting on this remark of mine you went on to say, 'I should like to know who are we.'

"This I conceive to be a very sensible question and one well worthy of an answer. From some of the observations in the course of your speech you appeared to be under the impression that 'we' only included a few hot-headed persons so insignificant in their number that 'a few grains of ridicule,' as you observed, would suffice to disperse them.

"From these remarks I am led to believe that you are labouring under false impressions which may ultimately lead you fatally astray on the Irish question, a disaster which might be avoided by accurate information. The object of the Ulster Convention on June 7 is to answer in a conclusive manner who 'we' are. But unfortunately the Radical papers will lay themselves out to mislead their readers, you amongst the number, as to the true character and magnitude of the meeting. . . ."

He therefore invites Sir William to come over and see for himself. Here is the reply:

"45, BROOK STREET, W., *May 29*, 1892.

"MY DEAR SAUNDERSON,

"Your letter of the 28th reached me simultaneously with its publication in *The Times*. Nothing could be more agreeable to me than to accept an invitation, whether public or private, which would give me the advantage of your society—a pleasure equally appreciated by your opponents and by your friends.

"I have never witnessed a good Belfast 'faction fight,' which I believe is about this time in season, and I am sure that under your proffered safe-conduct I should find at once an entertaining and instructive spectacle for those who, like myself, belong to the Party of 'Law and Order.'

"I have, however, at present a good many engagements, and am likely to have more next month in this duller corner of the United Kingdom. I understand that your June parade is rather in the nature of a preliminary review with a regard to future contingencies than an immediate call to arms with a view to instant hostilities. I must confess to you that I find reviews, whether in print or in the field, rather sad amusements. When your hypothetical insurrection is a little more advanced and war is actually declared, I may perhaps take advantage of your offer and solicit a place as spectator on your staff.

"I do not know if your plan of campaign contem-

plates a march upon London against the Crown and
the Parliament; if so, I might meet you half-way at
Derby, which was the place where the Liberals of the
last century encountered the 'loyal and patriotic'
Highlanders who disapproved of the 'Act of Settlement' and resolved to resist it.   They also were a
'powerful section' of the Scotch people who objected
to a transfer of their allegiance.   I presume that might
be the point where the rebel army would effect its
junction with the ducal contingent from Chatsworth
under the command of the Lord-Lieutenant of the
county.

"It must be a satisfaction and an encouragement
to you to know that the Prime Minister would regard
it as an outrage to oppose your progress, which will
secure you a bloodless victory over the Statute Book.
In the meanwhile I fear I must trust to the ordinary
channels for information as to the mobilisation of the
Orange array.   But I can assure you that I shall
watch your strategy with interest, and try to alarm
myself as much as I can manage.

"Yours sincerely,
"W. V. Harcourt."

That the Colonel was wholly unrepentant is proved
by a speech which he subsequently made in the
House of Commons during the debate on the Address,
after the new Parliament had met, and two days
before Lord Salisbury's Government fell.   He knew
not, he said, what Mr. Gladstone's Home Rule Bill
would be, but, he went on:

" I say that whether the House of Lords rejects this
Bill or does not, we reject it, and that although you
may occupy the House of Commons in years to come
with academic debates upon the value of this Home
Rule Bill, when all is said, and even if you pass this
Bill, I say in the name of my people, we will reject it.

"An honourable member :   Who are you?

"Colonel Saunderson :   No man has a better right
to say that than I.   I say, in their name, that we will
reject it, and that if you ever try to erect it in Ireland
we will crumble it into dust."

In April an Irish member had again inquired whether the Colonel was to be prosecuted for vowing hostility and resistance to any Government which might be set up in Dublin. Again the reply was that as there was no Irish Parliament in existence, it was impossible to speak treason about it.

At the same time he was interesting himself in the case of a woman who had been convicted of horrible cruelty to her child, and in whose favour some remission of sentence was foreshadowed. The nature of her offence was, to Saunderson's mind, so monstrous, that he determined to prevent any mawkish sentiment from prevailing in her favour; and so forcibly did he distinguish the culprit's character in a question which he asked, that the Speaker had to remind him that an expression of opinion was in that form out of order.

At the beginning of the session of 1892 he had introduced a Bill on behalf of the weavers in his constituency. Any one conversant with parliamentary procedure knows that nothing but the fortune of ballot enables a private member to pass a measure through its necessary stages; competition leaves the remainder still-born: but impatient constituents can never understand this. When the election came the Colonel was so fervent in his warnings against Home Rule that his election address contained an assurance that Mr. Gladstone was going to pay for the Irish vote by "the subjection of Ireland to the joint authority of the priests of the Church of Rome on the one hand and the authors and instigators of the crimes of the Land League on the other," but nothing about the unhappy weavers. For this he was taken to task, and had to face some discontent; but, being unopposed, he had no evil consequences to fear, and, secure in his election, remained steadfast to his great purpose.

The Belfast demonstration on June 17 was a triumph, so far as it went ; in magnitude and harmony it left nothing to be desired, and the Duke of Abercorn, as chairman, used a simple phrase which roused a tumult of enthusiasm : "We will not have Home Rule" became a party watch-word. Saunderson, on this occasion, shared in the tribute of acclamation, but was self-denying enough, to take no place amongst the speakers. Nothing, however, could avert the coming defeat. The Government, in the undoubted exercise of their rights, manœuvred business so as to dissolve on the most favourable day ; the Opposition, equally pursuing their recognised duties, did their best to thwart them. The Government had their way, and Parliament was prorogued on June 28 : Saunderson sought a final outlet for his feelings in a letter to *The Times*, with the extensive heading "Our Objections to Home Rule," as if they were not already familiar enough. Writs were issued at once ; the pendulum took its appointed swing, and Mr. Gladstone found himself in possession of a majority of 42 over all Unionists. Of the Irish party 9 seats were retained by Parnell's faithful few.

Mr. Gladstone's own majority in Midlothian fell from 4,000 to 600. Amongst the more notable Unionist defeats was that of Mr. Walter Long, in Wiltshire. In May Lord Salisbury had made some remarks in a speech at Hastings which were taken to be a yielding to the Protectionist element in the party. On the eve of the poll therefore a number of men were turned into Mr. Long's constituency to spread the tale that if the Unionist Government were returned there would be a tax on the food of the people, with divers false embellishments of a personal application which caused an excellent gentleman not only to lose his seat but to be subjected to much base calumny.

Lord Salisbury decided to meet Parliament. Mr. Asquith was put up to move a vote of censure ; the Opposition secured a majority of 40, the Government resigned, and Home Rule once more entered into the range of practical politics.[1]

[1] August, 1892.

CHAPTER XIII

1892—1893

THERE was the usual crop of rumours concerning the formation of the new Government. It was asserted, on the highest authority, that the Queen had positively refused to send for Mr. Gladstone; it was also alleged that he had been forbidden by his doctor to take office; it meant certain death. It was darkly hinted that he and Lord Rosebery had quarrelled in Scotland and parted in wrath. Nevertheless Mr. Gladstone became Prime Minister, and Lord Rosebery went to the Foreign Office. Lord Houghton[1] was made Lord-Lieutenant of Ireland, and Mr. Morley returned to the Chief Secretary's Lodge. In fulfilment of party pledges and professions, they proceeded to suspend such provisions of the Crimes Act[2] as were still in force, and to revoke the proclamation of the National League. Next a Commission was appointed, with Sir James Mathew as President, to inquire into the grievances of the evicted tenants who were calling out for their promised succour; but the atmosphere in which it opened appeared to be so much more political than judicial that the other commissioners, as well as the landlords' counsel, found themselves unable to discharge their respective duties, and the result of the appointment was nugatory.

Saunderson was soon at loggerheads with the new

---

[1] Earl of Crewe.   [2] Of 1887.

executive. Police notices were issued to the effect that protection for evictions and other purposes could only be afforded during the hours of daylight. Saunderson at once wrote to *The Times* to protest that this was putting a premium on outrages after dark. Mr. Morley replied that legal proceedings could only be taken during stated hours, and that to send armed bodies about at night was to give provocation for disorder. The Colonel retorted according to his wont:

" If Mr. Morley lived in Clare, and had he been fired at four times and wounded fifteen since 1887, he perhaps might . . . object as strongly as Captain Croker does to an order which states . . . that no protection will be afforded him except during daylight."

There was no autumn session, and therefore no Home Rule Bill to attack, but Saunderson found ample material for his platform campaign, and commenced an earnest remonstrance against the interference of the Roman Catholic clergy in Irish politics, and the combination of Home Rule with Rome Rule, making special allusion to Archbishop Walsh and Bishop Nulty. In due course this brought him into conflict with an eminent Unionist, a member of the Church of Rome. The Colonel's explanation was ingenious; in effect that he used the words Romish and Popish in an abstract sense, suggesting no opprobrium; and his offence was deemed to be purged.

During the winter Saunderson paid a long visit to Cannes with Mrs. Saunderson and some of his family. It was here that the present writer became intimately acquainted with him.

I had spoken to him occasionally, but our relations had been little more than official; from this time I date a firm friendship which endured to the end. A strong attachment on my side was repaid by constant and conspicuous kindness ; and I write as an avowed personal partisan.   No better idea of a first impression of the Colonel in private life can be offered than an entry in a private diary ; I therefore make no apology for quoting again from mine.

"*January* 27, 1893.—Dined last night at Dunleath's. Edward Saunderson is staying there, in great form, and full of stories.   He says he heard the late Lord ——, who was old and pious, put to shame.   He gave a tract to a young stranger, urging him to read it because doubtless he was a sinner.

"' Are you a sinner, too ?'

"' Alas, yes.'

"' Then let me tell you that at your age you ought to be thoroughly ashamed of yourself.'

"I reminded him of an amusing speech I heard him make in the House of Commons, when he called Labouchere one of the gargoyles of the Liberal party.[1] L. rose to order and S. gave way.   He says he did this too quickly, and L, detecting a trap, refrained. S. was going to explain that a gargoyle was defined in the dictionary as a grotesque gutter-spout.

"He is very Irish, and declared ' there is no man Gladstone fears as he fears me.'"

I think it was on the following day that the Golf Club held some formal gathering.   I drove out with the Colonel ; and his extraordinary gaiety and zest remain vividly in my mind.   Some distinguished individual was to drive the first ball ; but the Colonel, albeit a novice, took it into his head to volunteer.   He made a prodigious bad stroke, and sent flying quantities of turf.   Entirely unabashed, he turned to the expectant crowd with a shout of laughter, delighting in his own discomfiture.   There was little of the "cavernous eyes of the representative Cromwellian ": they were

[1] *Vide supra*, p. 126.

bright and ardent as a schoolboy's. His vigour and good humour were contagious.

Parliament met a few days later[1] and he went home. I was obliged to remain, and the following letters, written by other hands from the House of Commons, give some idea of the disposition of parties after the change of Government.

"M.P.'s are arriving in London with that usual air of responsibility that rests so heavily on the heads of those who have no responsibility. . . . There were some amusing incidents in the very early morn : several Irish Unionists put in an appearance by 6 a.m. to get seats, and soon after Tanner[2] appeared, who put several hats on our benches, took off his coat and waistcoat, and laid them on the benches. Waring told our men, as they came in, to put their hats in the same places. Tanner said he would sit on them, whereupon Waring said he would call a policeman, upon which Tanner shut up. I believe he began to take his trousers off so as to take more seats. The L.U.'s came early and took several seats on the Government side."

It is reported that the Colonel arrived at seven, by which time the crisis appears to have subsided. A later letter adds :

"Carson, the new Irish lawyer, made a distinct success [in the debate on the Address]. Mr. Gladstone . . . seems to have lost much in vigour, and goes away early. . . . Edward Grey[3] was a distinct success. . . . Randolph now sits on the front bench,[4] and is very docile."

Two comments arise on these reports, one ridiculous the other mournful. Nothing more unseemly and undignified can be imagined than the spectacle of grown-up men scrambling like urchins ; an extreme

---

[1] January 31, 1893.   [2] Dr. Tanner, M.P. for Mid Cork.
[3] Under Secretary at the Foreign Office.   [4] Opposition.

illustration was to come when Mr. Gladstone introduced his Home Rule Bill on February 13. The
doors, according to the rule then in force, were not
to be opened until noon, by which time the lobby
was crowded with impatient members. The moment
admission was allowed there was a rush. Saunderson
fought his way to a seat, and, throwing himself into
it, found himself sitting on somebody else's hat. An
altercation and collision ensued. The Colonel declared
the hat had been thrust under him as he sat down;
the owner vowed that it had been put there long before. The Colonel magnanimously yielded, and even
undertook to make compensation with a new hat.
Learning subsequently that the owner had made a
formal complaint to the Speaker, he indignantly withdrew his promise. If his rival got his seat, at all
events he had to pay for it.

Such are the ludicrous incidents of parliamentary
life. Altogether graver was the spectacle of Lord
Randolph Churchill. He had returned in an altered
frame of mind. He sat with his old colleagues; he
made friendly overtures to those from whom he had
entirely estranged himself; he set himself to take a
prominent part in opposing the Home Rule Bill in
the House and country. He attended a party meeting at the Carlton, and made a loyal speech. But
it was too late; the insidious mischief was at work;
he was a stricken man. The gates of destiny were
closed against him, and the political world, which
had rated him so high, and would have welcomed
him again so willingly, was to know him, as he had
been, no more. Life was to be spared him for two
years yet, but upon terms which compel nothing
but commiseration. As a political power his days
were already numbered.

Saunderson lost no time in giving the new Parliament a specimen of his style. On February 2 he spoke on the Address. After a preliminary skirmish round "the Roman Catholic hierarchy," and a recapitulation of his quarrel with Mr. Morley about police protection, he made an uncompromising attack on Mr. Justice Mathew, as a prejudiced politician. The Evicted Tenants Commission, he said, ought to be called the Members for Cork and Mayo[1] Relief Commission. The Commission was appointed, because those gentlemen "had got themselves in a terrible fix, and something had to be done to relieve them, they being the chief supporters of the right honourable gentleman the member for Midlothian."

Next he turned to the release of the Gweedore prisoners. In this case he declared murder had been perpetrated at the instigation of a priest. "This ruffian M'Fadden," he went on. There was violent interruption. "I will amend what I said," retorted the Colonel, "and say this murderous ruffian." Then there was an uproar. The Speaker, who did not condemn Saunderson, failed to calm the storm. Finally Mr. Gladstone and Mr. Balfour in turn appealed to the latter to modify his language. This had the desired effect. The Colonel amiably agreed to substitute for the words he had used, "excited politician." He did not fail to dwell on the divisions in the Nationalist party. Mr. Healy had spoken of "the jackasses of the Billy Redmond type;[2] and these were the men to whom Mr. Gladstone was going to entrust the government of Ireland." Those who listened to Saunderson for the first time heard one of his most

[1] Mr. O'Brien and Mr. Dillon.
[2] Saunderson made a point of quoting such instances of the "vicarious vituperation" amongst the divided Nationalists.

characteristic speeches. He makes no comment upon his own performance, but he pays a generous tribute, next day, to his new colleague who had taken the first step in his brilliant career.

"*February* 3.—Carson has just made a magnificent speech, which has completely vindicated all I said about M'Fadden."

On February 13, as we have seen, Mr. Gladstone introduced his second Home Rule Bill. He spoke for two hours and a quarter, which was a sufficiently fine effort for a man in his eighty-fourth year; but by common consent it fell short of his performance of 1886. In principle, he claimed, the Bill followed the precedent which he had then set up. The most notable contrast lay in the retention of the Irish members at Westminster. His original proposal to exclude them had driven away many doubting followers. His present scheme for preserving them, to the reduced number of eighty, but without power to vote on questions exclusively English or Scottish, was regarded as an unsatisfactory compromise, and eventually he agreed to remove all voting limitations.

"I scarcely see how a Cabinet could have been formed," he had written to Lord Granville in 1886, "if the inclusion of the Irish members had been insisted on; and now I do not see how the scheme of policy can be saved from shipwreck if the exclusion is insisted on."

Truly it was a dilemma beyond the wit of man, as he had said, to solve with entire success. Many remained who considered the removal of the Irish members the one redeeming feature of his proposals, and were therefore disgusted now. Saunderson spoke on the second night of the debate.

" He was not going to occupy the House with the details of the Bill," he said with candour, and indeed that was never his way : " he did not care, and his people did not care a farthing, about details. What they opposed, and had opposed all along, was the general principle of granting a Home Rule Government to Ireland, responsible to an Irish Parliament.

" Presently he paused to give a cuff to Archbishop Walsh, and then applied himself to Mr. Dillon, one of whose recent speeches he proceeded to quote :

" I have never hesitated to express my admiration for the men of '67 ;[1] and I declare that our movement is in all its main principles, and in the great issues at which it aims, the legitimate successor of that movement, as well as those of '48[2] and '98.[3] Our objects are the same although our methods may be different. Our chief object is the liberty of Ireland.

" He challenged the honourable member, if he took part in the debate and professed his readiness to accept this measure as a final settlement, to state to the House that the speech just quoted was absolutely devoid of foundation. . . . They might pass the Home Rule Bill, but they had not the power to make the Loyalists obey it."

In these sentences we have a typical exhibition of Saunderson's turn of mind, method of argument, and attitude of defiance. The Bill was read a first time three days later.

Irish Loyalists were at red-heat. At a Belfast meeting Mr. Johnston held up an open Bible whilst a vast audience repeated after him a solemn pledge of hostility to Home Rule. The talk of armed resistance became louder than before, and peaceful citizens joined English volunteer corps, so as to acquire some acquaintance with the art of war.

Mr. Redmond, indeed, declared that he and his friends would retain a free hand in dealing with the

[1] Fenian disturbances.
[2] Smith O'Brien and the " Young Ireland " party.
[3] The Great Rebellion.

various stages; but there was no doubt that the Bill had been accepted and would be pushed forward with pertinacity by the united forces of the Home Rulers.

Meanwhile Saunderson was to find the session full of storm and stress. Early in March the public were again reading of his personal entanglements. Mr. Russell had moved the adjournment of the House upon the state of Co. Clare; Saunderson seconded. In the course of his remarks he made his customary charge of complicity with crime against the Irish members. Mr. W. Redmond challenged him to repeat this outside. The Colonel accepted with alacrity and solemnly wrote to appoint a meeting in the lobby. An interview immediately took place, but it cannot be regarded as quite worthy of so grave an occasion. A dialogue something like this ensued:

"You challenged me to repeat in the lobby what I said in the House: I am here to do it."

"Do you charge me with being a murderer?"

"Whatever I said in the House I repeat here. I did not charge you with being a murderer."

"Do you accuse me of sympathy with murder, then?"

"I don't know what you sympathise with, nor do I care. I never said that you sympathised with murder."

"What do you charge me with, then?"

"I never mentioned you at all."

"Do you accuse the Nationalist members of sympathy with murder?"

"I did not even say that. What I did say was that John Dillon made a speech one Sunday and there was an attempted murder a few days later."

One cannot help quoting:

"No, sir, I do not bite my thumb at you, sir, but I bite my thumb, sir."

"Do you quarrel, sir?"

"Quarrel, sir? No, sir."[1]

[1] *Romeo and Juliet.*

And one is disposed to wish that the Colonel had clinched the argument with the historic " Never mind, sir !" of Mr. Peter Magnus.[1]

Together with the leading Loyalists of Ulster, Saunderson issued a manifesto inviting support of the Ulster Defence Union, and had within a few days to acknowledge contributions ranging from £50 to single shillings, subscribed by working men. He was indefatigable and unsparing of exertion. Amongst other places where he hastened to speak was Sheffield, of which a souvenir remains in an anonymous letter which says: "Unless you alter your views . . . I shall take your life with a knife or a pistol. . . . Should you oppose the second reading of the Home Rule Bill your days will be numbered."

Saunderson, indeed, shared the distinction attaching to ministers of becoming an object of concern to the police. He was advised to incur no unnecessary risks, and to carry a revolver; but it did not suit his temper to " blush unseen," and when he had to address a demonstration in St. James's Hall on one occasion he preferred to walk up Piccadilly deliberately and ostentatiously through the crowd.

During April numerous demonstrations were organised : in Belfast, where Mr. Balfour witnessed a march-past of 100,000 Loyalists ; at Hatfield, where the Colonel was " hoisted " by his admirers in the garden, and received other flattering attentions, as if he were to be regarded as the presiding spirit of the entertainment; at the Albert Hall ; and elsewhere. In May Lord Salisbury visited Belfast. In this centre the war movement was livelier than ever. Trade was said to be paralysed ; orders were being cancelled wholesale ; a rising was regarded as quite conceivable.

[1] " The Pickwick Papers."

"NEVER MIND, SIR!"

From the drawing by Sir F. C. Gould.

A private letter from Dublin early in April reported that there was not a single Home Ruler to be found, and that the Castle entourage looked upon their position as farcical; whilst the military authorities declared that if the Bill were to pass, civil war would inevitably ensue. A general officer was writing to *The Times* to urge that the position should be made clear and the contingency seriously contemplated. In March a retired cavalry officer had written to Saunderson that, in the event of an outbreak, he should at once advise his three sons to resign their commissions in the Army so as to escape the odious duty of fighting against Loyalists.

Much ridicule was, of course, thrown upon all this talk by the supporters of the Government, but the Ulstermen believed what they said; nor were men wanting on this side of the Channel to take them at their word.

Colonel the Hon. Lewis Dawnay, who had formerly served in the Coldstream Guards, and had sat in Parliament as member for Thirsk from 1880 to 1892, conceived the idea of raising a Yorkshire corps to join them in the field. Colonel Saunderson received the proposal with becoming gratitude.

" *Colonel Saunderson to Colonel Dawnay*

" HOUSE OF COMMONS,
" *April* 11, 1893.

" MY DEAR DAWNAY,

" I was extremely glad to get your letter to-day. I was expecting some such suggestion from this side of the water. I am persuaded that when England realises what Home Rule means, from an imperial point of view, the idea of enrolling volunteers over here will be widely taken up.

" If Home Rule was a policy only affecting Ireland, we might indeed expect sympathy and support. But being, as it is, a policy subversive of the integrity of the empire, it ought to meet with the sort of opposition you and your friends contemplate.

"It is well to remember that our proposed action in opposition to Home Rule is, so far as we can judge, in harmony with the wishes of the great majority of the English people.

"The stand I have taken in the matter has all along been a public one. The Ulster Loyalists, in whose name I am authorised to speak, have publicly announced their determination to resist the authority of a Home Rule Parliament by force—I echo their words.

"You can make any use of this letter you may think fit. Wishing you every success in a movement which will rejoice the hearts of the Irish Loyalists,
                                "Ever yours,
                                        "EDWARD SAUNDERSON."

This letter Colonel Dawnay circulated, covered by the following invitation :

                                "BENINGBROUGH HALL, YORK,
                                        "April 1893.

"DEAR SIR,
        "It is proposed to raise a Yorkshire Corps of Gentlemen Volunteers, with a view to rendering assistance to the Irish Loyalists in case of need.

"You will see by the enclosed letter that the idea meets with the cordial approval of the leaders of the Loyalist Party in Ireland. Do you feel disposed to join the movement ?
                                "Yours faithfully,
                                        "LEWIS PAYN DAWNAY."

Amongst the replies received many are instructive and noteworthy. Objections, of course, were obvious. Some officers of Yeomanry and Militia pointed out the impossibility of reconciling such action with their present obligations. Some observed that, as Justices of the Peace, they could not with propriety set out to resist the execution of any law which Parliament might think fit to enact. One wrote : "What do you propose to do if you find your corps in opposition to the Queen's troops?" Others confessed hesitation at the prospect of encouraging civil war. Several pleaded age and infirmity, and one distinguished Crimean officer frankly admitted that he had had enough fighting.

But there was plenty of response in a different tone. "Though now sixty-two, I shall be glad to join any mounted corps," wrote one who wore the Victoria Cross. "I have no hesitation in expressing warmest approval of your scheme," says one peer of the realm. "Body and soul I am with my kinsmen in Ireland," exclaims another. A surgeon and a trained nurse offered their services. Promises of assistance came from outside the county. One man was ready to join with three sons; another with two; whilst plenty of stalwarts sent a laconic assent, and begged to be enrolled.

The Bill was read a second time on April 21, and, in accordance with local traditions, riots broke out in Belfast.

With the Committee stage Saunderson's activity grew even greater than before. That he had little scruple in disregarding minute observances may be gathered from this interruption to his first contribution:

"The Chairman: It is not competent for the honourable member to discuss clause nine; this is an amendment to the first part of clause one."

One clause was as good as another for the Colonel's purpose, and he proceeded with the following comprehensive criticisms:

"If a Home Rule Parliament was established in Dublin . . . [there] would be a Government of robbery, jobbery, and beggary. . . . It might have been expected that the course of honourable members would be that which they followed, because theirs was essentially a personally conducted party . . . whatever [they] might think they would be careful to keep it to themselves."

Next day he was observing that—

" The proposal was to give some reality to the supremacy by the introduction of the word subordinate. The word was not altogether happy in its application; the word insubordinate would more accurately describe the Irish Parliament and people."

Next day, pursuing this theme, he further argued that the proposed second chamber would prove in operation to be no effective check on the other House:

" If we could conceive this metropolis having two chambers, one composed of burglars and the other of pickpockets, that would be an analogy to this proposal."

Not content with this, he was up again within forty-eight hours denouncing the—

" union of hearts, which was supposed to be the spontaneous action of mutual affection; . . . but he had always warned the Gladstonian party that the union of hearts was a very uncertain quantity; it was a union of conditional amorousness."

The Government began to grow impatient, and at the end of May Saunderson had to complain that they were not doing their full share of talking. The debates, he said, were lopsided; all the speeches came from one side. Singling out the Chancellor of the Exchequer (Sir W. Harcourt) he protested that the Committee, knowing what they did of his past history and his fame as a constitutional authority—

" Had a right to expect and hope that the right honourable gentleman would let loose the floods of information which he had boiling up inside him, and pour it out to satisfy a thirsty Opposition."

Presently he found one speech a day insufficient. When the character of Ulstermen was assailed, he was up at once.

" The honourable member for Kerry had accused the Ulstermen of being cowards. . . . They did not shoot people from behind hedges, or carry out the laws of the League by houghing cattle, firing into dwellings, or burning hayricks. . . . They in Ulster had not the courage to perform these acts. . . . Then the honourable member had said that the Ulster party was a revolutionary party. The usual idea of a revolutionist was a man who proposed to pull down the institutions of the country; they, on the contrary, desired and intended to maintain intact the institutions of this country under which they had thriven."

He had no faith in the promise of a benevolent Irish Government under which no weapons would be needed save "spades and shovels—and possibly blackthorns."

The situation was becoming critical. The Government could make little progress, and on June 28 they introduced proposals for the use of the guillotine. Determination was met by resentment; tempers were exacerbated. On July 11 there was a preliminary storm; on July 27 the Committee stage was completed, and that night the tempest broke in its fury.

It has been alleged that when the House is in an angry mood, the thermometers actually register a rise of temperature. It is an observed fact that when a wave of excitement is in motion, members—notably those from Ireland—may be seen fanning themselves with their order papers, as though they were physically heated. Nobody who has sat in Parliament can forget the consciousness of storm in the air when the current of human passion is running strong and high. Such was the condition of the House of Commons on the night of July 27.

So much notice was taken of the scenes which followed that it would be an obvious omission to ignore them here, the more so as Saunderson's name was much in evidence. Stated as briefly as possible, the story was this: a state of tension, already sufficiently strained, had been made worse by an Irish member, who persisted in shouting " Judas " at Mr. Chamberlain. Both sides had lost their tempers. Whilst the House was being cleared for a division, a Liberal member loitering near the front Opposition bench fell into altercation with one of its occupants. Resenting an intimation that his company was not desired, he proceeded to seat himself there defiantly; whereupon another member from behind pushed him off. Then began a scrimmage. The Irishmen surged up from their benches towards the gangway. Members were knocked down, hats crushed, there was indiscriminate shoving, and no doubt some exchange of blows. Saunderson was in the thick of it. His own version was that an Irish member " flopped down on the top of him," upon which he seized him by the collar, although he subsequently learnt that "the honourable gentleman had slipped and arrived there by accident." Then another Irishman from behind struck the Colonel on the forehead, leaving a visible mark. " Of course I returned the blow," said he, "and then the fight became general." He was accused in the Irish Press of assaulting a man who was known to be an invalid, which was nonsense. Saunderson attributed the outburst to the fact that—

" When the Irishmen below the gangway saw the scrimmage on the front Opposition bench, the natural combative instinct of Irishmen overcame all restraint. They were unable to resist the temptation of joining in, and they came in a sort of wave and threw themselves across the gangway."

He objected to being hit from behind; it was a cowardly blow—

" But fortunately my head is as hard as a brickbat. However, I don't think the Irishmen have any feeling [afterwards]; I don't, really, from my knowledge of the country."

The member who had shouted "Judas" wrote a sentimental and over-coloured description of the affair in one of the papers; meanwhile the following extracts from letters received from two eye-witnesses are rather contradictory :

" The reports of the row were greatly exaggerated," says one. " I fail to see the use of a scene unless some of the blows said to have been given took effect. Saunderson says he hit out, but confesses he hit no one." [1]
"Anything so scandalous as the scene here last week is beyond imagination," writes the other.

Finally, it ought to be confessed that the Colonel confided to the initiator of the scrimmage that it might all be very disgraceful, but that he was indebted to him for ten minutes of the best fun he had ever had in his life.

With a mass of angry men in violent contact, it is obvious that there was a serious, and might have been a disastrous, breach of the peace; but in order that there may be no appearance of an attempt to dignify the episode with any heroic character, the following

---

[1] In a subsequent interview, when he was asked if he hit anybody he said: "I did—several; but only in self-defence. My friend Mr. Burdett-Coutts defended my rear, so that I only had to keep my front clear."

ridiculous letter from an anonymous correspondent
may serve as an appendix :

" July 29, 1893.

" DEAR COLONEL,
    " I must congratulate you for the noble part
you took in the fight in the House of Commons.   You
are a gentleman.   It has given evidence that you will
die in the last ditch or any other ditch for the cause
of ould Ireland.   My friends and I have been pleased
to the soul ; that you are a broth of a boy, sir, is
without doubt."

There follows another page of panegyric, expressing
an opinion almost too good to be true, in language
a little too suggestive of the Irishman of melodrama ;
and it is rather disconcerting to find this sad falling
away at the close :

" Woe to the villains that dare to attack predjuce
[prejudice ?] and priviledge, and you are . . . well
calculated to represent the whole of the Humbugs
of Ulster."

CHAPTER XIV

1893—1894

SAUNDERSON was determined to neglect no expedient in pressing his onslaught. He had made speeches in abundance, and written a profusion of letters: now he was seized with an aspiration to appeal directly to the Sovereign. Everybody knows that a political appeal must be presented through the medium of the Secretary of State. Peers possess a technical right of access which apparently was still recognised at the beginning of Queen Victoria's reign,[1] but which is practically obsolete now; commoners and political bodies must memorialise according to etiquette and rule. But Saunderson was not to be deterred by custom; this was no ordinary case, and he was no ordinary man. He armed himself accordingly with a petition, and wrote to the Queen's private secretary to say that he wished to present it. The inevitable refusal had to be repeated before he would give up, as the following letters show; and the culminating note is a sad return to the realm of commonplace.

From Sir Henry Ponsonby

"OSBORNE, *July* 16, 1893.

"DEAR COLONEL SAUNDERSON,
"The Queen can receive no political petition or address without the knowledge of her responsible

[1] "The Letters of Queen Victoria," 1, 431.

advisers, nor can she reply to any such appeal except with their advice.

" It would be, I imagine, unconstitutional if such an address as you describe were privately presented to H er Majesty.

" The meaning of the petition is, of course, that the Queen should dismiss her present ministers, and you will understand that it would be impossible for Her Majesty to listen to such an Address without some responsible adviser being in attendance.   There is no difficulty in sending the Address to the Queen. The Secretary of State, whatever his opinion may be, will always submit petitions to the Queen—though of course the reply he will advise will not, I presume, in this case be very encouraging."

"Osborne, *August 9,* 1893.

"Dear Colonel Saunderson,
    "I think I explained in my last letter to you that the question of receiving political addresses depends entirely on the Queen's minister, and that I have no power to bring the matter before Her Majesty.

"Your request should be addressed to the Secretary of State, Home Office."

On August 28 Colonel Saunderson writes to his wife:

" There is nothing new going on.   Lord Salisbury is presenting the petition through Asquith."

The Report Stage of the Home Rule Bill was disposed of on August 25, and it was eventually read a third time on September 3.[1] Saunderson was enduring an arduous existence. In one of his last speeches he indicated the gloomy prospect awaiting landlords if Home Rule should ever come to pass. If they stayed at home they would run a good chance of being shot; if they became absentees they would be taxed beyond the possibility of existence.

Moreover it was a season of abnormal heat. On

[1] By 301 to 267 votes.

August 16 he writes from the House of Commons :
" Heat in the shade, 93°. Last night I was nearly
choked in my bedroom. To-night I sleep in the
tent" (at Holly Lodge). A few days later the ther-
mometer registered 98°.

At the end of the month he allowed himself a short
holiday for grouse-shooting with Mr. Rimington
Wilson :

" BROOMHEAD.

" *August* 31, 1893.—We had a tremendous grouse
shoot yesterday. After 4 drives, 9 guns, we had shot
1,912 grouse. We had 2 drives after lunch, when we
increased the number to 2,560. There has been nothing
like it in England. Rimington is in great force. . . .
We have a very nice lot of men : Lord Yarborough,
Lord Powis, Lord Throwley,[1] Savile Crossley, Mr.
Mason, and Mr. Pretyman. When the others went to
bed, Rimmy and I sat up and jawed. . . ."

On September 8 the Home Rule Bill was thrown
out in the House of Lords upon the second reading.
The debate lasted for four nights and gave occasion for
some fine speaking. Herein the House of Lords has
an advantage over the House of Commons : on an
occasion of this kind none but the shining lights
illumine the darkness of debate. There are not dozens
of insignificant gentlemen struggling to catch the
Speaker's eye, bent upon delaying business with an
uninteresting speech. Those who take part are men
whose views are awaited with interest, and who are
practised and capable speakers.

Every Unionist peer who could be found was brought
up to vote, regardless of infirmity or age. It was said
that only two were absent without valid excuse ; one
was shooting lions in Somaliland ; the other killing rats
at Reigate. But the character of the proceedings was
artificial. When the Bill left the House of Commons

[1] The late Earl Sondes.

Mr. Redmond had repudiated it as a final settlement of the Irish question ; it came up as surely doomed as the bull that enters the Spanish arena. The most eloquent of its advocates, Lord Rosebery, could scarcely bring himself to defend it with gravity and conviction. The division might, as usual, have preceded the debate instead of terminating it, so far as the result was concerned. The hostile majority was 419 to 41. Nor did the peers, thus flouting the decision of the democratic house, imperil for one moment their authority or their favour, such as it might be, in the eyes of men.

A fortnight later Parliament adjourned. Had Home Rule received a last and fatal blow ? No man can say That it has receded very far into the background amongst the principles of Liberalism is undeniable. It has long ceased to be adopted as a genuine and in-spiriting cry at elections. But after fourteen years an Irish party is still to be found extracting a proposal for local self-government from a Cabinet, in fulfilment of an oracular promise by which its president had bound himself, and then flinging it back contemptuously as wholly inadequate to meet its requirements. Whether the Liberal party will turn the other cheek and risk a further slap; whether they will take heart of grace and surrender everything ; or whether they will beat a general retreat and withdraw all their pledges and professions, time only can inform us. But one fact is patent: with the defeat of the Bill of 1893, Saunderson's labours in one sense were at an end. He was not to live to see another serious attempt to establish Home Rule.

As we shall see, he remained the leader and played a leader's part; but his best work was done in opposing Mr. Gladstone's two measures. It was a task for which he was exactly suited, and no man could possibly have performed it better. Intricate calculations and minute details were not congenial to one of his disposition. The spacious mind was fretted with technical limitations in discussion;[1] he needed ample scope. He was less a patient tactician than a bold and impetuous fighter. His idea of strategy was to engage the enemy everywhere simultaneously and with all his forces. The clear issue of Home Rule gave him every opportunity for warfare of this kind, and he will certainly be remembered best and with greatest admiration for his rushing onslaughts during that momentous period. His own appreciation of the case as it now stood is not quite clear. In October he spoke in Belfast at a meeting of the Ulster Defence Union : " Home Rule," he said, " was dead. It was dissected in the House of Commons, buried in the House of Lords, and even the Irish people would not take the trouble to give it a wake." Yet, he went on :

" The meeting had one object in view : that in case of extremity they should not be taken unawares. If the Home Rule Bill should ever be passed by the insanity of the British Parliament they should resist it to the bitter end."

Then, returning to his favourite theme, and employing his favourite term of opprobrium : " The most atrocious desperadoes on the face of the earth were the Irish Americans, and yet Mr. Gladstone had not scrupled to write a letter commending them." A few days later, at Derryadd, he was declaring that—

" They would in all probability have another turn at Home Rule. . . . Only the other day he received a

---

[1] *Vide supra*, p. 197, where he began discussing clause 9 upon the first line of clause 1.

letter from an [Orange] brother in British Columbia to say that they were willing to send over material when they required it to fight the battle of the Union.

Meanwhile the gentle protest which has already been noticed did not deter the Colonel from pursuing his denunciations against the Roman Catholic Church in politics. At Belfast he had said, "For the first time since the reign of James II. the English Government was maintained by men elected by the authority of the priests." At Portadown he declared that—

" they were opposed to the setting up in this country of a new ascendency, more hateful, more tyrannical and more detestable than any which had gone before, namely, the ascendency of the Irish Roman Catholic Church."

This was too much for another Roman Catholic Unionist, who sent a passionate protest to the newspapers. The Colonel, he declared, "wallowed in rant"; and whereas every priest was not a Dr. Walsh, every Unionist was not a Colonel Saunderson. The Colonel was incorrigible. Immediately afterwards at Lurgan—

" he admitted that every priest was not an Archbishop Walsh. Some were better, some worse; some were excellent men; some bishops had certainly condemned the criminal action of the Land League; but what did that matter if they had Home Rule? Who was the priest that would rule Ireland? Why, Walsh. He was the man who returned over seventy members to the House of Commons; he was the wire-puller."

And at Derryadd he observed that he did not want to insult any man's religion, but it was the priests who led the Land League, " that organisation which had marked with letters of crime and blood the history of their country"; which, if not an insult to their religion, was certainly not the language of adulation. In the course of the same speech he declared that Home Rule was not dead; it was put by in lavender for a time. Crossing next to Scotland, he assured a Glasgow audience that Home Rule was " so stale that it would not keep for another day "; nevertheless he seems to have arrived at the conclusion that after all it was scotched, not killed.

It was to be an abnormal session. Parliament had met on January 31, 1893. It had adjourned on September 22. On November 2 it met again, and, with three days' holiday at Christmas, it remained sitting until March 5, 1894, when it was prorogued, only to commence a new session a week later. The business of the autumn session consisted of the Parish Councils Bill and the Employers' Liability Bill. Neither of these concerned Saunderson closely, and he rested after his labours of the previous months. His annual appearance at Glasgow has been mentioned; again he was annoyed, if not disconcerted, by the excessive juvenile element in his audience :

"NEW CLUB, GLASGOW.

"*November* 4, 1893.—I had a great meeting last night; it went off well. There were many babies who squalled fearfully. . . ."

Returning to Belfast, he was detained by a reception which was being prepared for the Duke of Devonshire:

" BELFAST.

"*November* 5.—Our people here especially wish me to take part in the reception of Devonshire, so . . . I remain.

" *10th*.—The banquet was a great success. I am supposed to have made a very good speech. Londonderry was greatly pleased with it."

14

Subsequently he attended the House of Commons as the spirit moved him, but he had no part to play. Before the Christmas adjournment there was a full-dress debate upon the Navy, when Lord George Hamilton moved a resolution demanding increased preparations. Saunderson contemplated a speech, but he made none :

" *December* 17, 1893.—There will be a field-day in the House on Tuesday, when I hope to make a few remarks, to show that we Irish take a lively interest in all that affects the welfare of the empire."

Throughout his public life he had been a stout Imperialist, as the phrase is, and his sympathy on such a question as this was a foregone conclusion; but, in spite of his love of all things appertaining to the sea and ships, he never presented himself to the House as a naval critic.

It was not a time of ease for the Government. Their management of the Parish Council Bill was not entirely successful. Over the Employers' Liability Bill they came to loggerheads with the House of Lords. One of their own supporters in the Commons had moved an amendment in favour of contracting out; this was rejected. When the Bill reached the other House, Lord Dudley reasserted the principle, and his amendment was carried. The Bill went back to the Commons; the Government threw out the Lords' amendment by a majority of sixty-one, the original mover of the clause this time voting against it. The Lords stood firm, and a deadlock ensued. Trade was bad; revenue was falling; the Budget prospects were gloomy in the extreme, and prophecies of a dissolution were general. " The Government are in a hopeless muddle with their business," wrote one close observer at Christmas :

" I can't see any way out except an election. Indeed
it looked last week as if they were riding for one, but
it now seems as if things would run on a bit. Harcourt, I know, is much upset about his Budget prospects,
which are of the blackest. The revenues are very
bad, and the Navy people have to be satisfied."

In connection with the prevailing spirit of uneasiness,
occasion may be taken to insert a letter from Baroness
Burdett-Coutts which echoes the general tone. At the
same time it gives some insight into her most interesting personality, and illustrates her friendship with
Saunderson.

                              " Shenley, *October* 31, 1893.

" Dear Col. Saunderson,
       " Many an anxious thought has occupied your
mind and many an arduous day passed with you
since we all sat chatting and laughing on the lawn
of this pretty farm in the dazzling sunshine and
beauty of a summer which really seems loth to leave.
Ashmead and I drove over early to-day and he has
gone to make his rounds. I have not been here
since that bright day with you and some others of
our gay party, some scattered now—East, West, North,
and South—amusing themselves in other scenes. I
hardly know why that particular day has fixed itself
in my remembrance ; but it, for some reason, always
stands alongside of that sad day when we parted on
the edge of the stud.[1] You said, when you wrote,
you felt ' down on your luck' when you waved your
hand to us. And indeed we did the same, for we
both felt we were for a time bidding adieu to a dear
and kind friend ; to one whose friendship we value and
prize truly. And we could but think how much of
anxiety lay before you and speculate where and how
our happy intimacy may be renewed.
       " I have read constantly of the things so near your
heart, and we were nearly in your country. Ashmead
once thought of being at your great meeting, for he
must go over to Ireland to see after the Baltimore
Fishery School, of which he is trustee, and where he

---

[1] Mr. Burdett-Coutts's horse-breeding establishment.

has not been since Father Davis's death. I should have gone also; but the Committee Meeting was put off till later and I shall not come now.

"It is now very near the meeting of Parliament. It seems to me like the lifting up of a black curtain, and what is to be enacted now on that stage is a mystery. I see no gleam of light, and all the elements of confusion and distress are ready to work again. The strikes and their injurious effects on all, and their miserable results, go on. Suffering, wonderfully borne by those entirely innocent of and in no way connected with the strike, is beginning to be bitterly felt, and from its extent will be very difficult to meet.

"The weather has been and is a mercy. It has continued so fine, allowed so much work to be continued, and inspired a general cheerfulness greatly beneficial. Such an autumn has scarcely been seen. Its beauty was gorgeous, and our chestnut trees were like bronze gold.

"Ashmead has been shooting about and goes on Wednesday to Norfolk. I have been somewhat quiet, trying to get workmen out of my house. Those to whom you spoke[1] are cleared off; but I afterwards had some work done in Piccadilly which, less disastrous[2] and more quickly done, still takes up time. I suppose we shall get in some time in November, though I don't think we shall mind Parliament much. But it will be right to be at hand. What are you doing as to this matter?[3]—though we shall linger here perhaps as long as Holly Lodge is so beautiful. Don't forget the billiard table is there. About the 23rd November I go probably with Lady Margaret Howard and the Duke to a great meeting, on behalf of the Cruelty to Children Society, at Manchester.

"And now my dear and very true friend, good-bye. Give my love to Mrs. Saunderson and your cockatoo. My cocky looks out for you every day. I have never

[1] At that time a large number of workmen had been employed for many months on the house in Stratton Street, and before the main portion of them dispersed, Col. Saunderson made a speech to them.

[2] These words seem odd, but they refer to certain complications in the work which necessitated much of it being done over again.

[3] As to the possibility of his being likely to stay at Stratton Street when he came up for the session.

thanked you for the lines. My thorns and roses speak to me often.

"Yours very truly,
"BURDETT-COUTTS.

"Ashmead just in. Sends all the messages you would care to have. Some of our beautiful foals are a little poorly."

The year 1894 opened under gloomy omens. The problem of the unemployed was passing through one of its most acute phases; people were complaining that it was impossible to let houses, things were so bad in the West End. One Irish lady ended a letter with the summary, "There is a great lull over us in Ireland now, which is a great, great rest; but as a rule people here [in England] are ruined."

The House of Commons disposed of the Parish Councils Bill after prolonged labour, and then adjourned for a month whilst the Lords considered it. To this measure also they passed certain amendments. In the case of the Employers' Liability Bill the Cabinet refused to yield, and it was dropped: in the other instance they agreed, under protest. On March 1 Mr. Gladstone, in announcing this decision, made the following declaration:

"We are compelled to accompany that acceptance with the sorrowful declaration that the differences, not of a temporary or casual nature merely, but differences of conviction, differences of prepossession, differences of mental habit, and differences of fundamental tendency, between the House of Lords and the House of Commons, appear to have reached a development in the present year such as to create a state of things of which we are compelled to say that, in our judgment, it cannot continue. . . . The issue which is raised . . . is a controversy which, when once raised, must go forward to an issue."

It was his swan song. The "rising hope of the

stern and unbending Tories" was setting in stormy threats against the Conservative element of the Constitution. In the long series of stirring episodes which had marked his sixty years of political life, nothing more dramatic can be found than his secret passing. Antithesis gives it point. No emotional demonstration, no panegyrics, no cheers or lamentations, could have left a more forcible impression. The imagination lingers over the proud restraint of the weary old man who had uttered his last defiant message to his foes, and then, knowing that one word would have raised his legions about him in a riot of acclamation, preferred to make his exit unobserved.

Mr. Morley has told us[1] that the Prime Minister was in favour of a dissolution upon the issue between the two Houses of Parliament; his colleagues dissented. Rapid failure of power both in seeing and hearing warned him that his physical endurance could not long continue; moreover he was fundamentally opposed to a large expenditure upon Naval preparations such as the Cabinet were disposed to advocate. He had spoken against Lord George Hamilton's resolution, which had, indeed, been defeated; but he was not content.

"My name stands in Europe," he said, "as a symbol of the policy of peace, moderation, and non-aggression. What would be said of my . . . plunging England into the whirlpool of militarism? . . . I have uniformly opposed militarism."[2]

Early in February *The Pall Mall Gazette* staked its reputation for accuracy on an announcement of his impending retirement.

" 'Humph!' said Nicholas, 'that's an odd paragraph.'

[1] *Op. cit.*, vol. iii., chaps. vii. and viii. [2] *Ibid.*

" ' Very,' returned Crummles, ' I can't think who puts these things in. I didn't.' "

Mr. Gladstone might have made this denial with greater sincerity than Mr. Vincent Crummles. It was certainly not his wish that the news should get abroad; but some one in the secret had let fall an unguarded word, and some busybody had passed it on ; or some unscrupulous eavesdropper had fastened on it as a legitimate source of profit.[1]

On March 3, 1894, Mr. Gladstone resigned and Lord Rosebery became Prime Minister. On the 5th Parliament was prorogued ; on the 12th it met again to begin a new session. The new Prime Minister began with an indiscretion.[2] In outlining his policy, he declared that Home Rule could never be carried until the "predominant partner" in the Union of Great Britain and Ireland had been converted. The Irish took great offence, and refused to be pacified, in spite of Mr. Morley's assurance in the House of Commons that Lord Rosebery was only alluding to the action of the House of Lords. However, a speech at Edinburgh was devoted to soothing the irritation : Lord Rosebery here explained that he had only pointed

[1] Mr. Astor permits me to tell the following story : A stranger came to the office of *The Pall Mall Gazette*, anxious to sell this piece of information. Mr. Astor decided to see him, and, although there was little guarantee of truth, he was inclined to believe it. A stated sum was to be forthcoming if Mr. Gladstone resigned before a given date ; if not, then nothing. The resignation occurred a day or two after time. The stranger called again, admitted that he had lost his bargain, but appealed for a compassionate grant. Mr. Astor said that the terms had virtually been fulfilled, and therefore he intended to pay in full. The stranger professed great gratitude, and offered in return to impart another precious piece of information. This turned out to be the real truth about the Claimant. Mr. Astor answered that he would not give him five shillings for it ; and that was the end of their acquaintance.

[2] Some prefer to think that his indiscretion was in withdrawing, under pressure, anything he had said.

to the necessity of enlisting such general support in England that the House of Lords would be compelled to yield to the public demand; this was accepted as adequate, and shaken confidence was declared to be restored. It was not perhaps an entirely " regrettable incident"; it had the painful character of a honeymoon quarrel, but at all events it left the new leader at a considerable advantage. Mr. Gladstone had been pledged to Home Rule before all things; his successor had notified a distinct reservation, and to that extent he started with something like a free hand.

Another small embarrassment befell the Government in the House of Commons. On March 13 Mr. Labouchere moved an amendment to the Address in favour of the abolition of the House of Lords. With the echo of Mr. Gladstone's last speech still in their ears, it might appear that the party were in no position to refuse assent. But the Government were not going to be driven into hurried and undesirable commitments; they opposed it, only to become the sport of Parliamentary fortune. The Whips were caught napping; and although Mr. Balfour, Mr. Goschen, and others came gallantly to the rescue, the motion was carried against the Government by 147 to 145. This placed them in an awkward predicament: their Address was now unpresentable. Next day the Chancellor of the Exchequer moved a new Address in place of it. The House allowed it to pass, but not without a playful remonstrance on the part of Saunderson. His share in the two days' work may be told in his own words:

"*March* 14, 1894.—You will see that we had some fine sport in the House. The defeat of the Government, you will be surprised to learn, was due to me. I was dining in the House, and, as we sat there, most of the Conservatives rushed off to support the

Government, but I remained with those at my table ; so three of us refused to go in, which had the exact result of putting the Government in a minority of two. To-day we had a remarkable scene. For the first time on record the leader of the House got up to move the rejection of his own Address. After Harcourt had accomplished this feat, he rose with portentous gravity to move a new Address.   He evidently thought he would get over his disagreeable task with solemnity.   I rose to a point of order, and with great gravity asked the Deputy Speaker whether it was not contrary to the universal custom and practice of the House for the mover of the Address to make his motion without the uniform befitting his rank, and, if so, whether I should be in order to move that the House do adjourn for twenty minutes to enable the right honourable gentleman to assume the garb befitting the important position in which he stood.   The House on all sides roared, and Harcourt nearly burst with fury."

If this last comment be hyperbole, at all events the pages of Hansard suggest that the Colonel had wiped off the old score made by Sir William in the correspondence already recorded.[1]

Fortune never smiled very kindly upon the Government of 1894-5.   Their best asset was a rumour that the Duke of Devonshire was on very good terms with Lord Rosebery and might actually join him ; but this led to nothing but disappointment.   There was a demonstration against the House of Lords, elaborately organised, but if it demonstrated anything it was annoyance with the Liberal party for abandoning the Employers' Liability Bill.   The Lords' amendments were apparently condoned ; there was a strong demand for the measure.   Advocacy of Home Rule followed as a matter of less importance.

The principal Government Bill was destined to be rejected with undiminished resolution by the Upper

.[1] *Vide supra*, p. 179.

House ;[1] but even then the protests out of doors were not of the stern and menacing character which brings matters to a deadly issue.

Saunderson's correspondence at this time was cosmopolitan. A very old and dignified ecclesiastic of the Church in Australia chose him as the object of a long and vigorous protest against the injustice done to Irish Protestantism in Mr. Lecky's history. It was a remarkable composition for a man "far in his ninety-second year," and Saunderson may well have felt flattered that he should have been hit upon as fittest person for address.

An American journalist, of violent anti-Roman Catholic proclivities, wrote for sympathy and information :

"Unless our people become aroused, the destination of this republic is to be the home of the Pope," said he.

Exhibiting a not very flattering ignorance of Saunderson's principles, he makes the staggering request for a statement of—

"the grounds of opposition by the good people of Ulster to Irish national control. Do they fear despotic oppression by priestly Catholic antagonism ? Parnell was not a Romanist, yet he advocated Irish nationality."

One can only observe, on this, that American journalism is not always as enterprising and well-informed as we are usually given to believe.

From New Zealand came a notification that he had been appointed a delegate to represent their Grand Lodge at the forthcoming Orange Council in London. Nor was he without invitations nearer home. One of his colleagues, begging his presence at a meeting, baits his letter with the postscript, " The Colonel is next to the Queen amongst my constituents." He made several speeches in Ireland during the spring. At Lurgan, on March 31, this pronouncement upon Irish local government is worth noting:

" I would vote for a Bill of local government which will place Ireland exactly on the same level as the rest of the British Empire. I would not give Ireland more, I would not give Ireland less; and I venture to say that, when the working classes in this country have more to say to the erecting of labourers' dwellings and the granting of allotments, then we will see carried out in this country what we have seen to a certain extent in England—a great and growing improvement, with comfort in the dwellings of our working people, and affording to them on the land a power of cultivating small gardens, which un- doubtedly would be to them an unbounded blessing. As regards the land . . . I am happy to say that on my own estate I have not got one single evicted farm."

It was from Lurgan, at this time, that there came a trophy familiar to all visitors to Castle Saunderson—a big drum. In this unconventional form did the Lurgan Orangemen embody "a slight token of their respect and esteem," adding the spirited superscription " No surrender!" If ever a doubting Irishman had visited Lough Erne in search of evidence that there were signs of wavering on the part of the Loyalist leader, he might very likely have been undeceived by the spirited efforts of some member of the family, booming forth defiance and " No surrender!" It was a scene not easy to forget when the Colonel would hold forth under his own roof-tree upon his boasted crusade, whilst one of his devoted sons would whack the great drum as an encouraging accompaniment.

The Colonel continued to make lively speeches, and always upon the same lines. He cared not how, or in

what guise it came, anything which seemed to play
into the hands of the Irish Nationalists was to him
anathema. He could not refrain at a Diocesan Synod
from observing that their political opponents were " the
predatory party "; and when he opened a sale of work
he was moved to the reflection that opposing generals
of course believed that God was on their side. Sometimes God was on neither side; but in the present
conflict he was certain that God was with them
" because their cause was the cause of the liberty and
freedom of all men." He speedily undertook to
demolish Lord Rosebery, who, he said, "appeared to
him to know as much about Ireland as he did about
steering a Chinese junk."

In the early part of the session Saunderson took
little part in the business of the House. His most
conspicuous reappearance was caused by a Labour
member who opposed an address of congratulation to
the Throne upon the birth of a son to the Duke and
Duchess of York. The Colonel, incensed at any
language of disloyalty, gallantly moved " that the
honourable member be no more heard "; though he was
persuaded not to insist. When a Scottish Labour
Council wrote afterwards to say that they approved
of their friend's conduct, the Colonel replied that
" gentlemen in the truest and highest signification of the
term are to be found in all classes of the community,
from the highest to the lowest "; he had no right to
complain of the honourable member's principles, but
his methods and the spirit of his remarks had inspired
him with a disgust which he felt sure would be
shared by the vast majority of the working classes of
all shades of political opinion.

Late in July the Evicted Tenants Bill was before
the House, and Saunderson was fully occupied. In

moving the rejection of the second reading he epitomised his objections to it in this passage :

" Let them imagine that, ten or twelve years ago, a
landlord got rid of a tenant who owed him five years'
rent. The tenant disappeared from view, and another
tenant took that farm. A great many of those who
had come in had done very well. If this Bill
passed into law what would happen ? The tenant
came back from America, or, if he had died, his
representative might appear on the scene, and insist on
being reinstated on the holding. What would happen
then ? The new tenant would be evicted. This Bill,
therefore, was not only a reinstating Bill ; it was an
evicting Bill."

The following letters bear testimony to his diligence :

" *July* 27, 1894.—You will see that I had a go at the
Bill yesterday. I took a good rise out of the Government. They don't report me at length in *The Times* ;
but you will see enough to understand what I was
driving at. When we were fighting up to midnight,
I was thinking of how you were getting on.
" 31*st.*—I spoke twice on Friday. . . . I got the
House into a hopeless state of laughter at the Bill."

" HOLLY LODGE.

" *August* 1, 1894.—We had a very smart debate
yesterday. The Radicals are mad with me, and have
discovered that I am at the bottom of the course
pursued by Balfour and Chamberlain. I never knew
I was so formidable a personage. You will see that
we have chucked the Bill, and will take no further part
in debating it."

On July 26 Mr. Brodrick [1] moved in Committee to
limit the operation of the Act to holdings not exceeding £30. Mr. T. W. Russell, who was beginning to
follow a line apart from his colleagues, objected on
the ground that this restriction had not been introduced into the Unionist measure of 1891. Saunderson's

[1] Viscount Midleton.

"good rise" consisted in telling the Government that the Bill only aimed at "reinstating a certain class of tenants, namely Plan of Campaign tenants." In another speech he declared that it was "put forward to gratify Irish criminal conspirators, who were to be paid the wages of iniquity from funds supplied by the Church." And again, "the great necessity for the measure was to be found not so much in Ireland as in this House. Had not the right hon. gentleman on the Treasury Bench brought in this Bill they themselves would have become evicted tenants." No doubt he turned the laugh against the Government when he described how he had seen one of the new tenants working under police protection, and the landlords guarded by car-loads of constables, whilst the evicted tenant was to be seen placidly driving along in a carriage and pair.

On July 31 the Government brought in "guillotine" proposals for closuring discussion. The Opposition made their protest, and declined to take further part in the proceedings. Saunderson's contribution on this occasion was the assertion that "in accepting these proposals the House of Commons would be wiping out of the flag which the Liberal party, of all parties, was most proud to bear, the two mottoes, fairness of discussion and freedom of debate." He was, as he reports, accused in the House of conspiracy with the House of Lords to create a situation which would justify the rejection of the Bill in another place.

Being for the moment free, he hastened to indulge in his favourite pastime, and went down to Cowes.

"Cowes.

"*August* 4.—The *Vigilant* was too much for the *Britannia* in the reaching wind. On Monday I sailed round the island in the *Vigilant.* On Tuesday I have to go up to Stratton Street[1] to speak on the third reading debate."

The narrative proceeds :

"I, STRATTON STREET.

"*August* 8, 1894.—We had a good night of it in the House yesterday. I was afraid that some compromise might be arrived at which might have caused the Lords to pass the second reading, which would have been a disaster.

"I was to have spoken at 10, but Joe got up, so I gave way. He made a terrible onslaught. . . . I had a grand sail on the *Vigilant* on Monday. When we got near Ventnor we tried to get on the *Britannia's* weather, who luffed us. We thought, as she drew three feet more water than us, we could get by, but *Britannia* luffed away. Our pilot warned us that we were going for a ledge of rocks. Gould said he did not care, so on we tore, I waiting for the crash. Bang went *Britannia* on the ledge; up went her bow. We thought we were all right, but bang we went on the rocks. With a series of jumps we both shot over into deep water. There never was such a sight. We won by seven minutes.

"Just as I was going off to the *Egeria* the German Emperor came into the club. He was very friendly, and came to me at once. . . . I had some minutes' talk with him about boats and centre-boards.

"*August* 10, 1894.—I had a long jaw yesterday with the Emperor . . . . We were so glad that the Prince won yesterday. I am going to lunch with Ormonde to help him to entertain the Duke of York. I rather think the Emperor will build a big cutter for next year."

"HOLLY LODGE.

"*August* 12, 1894.—We came up yesterday. . . . Just before we went to dinner the Baroness came to me with a most sad face and said, 'There is a telegram which I have just received, and which I should like to suppress.' I got a great scare; I was afraid something had happened to you. It was a telegram asking me to dine to-night with the Emperor. So . . . I go

[1] Baroness and Mr. Burdett-Coutts's house.

off to Cowes again in quarter of an hour and back here to-morrow."

"*August* 13, 1894.—I dined with the Emperor yesterday. . . . Nothing could have been kinder than he was. He said had I not come he would have sent a squadron of cavalry to capture me by force. We did not get away till 12.30. Blowing a gale. Sir W. Harcourt has just made his speech, and as he has stuck to compulsion the fate of the Bill is sealed."

On the third reading Mr. T. W. Russell moved to make the provisions of the Bill voluntary. As the Colonel says, the Government refused, and its fate was decided. It passed the last stage in the House of Commons by 199 to 167. The House of Lords promptly threw it out on the second reading by 319 to 30 (August 14). A demonstration against them was duly organised, but their withers were still unwrung, and on the 25th Parliament was prorogued, after having sat almost continuously for eighteen months.

CHAPTER XV

1894—1895

IN September I paid my first visit to Lough Erne, arriving on the afternoon of a race-day. The Colonel had lately launched a new boat, and my first impression of him in his native place was gazing at his latest achievement enraptured. He had only finished second, but, as far as I could make out, he had beaten the rival which he had undertaken to out-class. "She's a terror," was his apostrophe, "a perfect terror. I don't believe a better boat was ever put into the water."

Crom Bay was, as usual, the rendezvous after racing. Competitors and spectators alike came ashore for tea, and the little community was to be seen in its most sociable and intimate phase. Nothing more pleasant and attractive can be imagined than the spectacle of Crom Bay upon those sunny afternoons : the modern castle confronting the neighbouring ruins, sloping lawns, wooded paths, and gay flower-gardens ; on shore animated groups ; on the blue lake a flotilla of dawdling yachts, punts, and canoes, with a steam-launch coming in from Castle Saunderson, Lanesborough Lodge, or St. Hubert's. The large company made a famous display of high spirits and good looks : the setting of the scene was romantic and appropriate ; and in the midst of so much youth and gaiety nothing was more conspicuous than the bold figure, the ringing voice, and the joyous laughter of " Colonel Ed."

After a few days I proceeded to Castle Saunderson, and I hope I violate no obligation of hospitality if I describe the ludicrous situation upon which I made my first entry. I was taken at once to the dining-room; but lunch had been interrupted, and I was enjoined to stand still and be quiet. A stag had apparently found its way down from the hills and was lying under a tree in the park: one of the sons at the window was on the point of firing. Neither the first shot nor the second took effect. The family pride was roused; the stag did not so much as stir. Firing might have gone on indefinitely if it had not occurred to somebody that the stately antlers were the branches of a tree—as indeed they were. Saunderson never objected to have the laugh against him; he was a genuine humourist, and saw as much fun in this fiasco as if he had set a trap for somebody else.

On a subsequent occasion I had to extricate myself from a facetious plot laid for me by some of his neighbours. The Colonel reproached me for my want of spirit: "If you had been an Irishman you would not have minded," he said.

"But you see I am not an Irishman," was my only excuse. Probably the idea of shyness or stiffness in such a predicament had never occurred to him.

I find my first impression of him in his own house noted thus: "Saunderson at home is immense: enthusiastic about everything he does or possesses." His two principal interests were politics and his boats. A lady staying on the Lake expressed a desire to pay him a visit: "She doesn't like to leave," he explained, "without seeing the Ulster leader at home."

His love of boats was absorbing. He not only

L.E.Y.C. A RACE.

found an insatiable delight in sailing, and a perpetual zest in winning races, he had the enthusiasm of a craftsman; his head was full of theories which he was never tired of putting into practice, and a full half of the attraction lay in his plans and drawings, to be followed by the models which he executed with infinite care.[1] Even when the weather was foul, even when the younger members of the household had sought distraction elsewhere, he instinctively found his way to the boat-house, and the progress of years left the same unfailing readiness to start directly after breakfast and return only in time for dinner. As a rule his crew on racing days was composed wholly or partly of his sons, and in submitting his achievements to the German Emperor, with whom he had many communications on yachting matters, he made the proud boast that he not only designed, built, and steered his boats, but had bred his own crew. A letter of this period conveys permission from Berlin to present to His Majesty a model which the Colonel had executed of the latest addition to his fleet.

He had recently taken to golf, and had laid out a links. He played with a will, and frankly admired the rapid progress which a man of his age had made in so short a time. Indoors he was the heartiest of men; his voice and personality pervaded the house. His habits were not sedentary; his writing-table was no model for a bureaucrat. What fate befell his letters I know not: many of them, instead of being answered,

[1] He once devised a plan for lowering his mast in order to pass more expeditiously under the bridge near Enniskillen. Something went wrong, and the mast came down with a crash. A young lady on board, thinking that all was not right, inquired, "Oh, Colonel Saunderson, is that the best way of lowering your mast?"
    "No; but it is by far the quickest."

served as sketching-blocks, and were probably carried off by somebody for the sake of the caricature which he had felt moved to perpetrate. Amongst the litter, matches at one time predominated. Finding himself with no means of lighting his cigar one day, he ordered a gross of boxes, so as to be on the safe side; and for some time his writing-table resembled a shop counter.

One remembers him arrayed, as a rule, in a blue flannel suit, flannel shirt, red necktie; probably a jersey, showing his yacht's monogram; a yachting-cap on his head, and, during a considerable portion of the day, a long thin cigar in his mouth. He suffered fools gladly. One stormy day he allowed the present writer to offer entirely ineffective assistance on board. An unmanageable mackintosh made confusion worse confounded. The Colonel, who had probably never before carried a mariner in such a garment, had nothing worse to say than "That is the most omnipresent coat I ever saw."

On Sundays his personality became even more distinct. After luncheon he would be seized with a whim for riding a steeplechase round his billiard-table on a bicycle, with one hand on the table-edge, the obstacle being his granddaughter, who lay prone across his course, and who seemed to find it an extremely amusing occupation, with no inconvenience whatever to her small person. In the Church, beyond the garden,[1] he would in the afternoon conduct the service and preach the sermon, not caring for assistance even in the reading of the lessons. It is no small testimony to the excellence of his preaching to record

[1] This was a private chapel and not consecrated. It was attended by neighbours as well as by the household. On two Sundays in the month the rector or curate came from Belturbet (four miles) to hold a service. The Colonel would assist them; or, in their absence, conduct the service himself.

FATHER HEALY.

COLONEL NOLAN, M.P.

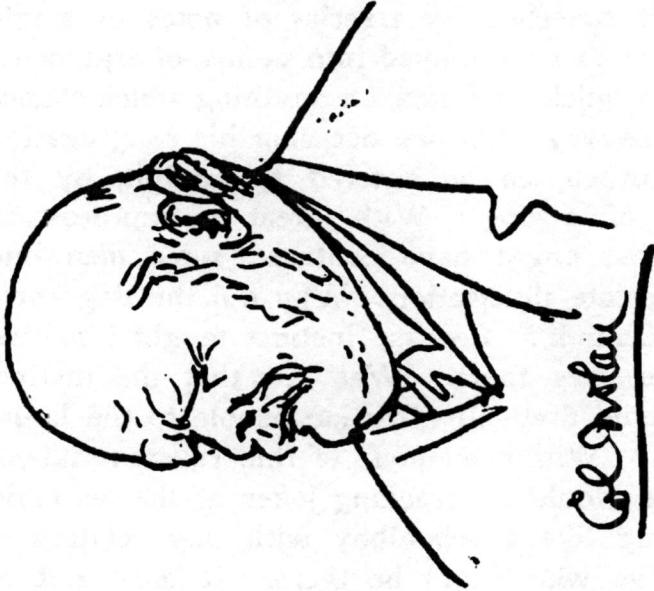

THE RIGHT HON. JAMES BRYCE.

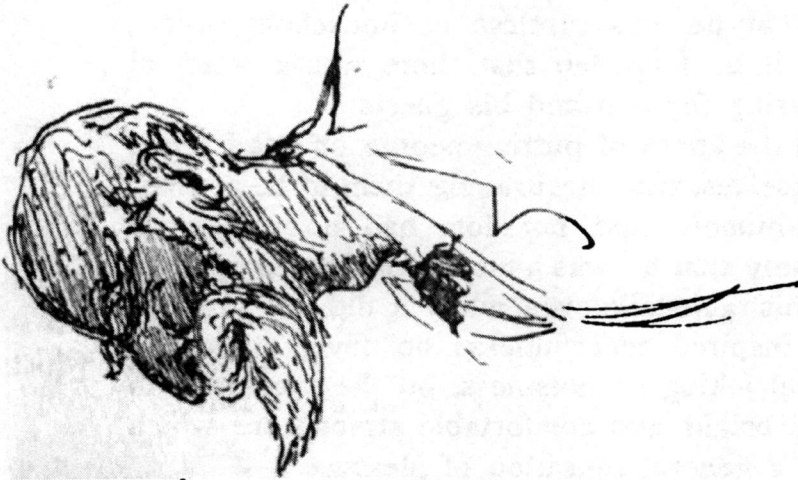

that one sermon in particular remains a vivid memory, after the lapse of so many years. " Whose is this image and superscription ? " Upon this text he hung his exhortation to generosity : every man and woman, no matter how degraded or depraved, was made in God's image, belonged to God, and should be treated as God's creature.

It was his practice to prepare his sermons, as he did his speeches, by a series of notes or single words, each to be amplified into points of argument ; but he was quick to fasten on anything which chance threw in his way. On one occasion his congregation were disturbed, as he entered the pulpit, by the intrusion of a dog. With great promptness he turned what might have confused some men into an appropriate illustration. Why did the dog come into the Church ? Because instinct taught him that his master was there. Was not that the instinct which should draw all Christian people to the house of prayer ? Within an hour of this reverent labour of love he would be cracking jokes at the tea-table, or romping like a schoolboy with any relation of suitable age who might be there. It must not be inferred that he was careless of household order ; nor must it be forgotten that there was a watchful hostess caring for him and his guests.

He had the knack of putting people on good terms with themselves, and encouraging them to be at their best. Ill-humour and boredom had no place. It was not only that he was a most amusing companion and that his table-talk, even when it did not provoke laughter, inspired cheerfulness ; he never descended to practical joking or noisiness, but he succeeded in creating a bright and comfortable atmosphere which produced a general sensation of pleasure.

During his autumn campaign Saunderson was unable to ignore a divergence of opinion between one of his ablest colleagues and the remainder of the party which he led. It will have been noticed that on previous occasions Mr. T. W. Russell had shown an inclination towards independent action. His views upon land legislation were at no time formed by motives and principles identical in all respects with those of his friends, and some of his recent speeches appeared to Saunderson to require notice. It will be seen that he adopted no tone of dragooning, and his criticisms were temperate and good-natured.

"Mr. Russell was one of his most trusted friends and colleagues," he had said in an earlier speech. "There were differences of opinion, no doubt. They had freedom in the Unionist camp. Mr. Russell held very advanced views on the subject of the tenure of land. He was a tenant's man, and on that point there was a divergence of views between him and the party he [Colonel Saunderson] had the honour to lead. But upon the great question of the Union, Mr. T. W. Russell and his colleagues had ever marched shoulder to shoulder, and did so still."

At Portadown, on November 6, he said :

"He saw his friend Mr. Russell had made some eloquent speeches in Ulster. In one speech he made the other day he said he stood with his back against the wall. He did not know what wall it was. And Mr. Russell further said he was ready to fight to the death. He did not know that anybody desired to slaughter Mr. Russell. The landlords did not approve of his land policy ; he could not expect them to ; yet they manfully supported him because they looked on him as an able defender of the Union. The Nationalists did not want to slaughter Mr. Russell because they looked on him as one of their chief friends standing against the wall. Yes, but he saw faces grinning over the wall. . . . Mr. Michael Davitt, Mr. William O'Brien, and Mr. Healy. Well, he did

not like that company. Mr. Russell . . . practically
advised the Ulster constituencies to force their
members to do two things—to back up Mr. Morley in
the future session, and to bring about compulsory
purchase in Ulster. That was to say, kick the landlords out, whether they like it or not. . . . Well, he did
not believe that in any constituency in the whole of
Ulster would the electors be found . . . mad enough
to pursue a course which was an entire approval of
the Nationalist gentlemen to whom he had alluded. . . .
They might sweep them away; they might put in
their places new landlords; but as sure as the sun
rises a new agitation would arise. They would have
no more right to their property than he had to his.
The labourers and working classes would argue that
as the State took his property and divided it with
[the new owners] so they would expect the State to
take it away again and divide it with them."

The Land Bill was to be for Ireland the centre of
interest in the coming session. The tenant farmers in
the Colonel's constituency were sufficiently sanguine
to call a meeting in anticipation for the purpose of
strengthening the hands of the Government. This took
place near a house called "The Birches," and gave
rise to lively scenes. The Government was called upon
to pass a Bill for compulsory purchase on just terms,
excluding the tenants' interest from the landlords' price,
and their member was requested to assist towards
this end. The Colonel's friends had, however, come to
the meeting, and began by raising loud cheers for the
abstract negative of "No Home Rule." According to
a poetical reporter, the speaker "might as well have
tried to make himself heard above the music of the
ocean breakers." The interrupters having stormed
the platform, one of them "executed a *pas de seul* (sic)"
accompanied by a shout of three cheers for something
concrete and positive this time, namely Colonel
Saunderson. His friends apparently proceeded to

join him in the dance, for we are told that they "elevated their pedal extremities," whilst the police, to their shame it is recorded, remained aloof, " as firmly implanted, for all practical purposes, as the birches in the neighbourhood."

Charged with this disputed mandate, Saunderson was in his place when Parliament met on Feb. 5, 1895. Again he brought in a Bill in the interests of his weavers, but fortune had nothing to bestow, and again his efforts were thwarted. Mr. Redmond moved an amendment to the Address in favour of a dissolution of Parliament. The Colonel was quite ready to support this. He had something to say about Lord Rosebery's recent querulous attacks on the House of Lords, at whose door he laid the difficulties which beset the conduct of affairs by a Liberal Government. Neither argument nor answer need be examined, because they are evergreen, and the Colonel's confident prediction that the peers would long be left as a buttress to withstand revolutionary legislation is not yet part of a forgotten controversy. With regard to the Land Bill he contented himself with the prophecy that it would prove to be nothing but a " Home Rule dodge." An Irish member had declared that it was going to be a scorcher : he imagined that the scorching was intended to consume Irish landlords.

The Bill was introduced on March 4. Saunderson, speaking on the first impulse, said that—

" The part to which he objected was that which proposed, if he understood it aright, to give the tenant not only security for the money he had laid out on his holding, but to give him also the whole value of the farm acquired by that expenditure. That would give the tenant a distinct ownership in the soil, and against that he protested. . . . As far as he was concerned," he said in conclusion, " he should give the

Bill fair consideration, but he was afraid that if it remained unaltered . . . he should be compelled to oppose it, though with great regret."

Reflection and examination clearly strengthened his unwillingness to have anything to do with it, and his desire to move its rejection on the second reading. Eventually he sought counsel from Lord Salisbury, and received the following letter:

"20, ARLINGTON STREET,
"*March* 20, 1895.

"DEAR COLONEL SAUNDERSON,

"I beg to acknowledge your letter with reference to the Irish Land Bill. Though I take the strongest possible objection to some of its proposals, I do not look upon it as a whole precisely in the same light in which it presents itself to you, and I do not concur in your view as to the most judicious mode of dealing with it in Parliament. If you had not written to me, I should not have ventured to offer any opinion as to the course that ought to be taken in the House of Commons, for it depends on many considerations of which I am only imperfectly a judge. But regarding principally the effect which the course taken in the House of Commons will afterwards have upon the action of the House of Lords, I am clearly of opinion that we should be hampered and not assisted by a division against the Bill upon the second reading in the House of Commons.

"In my opinion it is impossible to divide against the principle of the Bill, because the Bill has no principle. It is an omnibus Bill, containing a large variety of separate propositions . . . having no further connection with each other than the one fact that they all, in some way or other, concern the land of Ireland. If this view be correct, a division against the second reading is an improper way of dealing with the Bill unless you say that you have a strong objection to *all* the clauses it contains. The ordinary way of dealing with an omnibus Bill, to some of whose clauses you object, is to pass the second reading and strike those clauses out in Committee. I can hardly join in the view that *all* the clauses of the Bill are objectionable in a high degree. The 2nd clause almost entirely and the greater part of the 5th clause are very objectionable indeed, and I had much rather that the Bill were lost than that those clauses, in their present form, should pass.   But it is impossible to use such strong language with respect to other portions of the Bill.   It is quite possible to object to the term of ten years, or to the restriction of the right of appeal, or to the abolition of the right of pre-emption, or to the legislation with respect to future tenancies ; but I think it would be using excessive language to speak of any of those provisions as objectionable in a very high degree. They are proposals for discussion in Committee, and are no doubt capable of very considerable amendment.

"The clause of the Bill which re-enacts the 13th clause of the Purchase of Land Ireland Act of 1891, though capable of certain amendment, is on the whole a clause which I think it expedient to pass. . . . There are some other clauses which are doubtless capable of amendment, but are hardly good ground for rejecting the Bill altogether.

"Now, the great practical objection which exists to rejecting the Bill as a whole, on account of the abominable proposals in clause 2 and clause 5, is that you will exasperate not only the supporters of clause 2 and clause 5, but also the supporters of the other clauses. . . . Whatever assistance may be given to us in the House of Lords by the authority of those who have resisted the two clauses in the House of Commons, will be so far diminished by the fact that they have taken equally drastic measures to destroy the other clauses, which everybody knows to be comparatively harmless.

"I have not ventured to touch upon the question of the effect of your action on public opinion in the North of Ireland ; but the fact that a notable number of the small body of Unionist Irish members will either vote against you or refuse to vote with you, will, I cannot but think, injure the position of our party in the Ulster constituencies.   Of that, however, you are a better judge than I am.   My observations have been mainly directed to the question as it appears to me from the standpoint of the resistance in the House of Lords.

"Yours very truly,
"SALISBURY."

Saunderson yielded to advice. The second reading was moved on April 2:

"*April* 2, 1895.—I don't know whether I shall have to speak to-night. I shall do so, I think, because I shall wish to make my position clear as soon as I can. I don't like the job.

"I dined with —— last night. . . . He made me play a farewell game of 500 up. I beat him by 160 points.

"*April* 3.—I am to speak to-morrow. I hope to rub Morley down. He trailed his coat before us yesterday."

On April 4 he followed Mr. T. W. Russell, who supported the Bill. He quickly showed that he had not become reconciled to its provisions. "At the very starting-point," he said, "the Chief Secretary executed a kind of oratorical war-dance before his enemies." He quoted Mr. Morley freely, and proceeded:

"Why did the right honourable gentleman call the landowning representatives . . . unteachable? There were lessons which it was hard to teach to Irish landlords—say, for instance, that it was a pleasing process to be skinned. . . . The prairie value within the meaning of this Bill was the value of the game on the land in the days of Brian Boru . . . that threw some light on the practice of valuing land in Ireland. They never understood how it was done. They knew that two or three men came to the land; they looked at it, sometimes they tasted it, they invariably smelt it, and having done so, they decided, according to the humour they were in, on a reduction of twenty-five, thirty, or even thirty-five per cent. . . . He looked upon this Bill as robbery dressed up in the flimsy covering of an Act of Parliament."

Had the Bill survived all its stages in the House of Commons it is not unreasonable to surmise that it would have been extinguished in "another place." Lord Salisbury's letter indicates that, so far as he was concerned, the Unionists there would not have been deterred by any scruples from "filling up the cup." But their resolution was not to be tried. In June the Government were beaten on a vote for cordite in the Army Estimates, and immediately resigned. One may be forgiven the cynical observation that the Secretary of State began the day by announcing the resignation of the Commander-in-Chief of the Army, and finished by offering his own. Everybody knew that in the former case the Duke of Cambridge was guided by exigencies of an official character rather than by personal inclination. We must wait for the publication of contemporary memoirs before we can be sure what motives inspired the Secretary of State. Every Minister is capable of an error of judgment, and liable to desertion by his followers; but there is a well-recognised resource for all Governments in adversity, known as "riding for a fall." It was generally understood that the existing Cabinet were not in a very happy condition, and the prevailing impression that they welcomed a plausible excuse for resigning implied no reproach. It was indeed made a reproach on the part of the Opposition leaders that the Government should have resigned instead of dissolving; but they were masters in their own house, and so long as somebody else could be found to accept office, there was nothing to prevent them retiring as they pleased. The gossips were busy asserting that Lord Salisbury had declined to take office again and that the Duke of Devonshire was to be Prime Minister; but they were no nearer the truth than usual.

Lord Salisbury returned to power and achieved the distinction, probably without parallel, of presiding over a large Cabinet which endured for five years unchanged by death or resignation. Lord Cadogan became Lord-Lieutenant of Ireland, and Mr. Gerald Balfour Chief Secretary.

Parliament was dissolved without delay, and the elections resulted in a majority beyond the expectation of the most sanguine Unionists—152.

Saunderson was returned unopposed. He had recently recovered from one of those attacks of influenza to which he usually fell a victim whenever the malady became prevalent. Writing from London to his youngest son, who had also been seized, he says :

"Oh, poor Johnit! it is too bad that you should have fallen a victim. And your miserable old father has also had five weeks' bad time, so you see we are a decomposed family. When you are able to come up a change will do you good. We can bicycle in Battersea Park. . . ."

In June he had resigned his office as Grand Master of the Orange Order in Scotland on the ground of the pressure of his parliamentary duties. He suggested the propriety of appointing a Scotsman as his successor; this was done, and ample acknowledgment was made of the time and labour which he had bestowed upon the discharge of his duties.

He was present at the annual Orange demonstration at home previous to his election :

"PORTADOWN.

"*July* 12, 1895.—I have just returned from a great gathering, and the day is magnificent.

"I blathered away against many big drums, which nearly blew me inside out.

"13*th.*—I believe there will be a contest, but it is impossible to be quite sure till Tuesday next. . . . We shall be all ready for the fray, but it is a bore. They are not going to fight any one else."

"WARINGSTOWN, CO. DOWN.

"*July* 17, 1895.—I felt a longing to get some sea air, so I am going to have a sail in the *Egeria*. We had a great meeting last night at Lurgan. I said a rather smart thing—that the only difference between Rosebery and Harcourt was that Rosebery had won two Derbys, and Harcourt had lost one.[1] I am sure you were relieved at hearing that I was returned unopposed. Fancy the bother and expense.

"*18th.*—Here I am again M.P. . . . Now I am off to Bangor to look for the *Egeria*. . . . There was a great meeting in the Town Hall, Lurgan. Walking home I was nearly devoured by the women. That was the audience [picture.]"

When the new Parliament met on August 12 there were three notable changes in the personnel of the House of Commons. Mr. Gladstone was no longer a member. In January Lord Randolph Churchill had died. Enough has been said of his connection with Saunderson in affairs as they developed after the general election of 1885, but before his figure passes finally out of this narrative, occasion may be taken to relate the circumstances which first brought them together. During the general election of 1885 Saunderson, in the course of a speech in the small town of Belturbet, had declared that although the Ulster Loyalists were few in number they would exert a powerful influence on the conduct of the Conservative leaders; it was to be a case where the tail wagged the dog instead of the dog wagging the tail. Lord Randolph, being in Ireland, read a report of the speech, and was so much taken with it that he desired to meet the speaker. Saunderson was asked to go to Dublin, where Churchill was staying, with Lord Justice FitzGibbon. When he came home he was asked what the great man had said. "He said

[1] Sir William Harcourt was defeated at Derby in the general election.

very little ; he hardly spoke." "What did you say?" "I said, Lord Randolph, there is one member of Her Majesty's Government [1] we don't trust, and that is yourself." It was not a promising overture ; and, as we have seen, he never truckled to Lord Randolph when he became leader of the House of Commons ; yet, as we have also seen, there did exist between them a mutual sympathy and attraction. Lord Randolph's death was a lamentable extinction of illustrious promise, and politicians of all denominations sorrowed when the "bright political star" came to its untimely setting.

The other great change was in the Speaker's chair. In April Mr. Speaker Peel had resigned, and the succession was hotly disputed. The Unionists put forward Sir Matthew White Ridley.[2] It was understood that the Government nominee would be Sir Henry Campbell-Bannerman ; but the name submitted was that of Mr. Gully.[3] He was opposed mainly on the ground that he was an unknown member. He was elected, but only by a narrow majority of eleven. When the Unionists returned triumphant in July, it was expected that they would put their own man in the chair: rather a defiant tone had been adopted ; but temperate counsels prevailed, and Mr. Gully was allowed to continue in his distinguished office.

In the summer of 1895 Mr. Horace Plunkett, M.P.,[4] determined to call into existence a conference between Irishmen of all shades of politics with a view to advancing the material interests of the country, regardless of Home Rule. The story of this enterprise and its

[1] Lord Randolph was Secretary of State for India during Lord Salisbury's short administration in 1885. *Vide supra*, p. 82.
[2] The late Viscount Ridley.
[3] Viscount Selby.   [4] Sir Horace Plunkett,

sequel he has related in a volume published nine years later.[1]   The difficulties of his task, he there says, were aggravated by the action of Colonel Saunderson, who wrote at once to the Press to say that he was not prepared to sit on a Committee with Mr. Redmond

The truth is that Saunderson and Mr. Plunkett approached the parliamentary position from different points of view. This is amply proved by the assertion in the book that—

" the Unionist party . . . adopting Lord Salisbury's famous prescription, ' twenty years of resolute Government,' made it what its author would have been the last man to consider it—a sufficient justification for a purely negative and repressive policy."[2]

Further on he pauses to—

" note in passing, with extreme gratification, that at the recent Land Conference it was declared by the tenants' representatives that it was desirable, in the interests of Ireland, that the present owners of land should not be expatriated, and that inducements should be afforded to selling owners to continue to reside in the country."

One may be forgiven for suggesting that Saunderson would have noted any such declaration with extreme suspicion. He held, beyond the possibility of dissuasion, that the Nationalist party sought before all things to destroy the landed interest and expel the landlords.   His speeches make this abundantly clear ; and any such overtures he would have shunned, mistrusting their advocates, whose words were of peace. His policy was negative and destructive only to this extent : his whole heart was set upon preventing Home Rule ; in the annihilation of this principle lay, in his belief, the only road to the salvation of Ireland.   Mr.

[1] " Ireland in the New Century " (John Murray).
[2] *Op. cit.*, p. 64.

Plunkett, so the Colonel may have thought, was for killing Home Rule by kindness; Saunderson believed that the only kindness was to kill Home Rule. The situation is further illuminated by subsequent allusions to—

"the extraordinary misunderstanding of Mr. Gerald Balfour's policy to which the obscuring atmosphere surrounding all Irish questions gave rise . . . yet his eminently sane and far-seeing policy was regarded in many quarters as a ·sacrifice of Unionist interests in Ireland. . . ."[1]

"Time will, I believe, thoroughly discredit the hostile criticism which withheld its due meed of praise from the most fruitful policy which any administration had up to that time ever devised for the better government of Ireland."[2]

Saunderson was no reactionary, but nobody would expect him to be in unreserved sympathy with Mr. Horace Plunkett's daring scheme. Nor would it be just, on the other hand, to pass on without recording the fruit of these endeavours.

Mr. Plunkett submitted his proposal in a letter to the Irish Press dated August 27, 1895. Starting with the admission that he was opposed to Home Rule, he laid it down that if the average Irish elector were as prosperous, industrious, and well-educated as he was intelligent, the experiment of Home Rule would very likely be made. On the other hand, by acquiring these advantages, he would very likely see the futility of his demands and presently abandon them. At all events, the discussion was to be undertaken without prejudice to either party. Saunderson, as we have seen, immediately dismissed the idea as impracticable. Mr. Justin McCarthy, for a similar

[1] " Ireland in the New Century," p. 225.
[2] *Ibid.*, p. 238. It is not necessary to dwell upon the " hostile criticism " to which the Chief Secretary was subjected.

reason, declined to move; he objected to the suggestion that the Irish people would ever "cease to desire Home Rule." Mr. Redmond, however, consented; and a remarkable body, to be known as the Recess Committee, was formed. There were Unionist members of both Houses of Parliament, Mr. Redmond and some of his colleagues, Orangemen, Roman Catholics, the Lord Mayor of Dublin, merchants, manufacturers, railway men, shipping men; it was representative of commerce as well as politics. Their deliberations were energetic and practical; within a year they reported; and the upshot was the legislation to which Sir Horace now points with pardonable pride, including as it did the creation of the Department of Agriculture and Technical Instruction. Over this department he presided from its formation in 1897, until the exigencies of politics required his supersession in 1907, and nobody need grudge him the honour and praise which his services to his country have established as his due. Saunderson did not like the idea in its inception, nor was he a cordial admirer of the policy of the new Chief Secretary at a later date, as the next chapter will make clear.

CHAPTER XVI

1895—1897

PARLIAMENT sat no longer than was necessary for the completion of outstanding business, and was prorogued on September 3, 1895. Saunderson was able to rest at his ease; an overwhelming majority opposed to Home Rule had been returned to power, and he had no occasion to spend the autumn in hard work. He wrote a long letter to *The Times* concerning the grave crisis in the ship-building trade caused by a stubborn strike, and this led to some comment and correspondence. He was beginning to concern himself with the financial relations between England and Ireland, of which more was to be heard later on. He informed a correspondent that one reason why he would not sit on Mr. Plunkett's Committee was that Mr. Redmond and his friends avowedly rejoiced in England's difficulties abroad, and that he would have nothing to do with men who aimed at the downfall of the empire, and, under pretext of seizing Ireland's opportunity, were really working for Ireland's ruin.

The first session of the new Parliament was to provide him with plenty of work; nor was it to be entirely serene. The thorny subject of Education caused awkward entanglements. A meeting of the party at the Foreign Office in June displayed a surface more ruffled than was right so soon after an auspicious send-off. Later on, the Irish Land Bill caused severe friction between the two Houses, and it was melancholy to find Irish Loyalists who had exulted over the victorious election in July, 1895, hurling anathemas in private life at the Government twelve months later.

Saunderson went to his friends in Stratton Street for the opening of Parliament. On the first day he writes :

"*February* 11, 1896.—I was so sleepy last night that I absolutely refused to go to Devonshire House, but in the end I was forced by the Baroness, so I went. I saw every one I knew, and got my wrist injured by shaking hands with some three hundred people. . . . The debate has been disappointing. The proposer [1] and seconder [2] have made by far the best speeches up to the present. None of the speakers appear to have realised the extreme gravity of the situation. To my mind it is portentous."

His anxieties were aroused by the situation abroad ; not, for the moment, in Ireland. At the end of 1895 the American President had addressed a message to Congress upon the situation in Venezuela which fell upon the world like a bomb. So arbitrary was its tone in dealing with the local interests of Great Britain that both nations were excited to a dangerous degree. At the opening of the new year came Dr. Jameson's ill-starred and fatuous exploit, followed by the German Emperor's telegram of congratulation to President Krüger. In Egypt there were prospects of further trouble ; the condition of Armenia was a standing menace to the peace of Europe. We seemed to be only emerging from one war-scare to tumble into another. "The British Empire was undoubtedly passing through dangerous complications," said Saunder-

[1] Mr. George Goschen, M.P. (Viscount Goschen).
[2] Sir John Stirling Maxwell, Bart., M.P.

son in the debate on the Address.   He killed two birds with one stone by quoting Mr. Redmond to illustrate the situation and to point out the light in which the Nationalists regarded it.   Great Britain, according to Mr. Redmond, " has the German Empire arrayed against her ; in the East she is afraid to stir hand or foot to redeem her promises to the Armenians ; in Egypt she is menaced by France ; in the Far West she has alienated the good will of the United States."

" Honourable gentlemen," exclaimed the Colonel, "cheered these things, and this is the Union of Hearts. . . . Whatever honourable gentlemen might say about the condition of the British Empire, and its relation to foreign Powers," so ran his peroration, " the nations of the world had learnt in the last two months that Great Britain meant something more than these islands.   It meant an empire greater and stronger than had ever been ; and the sense of patriotism of the British people, having cut out the Home Rule dry-rot that threatened to invade the whole Constitution and bring it crumbling to the ground, now at last stood forth as the greatest, the strongest, and the most united people the world had ever seen."

A day or two later we have this note :

" *February* 15, 1896.—My speech has made more sensation than I expected.   Everybody is pleased with it.   Chamberlain made a first-rate speech last night. To-night we have the dynamite prisoners before us, as usual."

On February 14 Mr. Harrington moved an amendment[1] to the Address in favour of liberating the men in prison convicted of dynamite outrages.   This was supported by two Unionists, Mr. Plunkett and Mr. Lecky ; the former on the ground that a Government with a majority of 150 could afford to be generous, the latter for the double reason that the men had

[1] Rejected by 279 to 117.

acted under ungovernable impulse and had been sufficiently punished; further, that Ireland was now in a tranquil state, and the moment was auspicious. It was Mr. Lecky's maiden speech, and his distinguished position in literature perhaps put him outside the ordinary political pale; but the other colleague had shocked all strict and determined Irish Unionists, and the leader had to make this unpleasant comment:

"*February* 20, 1896.—I have rather a disagreeable letter to write to Horace Plunkett on the part of the Unionist party about his speech about the dynamiters. We met to-day and considered the matter. . . . The Baroness is coming to the Aquarium with us to see the performing elephants."

A few days after this he was the guest of the Lord-Lieutenant in Dublin.

"THE CASTLE, DUBLIN.

"*February* 24, 1896.—I arrived this morning at six, and went to bed for two hours. I have been in a stew about leaving London, as there is an important question about the new rules.[1] I wired to find out if they had got a pair, but I find they have not, so I shall have to go back to London on Thursday morning.

"*February* 25.—I have caught a cold, and don't think I shall go to London. . . . There is a pleasant party here. I like Cadogan very much. . . ."

A previous letter has included a reference to bicycling. All London had gone crazy over the latest whim. What had hitherto been regarded as an ignoble method of locomotion suddenly became the chosen recreation of the shining lights of fashion. The London parks were crowded every morning, and the few existing restaurants reaped a rich harvest at breakfast-time. The passion was too violent to

---

[1] Mr. Balfour had proposed further alterations in the rules for parliamentary procedure.

endure, and within a few months it was completely extinguished; but its progress was fully recorded in the social gossip of the newspapers, and Saunderson was declared to be very regular in his exercise. As a matter of fact, he had ridden an old-fashioned high bicycle in Ireland when such things were hardly known,[1] and had terrified the peasantry, one of whom, meeting him at night with a lighted lamp, went home and declared he had seen the devil on wheels. Nor was he the only eminent politician who now came under the spell of an excellent pastime. The advent of motors has been so recent, and at the same time so overwhelming, that this piece of news reads like some fragment of ancient history:

"*March* 20, 1896.—Balfour had a frightful cropper on his bicycle yesterday, and sprained his wrist, which he carries in a sling."

Early in March Saunderson had to join issue again with Mr. Plunkett on the subject of evicted tenants. In a letter to *The Times* he deprecated his friend's proposals for reinstating evicted tenants by means of a national subscription. The Colonel protested that a Nationalist subscription would be more appropriate; the Nationalists had called the tune, and he did not see why Irish Loyalists and landlords should pay the piper. His advice was to wait a while: there was evidence that the tenants were gradually coming to terms with their landlords. He hoped that the forthcoming Land Bill would expedite matters, and that the sufferings which they had been obliged to endure would serve as a salutary lesson for the future. Mr. Plunkett sent a spirited rejoinder to *The Times*, declaring that this was no occasion for

[1] *Vide supra*, p. 14.

scoring a party victory; that it was bad tactics and bad statesmanship to increase the existing bitterness by raising the cry of *Væ victis*.

So matters stood when Mr. Gerald Balfour introduced his new measure on April 13. It was a far-reaching scheme, covering the payment of annuities by purchasing tenants, the freeing of estates from the Cumbered Estates Court, readjustment of rents, the valuation of improvements, the treatment of evicted tenants, and divers other proposals, raising financial problems and social issues of the most intricate and controversial kind. Some cynic was heard to say that it must be a good Bill, because it satisfied neither the landlords nor the Nationalists.

On May 16 a letter appeared in *The Times* signed by the Duke of Abercorn, Lord Londonderry, and Saunderson amongst others, entering a caveat against the allegation that the Irish landlords saw no harm in its provisions. On behalf of the Irish Landowners' Convention and the mortgagees of Ireland, they declared that, whilst some of the proposals were beneficial, and even necessary, the general tendency was to take away the few remaining property rights untouched by the Acts of 1881 and 1887, and they demanded reservation of judgment pending full examination and debate.

On June 6 the same gentlemen sent a further communication to the Press. They desired " distinctly to state that we do not write as opponents of the Bill," but they had to point out numerous clauses which they must steadily oppose. Their principal objection lay in the fact that various acts of grace or tolerance on the part of landlords in past times were now to become obligations prejudicial to their interests, bestowing as they did on the tenants a right where they had hitherto enjoyed a favour. What was known as the turbary clause gave special offence, and was to become a prime cause of conflict. As one indignant landlord elsewhere said, it was like forcing an English coal-owner to give all cottagers the right to extract as much coal as they liked from his pits. The second reading was fixed for June 8, and Saunderson spoke in a tone of marked hostility. He renewed his criticism of Mr. T. W. Russell's policy :

"In a speech at Cloyne the honourable gentleman gave a description of how this Bill was constructed. The only objection he had to find with his honourable friend was that in that very able speech he did not give any credit to his colleague,[1] the Chief Secretary, but to the right honourable gentleman the member for Montrose (Mr. Morley) and himself. . . . He denied that there was any such thing as dual ownership of land in the country ; it was a mere slipshod phrase, without any foundation of fact ('Oh, oh'). When Mr. Gladstone brought in the Bill of 1881 he emphatically represented, on this point, that he did not destroy the rights of property of the owners of the land, and showed that in his view there was no such thing as dual owner-ship. But the view of the Government was that there was dual ownership, and that the present land-lords in Ireland should be got rid of. They did not, he presumed, propose to do away with landlordism altogether, but to replace the present landowning class by another landowning class. How extremes sometimes met ! . . . There seemed to be a common agreement between the bitterest enemies of England and Ministers of the Crown that the proper thing to secure for the peace, happiness, and prosperity of Ireland was to sweep away the very class who, it was admitted, had been the strongest supporters of the authority of Great Britain in Ireland."

His conclusion, therefore, was less uncompromising than might have been expected :

[1] Mr. Russell was now Parliamentary Secretary to the Board of Trade.

" He supported, and intended to support this Bill, but at the same time he was bound to confess that it had disappointed him."

When he sat down he said to his colleague beside him, as a speaker often does, " Was that all right ? "

" Excellent," was the answer; " but you might have said something about the Bill."

" How could I ?   I never read it."

This was perhaps a figure of speech, but it illustrates the Colonel's method of attacking general principles and large issues, instead of dwelling on subtle analysis of detail, in which practice he closely resembled, as has been suggested, his old adversary Parnell. He was determined, at all events, that such analysis of detail should be forthcoming. It was rumoured that the Government intended to push the Bill through by suspending the standing orders and making time by means of all-night sittings. A remonstrance was accordingly addressed to the leader of the House, which called forth this temperate and conciliatory reply :

" *Private.*   " 10, DOWNING STREET, S.W.
                                       "*June* 11, 1896.

" MY DEAR SAUNDERSON,
        "Your letters of June 10 appear to be, to a certain extent, written under a misapprehension. There is no idea of an 'all-night sitting' to force the Irish Land Bill through, though I think it would be desirable to suspend the 12 o'clock rule on Friday and somewhat prolong the ordinary sitting of the House.

" The request that I should do so comes, no doubt, from the other side ; but it could hardly be refused without throwing a natural suspicion upon the sincerity of our desire to pass the Bill. I am afraid I shall have to ask the House to make a similar sacrifice, not unfrequently, on the Education Bill, and I could hardly enforce the demand in the one case and refuse it in the other.

" May I, in this connection, express my earnest

hope that you and the gentlemen on whose behalf you write will do all that you *conscientiously* can to promote the passage of the Bill during the course of this Session. I am firmly convinced that it is in the interests of the landlords as much as of the tenants, that the question should be got out of the way, and got out of the way while Ireland is peaceful and contented, and our Nationalist opponents divided and disheartened. I do not dwell further upon this part of the question, though I feel strongly about it ; but if you and any of your friends would care to see me, I am entirely at your disposal.

"Please communicate the contents of this note to the signatories of the second letter of yesterday.

"Yours very truly,

"ARTHUR JAMES BALFOUR."

If Saunderson had indeed neglected to read the Bill, he proceeded now to do so, and to master its contents ; for during the Committee stage he took his full share in debate. His mainstay at this stage, as indeed at all times, was Mr. Carson,[1] whose keen intellect and trained habits of examination were invaluable in minute criticism. On July 16 a whip was sent out, signed by them and four or five others, urging all Unionist members to attend in view of "most important amendments" having for their object "the protection of the interests of property in Ireland." On July 20 the Colonel was still professing that he was as anxious as honourable gentlemen below the gangway opposite to see the Bill passed, but he found himself obliged to vote against Mr. Balfour's motion to suspend the 12 o'clock rule and take a late sitting :

"If this Bill was hurried through it would not require great ingenuity to prophesy what would be the position of the Irish landlord in the immediate future—he would become a melancholy spectacle, attenuated by the enforcement of the provisions of drastic Land Bills administered by predatory land

[1] The Right Hon. Sir Edward Carson, K.C., M.P.

commissioners, who would wander over what was once his property in search of his incorporeal hereditaments."

The House did sit late—until five in the morning. It was recognised that if the Bill was not treated expeditiously it would have to be dropped for lack of time, and it was briskly pushed through.   On the third reading Mr. Davitt condemned it as a landlords' measure ; Mr. Smith Barry moved its rejection for the contrary reason.   Saunderson uttered a final protest with a poetical parody :

> Rattle his bones over the stones,
> He is only a landlord whom nobody owns.[1]

But it was passed without a division, and went to the Lords.   Here it received some rough handling ; Lord Londonderry led the attack on behalf of the landlords, although he too deprecated the idea that he wished to wreck the Bill.   Amendments were carried against the Government, and it seemed at one moment as if the measure must be sacrificed. Going back, as amended, to the House of Commons, it was restored to its former condition.   Practically all the Lords' amendments were rejected, with the notable exception of Lord Lansdowne's new turf-cutting clause.   Saunderson, as this letter shows, was ready to fight to a finish :

"*August* 13, 1896.—I had a hard day yesterday, as you will see. We nearly got the Bill right, but in the end we broke down. It now remains to be seen what will be done to-day in the Lords. Carson and I are going to be photographed together to-morrow."

But, as is not unfrequently the case, there was a sudden cooling and collapse in the ardour of the

[1] He made the pardonable blunder of ascribing these lines to Hood. They are Noel's in the original version.

conflict. The Lords gave way, and the Bill was passed into law.

"*August* 14, 1896.—Carson and I went to get photographed this morning. So the Land Bill is over! . . ."

Parliament was prorogued on August 14, the day foreshadowed as far back as June; and this without the surrender of any important work, except the Education Bill, which had been withdrawn. Seven measures promised in the Queen's Speech had been passed into law, so that the labours of the session had not been nugatory.

Saunderson had availed himself of certain intervals to do some yachting. His movements are recorded in these extracts:

"OAK VILLA, COWES.

"*May* 20, 1896.—I have just steered two races. One in a new 2½ called the *Tatters* which I won by 8 minutes. In the first race she was beaten, so the owner and crew were delighted. Yesterday Charlie Orr Ewing's boat *Heartsease*, 5-rater, against two other new ones. I won by 7¼ minutes.

"*26th.*—I sailed a great race yesterday steering the *Heartsease*. I was beaten by Wood in the *Silver* by 15 secs. I was delighted he won: he is such a good chap, and it was the first race he had won."

"COWES.

"*August* 2, 1896.—I met H.R.H., who asked me to sail with him some day.

"*4th.*—I have just come in after an amusing sail in the *Meteor*. We came in first, but did not win. I feel as fresh as paint to-day.

"*5th.*—I have just returned from sailing a fine race in the *Ailsa*. We won, beating *Britannia* by over 9 mins."

He was once more in his element on Lough Erne. Personal recollections must now be readmitted. I still possess a letter from the Colonel bidding me

THE COLONEL AT HOME.

welcome back to "this remarkable location," and saying that he hoped to see me at Castle Saunderson. This was correctly addressed to one of the neighbouring houses, but instead of my name, the envelope bore what I take leave to hope was a libellous caricature of myself.

One observation of his at this time I recollect. I had said that somebody was a cold-blooded creature, who had probably never been excited nor sworn an oath in his life. "I admire him for that," said the Colonel; "I don't like men who swear."[1] Throughout our acquaintance I can call to mind no occasion on which his conversation or language was unfit for use in the strictest company—with a single exception. One Sunday, at Cannes, the Colonel, during lunch, told a story of a speaker whom he had once heard in Hyde Park. "What am I doing here?" had been his cry; "what am I doing here? What am I doing on this here platform?"

"Making a damned fool of yourself," had been shouted by some one in the crowd. A lady, possibly because of the day, and the fact that she was on the point of going to church, professed her disapproval.

"Have I shocked you?" exclaimed the Colonel. "I am very sorry. I would not have done it for worlds." But it must be confessed that his sense of humour seemed to predominate over his remorse.

My visit was made memorable by one curious incident. Emulous of becoming a raconteur, where story-telling seemed to be the popular custom, I ventured on some experiments of my own. The Colonel frankly admitted that he could see no point in any of them, and encouraged me to try again. In

---

[1] He once said to a friend, "I am glad to think that the deck of my boat was never sullied by an oath."

vain I paraded the most admired veterans; my failure was complete and contemptible. Indeed the Colonel announced to the assembled company on the Lake that I was a most remarkable man: I had been telling stories incessantly for three days, and had not produced a good one yet.

That evening I narrated what I believed to be a fact, not humorous in itself, but adorned, as it happened, by the use of a dialect belonging, I confess, to no known region of the earth. The Colonel was enraptured; it was declared to be the best story that had ever been heard. He might have said, as Don Quixote did to Sancho: "Verily you have told one of the rarest tales, fables, or histories imaginable, and your way of telling and concluding it is such as never was nor will be seen in one's whole life"; and the praise would not have been less surprising. To every new-comer the story must needs be repeated; it became an accepted classic, never to be too often revived, never to be forgotten. It is no exaggeration to say that through all the ensuing years I hardly ever met the Colonel without his saluting me with one phrase or another out of this ridiculous tale.

They were pleasant days, and mine were prolonged beyond expectation by the allurements of the Lake hospitality. It was during this autumn that Baroness Burdett-Coutts, despite her burden of years, made the journey to Castle Saunderson, accompanied by her husband, in order to open a local bazaar. It probably gratified her to testify in public to the high opinion which she had entertained for the Colonel from the outset of their acquaintance,[1] whilst he was glad to show his ap-

---

[1] This dated from 1885, and arose out of the friendship which her husband formed with the Colonel as soon as they met in

preciation of so fine a character, and to pay his tribute
of respect to one whose noble life was destined in the
end to be commemorated by the supreme honour of
burial in Westminster Abbey. Her kindness and
affectionate regard he always repaid with a grave
courtesy and devotion, and this ceremony was distinguished by an interest and dignity not generally
achieved on similar occasions.

In the course of his speech Saunderson dwelt on the
urgent need of restoring order in Armenia, where
outrages and disturbance had been causing dismay.
He had a bold scheme for coercing the Sultan without
risk of a European war : England should withhold the
tribute due on account of the occupation of Cyprus,
and an embargo should be laid on the tribute paid by
Egypt. This money should be diverted to the relief
of distressed Armenians.

He kept a constant watch on affairs in the near
East. In the following March he was to speak in
Parliament on the condition of Crete, condemning the
Concert of Europe for not interfering to better purpose. As far as he could see, the Powers were
governed by two motives—suspicion of each other,
and self-interest. Meanwhile he had no confidence
whatever in Turkish police or in Turkish officers. In
fact he was heartily in favour of drastic measures for
the protection of the Christian communities from
Turkish misrule.

During the autumn (October 10, 1896) Lord Rosebery

Parliament after the General Election. The Baroness had long
taken a practical interest, as is well known, in the condition of the
people living on the South Coast of Ireland, and with this work
Saunderson was naturally in entire sympathy. He was deeply impressed by her personality, and she never ceased to watch his career
with friendly solicitude. To her care and hospitality at Holly Lodge
he was indebted, year after year, for the strength and health to endure
the physical strain of existence in the House of Commons.

17

made a memorable declaration at Edinburgh.   He was tired of being nominal leader of a party which gave him feeble support, and was distracted by dissensions and disloyalty.   Moreover, he had to differ from Mr. Gladstone, whose instincts and traditions moved him to demand prompt action in Armenia. In Lord Rosebery's opinion any man who would put the country in jeopardy of war, except under absolute compulsion, would be guilty of a crime. Recognising Mr. Gladstone's " matchless authority," he could only surrender his position and dissociate himself from further responsibility.

It was a significant speech. The condition of the Levant might be regarded as one of chronic confusion with intermittent crises. The condition of the Liberal party was one of passing disturbance of a different kind. That the situation in the latter case would eventually be made smooth, no partisan need doubt. Yet for the time they were a broken army.

It may have been the temporary security afforded by this disruption that induced Saunderson to take a step altogether outside his customary path.   The question of the Irish financial relations has been mentioned. What happened was this : Irish members had long complained that Ireland paid a contribution to the Imperial Exchequer[1] altogether out of proportion to her means. Attention to this grievance had long been promised, and under Lord Rosebery's Government a Commission had been appointed to inquire. In 1896 they reported. Their decision was, on the whole, an acknowledgment of injustice. A Home Rule flavour was imported to the extent of a declaration that for purposes of taxation England and Ireland should be regarded as separate entities;

[1] The English and Irish Exchequers were amalgamated in 1816.

but it was agreed by all the commissioners, save two, that Ireland was contributing one-eleventh of tax revenue, whereas she should in equity be required to find only one-twentieth.

Fortified by this confession, Irishmen of all classes united to extract relief from the Government. On December 28, 1896, the Lord Mayor of Dublin presided at a meeting where Mr. Ion Trant Hamilton,[1] the Unionist Lord-Lieutenant of the county, moved a resolution demanding legislation. Next day Lord Dunraven and Mr. John Daly, who had suffered imprisonment as one of the most active of agitators, were side by side upon a platform at Limerick. On Christmas Eve Saunderson spoke plainly at Belturbet : England had overcharged Ireland upwards of £2,000,000, and she must make restitution.

For the sake of clearness we may complete the story. When Parliament met early in 1897 the Government announced their intention of appointing a new Commission to clear up several points which in the recent report seemed confusing and inconclusive. This did not suit the impatient claimants, and, in order to press their suit, a movement was made to form a Committee of Irishmen of all parties. It will be remembered that Saunderson had refused to join Mr. Plunkett's Recess Committee on the ground that he would have neither part nor lot with Home Rulers. Now he waived his scruples and the strange spectacle was beheld of the Colonel elected to the chair of an assembly composed, amongst others, of Mr. John Redmond, Mr. Healy, and Mr. Dillon. It has been recorded that, whatever may have been the value of their deliberations and exertions, nothing could have been more satisfactory than the personal relations which marked these proceedings.

[1] The late Lord Holm Patrick.

Beyond this pleasant interlude in the long catalogue of combats there was no great achievement to boast. Colonel Saunderson, Mr. Lecky, Mr. Healy, and Mr. Clancy became a sub-committee to arrange details. The Government gave an opportunity for discussion, and on March 29 Mr. Blake was deputed to move a resolution setting forth that the Report had established the fact that Ireland was overtaxed, and demanding instant legislation. Mr. Redmond seconded :[1] Saunderson spoke on the second day of the debate. He declared that he had been proud to preside over the united committee of all Irishmen. There was not a constituency in Ireland where their action was not warmly approved. At the same time he repudiated the insinuation that the sacred principles of Union had suffered a moment's derogation. He enlarged on the various high-handed methods which had been used in dealing with Irish finances. For instance : " They had disestablished the Church and sold her possessions. They had converted Protestant bishops into tramways and light railways."

He made a point of the exclusion of Ireland from the benefits of the recent Agricultural Rating Act : so long as Ireland was regarded as part of a common community, she ought to profit by all benefits conferred on other parts of that community. Here he seemed to perceive that he was treading on delicate ground, and the impression made by his speech is that he still placed his hostility to Home Rule before any other considerations, no matter how weighty. The motion was rejected by 317 to 157 votes, and with

[1] An English member moved a hostile amendment on the ground that, so long as England and Ireland were united, they must be regarded as one unit for financial purposes. He was seconded by Colonel Waring, an Ulster stalwart.

THE JOINT COMMITTEE.
Col. Saunderson. Mr. Healy. Mr. Lecky.
From the drawing by Sir John Tenniel.

its defeat there disappeared the occasion for conjunction between traditional opponents.

The session of 1897 opened with a lavish promise of legislation, which was not destined to failure. When Parliament was prorogued on August 6 the Government could claim to have passed thirty measures, including an Education Bill and a Workmen's Compensation Bill.

Meanwhile there suddenly fell upon the House of Commons a spirit of repose. Laziness and indifference characterised debates, and the House was constantly counted out. One veteran member declared that he had never seen it so demoralised ; and for no reason.

Saunderson, as we have seen, devoted himself to the labours of the Financial Relations Committee. Beyond this he had no inducements to resist the prevailing impulse, and his parliamentary record, for the moment, was not heavy. He gave a good deal of his time to playing golf—principally at Deal ; and he attended sittings of the Synod of the Church in Dublin.

"*April* 28, 1897.—I have just come from the Synod. It is rather sad to miss so many old friends who fought by my side in old times."

But the engrossing interest of the year was Queen Victoria's second Jubilee, and it seemed as if neither politicians nor the public could spare attention to events of a less dramatic and stirring description.

Saunderson's energy found some outlet in Ireland. At the annual Orange celebration, on July 12, he delivered in Dublin a lively diatribe against the evil results of Roman Catholic domination :

"What would have happened if William III. had been defeated by James and Louis XIV. ? Look abroad at what happened in Roman Catholic countries. Look at France, with its Edict of Nantes, and the absolute destruction of liberty which culminated in the Revolution. What is the result in France to-day? . . . Practically speaking, the great majority of her people had rejected the Christian religion altogether. . . . There was one rock ahead of the Government at present, and that was with reference to the Roman Catholic University question. It would be an infatuated blunder to bring in a Roman Catholic University Bill, and he did not say that in a spirit of bigotry. Indeed, a Roman Catholic gentleman had said to him that, whatever he did, he should prevent the establishment of such a University here. Archbishop Walsh and the bench of Bishops had no doubt announced that . . . Roman Catholic laymen would be predominant, but what layman would dare risk the condemnation of the hierarchy?"

During the following week he explained at Lurgan his action in associating himself with his political opponents:

"Well, I was not a bit ashamed of doing that. I am never ashamed to join any man who does what I believe right for Ireland. . . . The thing that surprised me was that I was chosen chairman—the reason was that they could not get anybody else. If they had chosen a member of Mr. Healy's party, none of the others would have been in the room. . . . I walked into that Committee-room with my friend Mr. Lecky, with Mr. Carson, and Mr. Horace Plunkett, who were the only Irish Unionist members who could harden their hearts to sit in such company. . . . I will say this, that in no meeting was I ever treated with more respect or more willingly obeyed. . . . Then, on another occasion, I found myself, with great satisfaction, to be entirely of one mind with my Nationalist opponents. The British House of Commons voted two millions of money to pay half the rates of the agriculturists of England, and they refused to give it to Ireland. . . . We succeeded in showing the Government that if they did not give us what we wanted we would make it hot for them in the House of Commons. And we got it! Now half the county rates will be paid out of the Exchequer to the amount of almost £800,000 a year."

In the House of Commons he spoke on the subject of the South African Committee, the body to which had been referred the issues raised by the raid and the subsequent action of the Government of the South African Republic. He entirely condemned Mr. Rhodes in so far as he had been concerned in the project; but he exonerated him from mercenary and stock-jobbing motives, and urged in extenuation his previous patriotic services. He objected to the excessive punishing of the British officers implicated, inasmuch as they had only obeyed orders. Summing up the position, he declared that if Mr. Rhodes had sinned, this country had forgiven him; and as for the people of the Transvaal, they should entertain no sentiments but those of gratitude, for since the raid they had been able to arm themselves to the teeth without interference on our part—an observation of shrewd and mournful presage that had not long to wait for its justification.

In spite of any contumacious conduct of which he may have been considered guilty, his private relations with the Chief Secretary remained amiable enough, as this extract from a letter shows:

"CHIEF SECRETARY'S LODGE.

"*August* 26, 1897.—I shirked going to the ball last night, and went to bed instead. The Royalties[1] are in high good humour. . . . I must go to meet them in Cavan, although they don't come into the station."

-[1] The Duke and Duchess of York visited Ireland in August.

CHAPTER XVII

1897—1898

THE autumn on Lough Erne was clouded by a deplorable event. In the house of Saunderson's kinsmen, the title of Lord Farnham had not descended regularly from father to son. This year had witnessed family rejoicings over the coming of age of the Hon. Barry Maxwell, eldest son and heir of Somerset, tenth Baron.[1] Early in September there was dancing one night at Crom Castle. On occasions of this kind the lake is the highway for such levies as the other houses have to contribute. It is not an unknown experience, indeed, for unwary ladies, rejoicing in the cool night air and a romantic contemplation of the starry firmament, to repose unconscious of the fact that their elegant gowns are being steadily sprinkled by the black and sticky exhalations from the funnel of the launch. However that may be, the company is limited to the inmates of the house and the passengers from two or three steamers. It can easily be believed then that the absence of any one contingent is very quickly detected. On the present occasion it was soon apparent that the *Filibuster* had not arrived. Manifestly something had happened. It was a depressing discovery: apart from the loss of good company, there

---

[1] He had succeeded his uncle, James, ninth Baron, *vide supra*, p. 24. The ninth and eighth Barons both succeeded brothers. The present, eleventh, Baron succeeded his father, 1900.

was an uneasy suspicion of misfortune. However, there was nothing to be done except to hope that something had gone wrong with the machinery and the party had been prevented from starting.

Next morning we were sadly undeceived: Mr. Maxwell had been terribly injured by a fall from his bicycle. In front of Castle Saunderson a steep and wide descent of grass runs directly to the boat-house. Beside this a winding footpath through trees leads to and from the castle. For some reason, which could never be discovered, Mr. Maxwell appears to have tried to ride his bicycle down the grass. Unhappily he succeeded in reaching the bottom, only to be dashed against the building. It would perhaps have been less distressing if the result had been immediately fatal. As it was, he lingered some days, beyond all hope of recovery, until death completed a catastrophe which the circumstances of the sufferer and of the occasion combined to render peculiarly afflicting. I was to have proceeded to Castle Saunderson, but, in consequence of this, I left Lough Erne without being the Colonel's guest.

In October he sailed for South Africa. There were to be celebrations at Buluwayo in connection with the completion of the Bechuanaland Railway, which now extended 1,350 miles beyond the boundary of Cape Colony at Vryburg to the new terminus. Some members of Parliament had been invited to go out as guests of the company. The Colonel went, accompanied by Mrs. Saunderson and his third son, Armar. The other members of the House of Commons were Mr. (Sir) H. M. Stanley, Colonel Llewellyn, Mr. J. A. Pease, Mr. Hayes Fisher, and Mr. J. M. Paulton.

After reaching Capetown the Colonel and his wife parted company; she refrained from undertaking the fatigues of long and frequent journeys, and stayed behind at the Vineyard Hotel, Newlands. Consequently the letters which he wrote to her supply his itinerary.

"ORANGE RIVER, 10.45 p.m.

"*November* 1, 1897.—We have had an excellent journey. The food is very good, and we are very comfortable. I dined with Miss Rhodes last night,[1] also this. The air here is quite wonderful; quite warm and absolutely dry. You could lie down in the open, and wake all right. I have made some sketches which will give you an idea of the country. Dry as a bone; all covered with tufts; yet sheep live on it, and thrive. . . . We have a very nice party, especially Dr. Gill,[2] the astronomer."

"THE PALACE HOTEL, BULUWAYO.

"*November* 6.—I don't think you would have liked this place. The country for miles round is nearly bare of trees, and is of a reddish-brown colour owing to the absence of rain. The soil is excellent, and the climate splendid. It is hard to realise, when you are looking at the landscape, that you are not in England. . . . I went to see the Fawleys, who live two miles out of the town. . . . The tree is in the garden under which Lobengula executed justice four years ago. The streets are very wide, and are to have trees planted; at present most of the houses are of a temporary character. . . . The difficulty here appears to be to keep animals alive. The cattle have nearly all died of rinderpest; the pigs also. The chickens have a habit of falling down dead without provocation. Then the white ants eat the young trees, and the locusts devour the leaves. So altogether it is not at present a country fit for farming. Its future depends on finding gold in paying quantities. The admiral[3] is such a nice man, also Captain Egerton."

"THE SANATORIUM, KIMBERLEY.

"*November* 13.—I had a tremendous reception at Buluwayo after I sat down: I worked them up to a

---

[1] In the train.
[2] Astronomer Royal, Capetown, now Sir David Gill, K.C.B.
[3] Sir Harry Rawson, G.C.B.

high pitch. We had a hot journey down. . . . I was in pyjamas and slippers without stockings all day. . . . We are in clover; everything done as in a first-rate country house. . . . I do not know whether we are guests of the De Beers Co. or not; I should not be surprised if we were. . . .[1] The railway have shunted a sleeping-car off the train we came in to take us up to Johannesburg at 4—fifty hours' journey. Then we go to Pretoria; then to Pietermaritzburg and Durban. Then to East London by boat, . . . then across to Port Elizabeth, and so to Capetown. . . ."

"THE SANATORIUM, KIMBERLEY.

Undated.—" We had a most interesting day; we visited the diamond mines. They are quite wonderful. It appears that at some distant time there was a terrible convulsion of nature, and an eruption took place from the centre of the earth, driving up a funnel—1,000 yards across. . . . It never spread over the surface. How far it goes down no one knows. I went down 1,520 feet and saw the working, . . . all lit by electricity. As a favour they allowed me to buy a small diamond, which I shall have cut for you. The price was £6 10s. . . . We have fared sumptuously here; whether as guests or not, I don't know; anyhow we have been most comfortable, the cook first-rate, and the liquor admirable. This is a wonderful climate; the air is so pure. . . . I have a longing to see you again."

"ZOCCOLAS VILLA,
" Eight miles from Johannesburg.

" *November* 21.—We went yesterday to Pretoria. It is a most curious town—all houses and trees, with some good buildings and most terrible streets. We were entertained by Conyngham Greene,[2] a most charming Irishman, brother of Plunket Greene, the singer. I failed to see old Krüger, as when I went by appointment at 12-15 he was at dinner, and asked me to come back at four; which I declined to do. . . . I am longing to see you again, and get some rest. We dined last night with a lot of Reform men and had an

[1] The Colonel and his family were guests of the Company everywhere.
[2] British Resident.

interesting discussion. To-night we dine again and meet some more. It has made a good impression: they were in want of men with their heads screwed on the right way. . . . Last night I found an elaborate bouquet on my table; from whom it came I don't know."

"DURBAN CLUB, NATAL.

"*November 25.*—We had a hot journey, 106° in the shade; but, as the air was dry, I did not mind it. . . . Natal is a lovely country, so green after the veldt, where all was brown. The rail down to Maritzburg is quite wonderful, and I longed for you to be with us. . . . All kinds of tropical flowers and fruit; field after field of pine-apples and bananas, with tree-ferns waving in the air; also hedges of hibiscus. . . .

"I had a terrible disaster at Johannesburg: I lost my purse, with my rail passes, and £4 in money. . . . Here we have been royally entertained by Mr. Greenacre, the Mayor, and others. Nothing can exceed the hospitality we experience. Last night I went to an Irish smoking concert; all kinds of Irishmen; and when I got seated up got Mr. O'Hea, who used to sit for Donegal, and proposed a vote of welcome to me in a speech full of tremendous flattery. Then I spoke, and received a tremendous reception from Home Rulers and the rest. The Zulus are a magnificent race; you ought to see them running about the town dragging the rickshaws; I have been photographed in one. . . . The way we got on board the steamer is original. There is a huge basket into which the passengers get, then they are hoisted up on board, luggage and all."

He kept a pocket-book in which he wrote down his impressions as we find them here, with many sketches and some notes for speeches. One entry is:

"Mafeking looked like an English village. Crowds of people, fine-looking. It strikes me more and more what a wonderful people the English are."

Concerning his talk with the Reform men, of which he speaks, this is entered:

"Reformers made out their case and heard our

views. We don't go far enough for them. I told them they could not expect England to go to war because they were only making 15 per cent. instead of 20 or 30, which they might if Krüger treated them better. They appeared to understand this argument."

Writing to his son John he says :

" I saw a good deal of the Matabele up-country and did not think much of them, either men or women. This is Secombo, their leading chief [picture], a great scoundrel. He ought to have been hung, but got off. I went to the prison and saw fourteen Matabele who are to be hung this week for murders before the last war broke out. They did not appear to mind. We have free passes over all The Cape Railways for the whole party; so we go about in state. The ladies are not attractive, as you may imagine. I wonder what they would think of this one at Belturbet [picture]."

In another letter he makes the pregnant observation : " The Boers hate us like poison, and the Dutch in the colonies don't like us much. The English people out here are intensely loyal."

There is something characteristic in the Colonel's haughty refusal to dance attendance on President Krüger when he failed to keep his appointment. It would have been a curious meeting, although one can hardly think that there would have been a fluent or sympathetic flow of conversation. It must not be forgotten that the Colonel had been denouncing the President and all his works. It is therefore conceivable that the fixture of his dinner-hour on this particular day was an instance of Mr. Krüger's notorious slimness. It is even alleged that his excuses were conveyed in such terms as to bear with them a veiled reproach. Upon this we need not dwell with too much curiosity; but it is fair to say that perhaps the Colonel had not duly considered the difference between the head of a more or less independent republic and the leader of an Opposition at home.   He could have tea on the terrace with Mr. Gladstone, or sit on a Committee with Mr. Healy, in spite of his furious denunciations; but Mr. Krüger was President of the Transvaal Republic; not a fellow member of Parliament, and he may have looked on the Colonel's criticisms from a different point of view.

Saunderson's reputation had preceded him.   He tells his son that he appears to be as well known in Capetown as Belturbet.   He was met on arrival with a request to address the Young Men's Christian Association at Johannesburg.   The employés of a boot company presented him with a pair of Veldt Schoon, and expressed a hope that he would use them to kick certain political opponents.   Needless to say, his tour was punctuated with frequent speeches. At Buluwayo he made what may be called a rattling one, full of spirited appeals to patriotism, local and imperial.   He spoke of the country in optimistic language: the railway was to be carried on to the Victoria Falls, opening up vast coal-fields; then, said he, with gold, with coal, and with money, with a magnificent soil—what more did they want? He would tell them—they wanted a fine, vigorous, power-ful, courageous race; and they had got it.

It may easily be believed that, as he passed through the country, his proclivities hardened into firm con-victions, and that he had no intention of disguising them.   When he was interviewed at Maritzburg he paid no compliments to President Krüger, whose treatment of him, he confessed, had not been civil. He likened him unto the Sultan of Turkey: as one had been given a new term of credit by the attack made upon him by Greece, so the other had been rehabilitated by the Jameson raid.   At East London he spoke out plainly: forts existed at Pretoria and Johannesburg, he said; the Boer population was armed to the teeth, and policemen went about with rifles and fixed bayonets among the unarmed Uitlanders, who were composed almost wholly of British subjects. Undoubtedly the forts were meant as a menace to Great Britain. If war broke out and Great Britain was hard pressed elsewhere, it would be a question whether the Briton or Boer was to rule in South Africa. It was therefore the imperative duty of the British people in South Africa to be ready if called upon to assert with their own right arms the supremacy of the Crown.

The Colonel's forecast was only at fault to the extent that it required no complications elsewhere to afford Great Britain a critical ordeal when the appointed time came. The final injunction sounds like a true echo from Ulster, and he naturally dwelt continually on the analogy between the Loyalists of Ulster and the Uitlanders in the Transvaal. He did not point out, nobody ever seems to have pointed out, that President Krüger might have yielded all that the Uitlanders professed to desire and yet have retained power in his own hands. It is easy enough now to ask why he did not, and to wonder whether in that case the war would ever have been necessary. Saunderson perceived, as did most observers, that the President meant to be stubborn; what he and his friends called defence Saunderson dubbed defiance. It was manifest that a collision must ensue if the two forces, starting from opposite standpoints, were equally determined not to give way. His only care was that when the crash came, the party with which he sympathised should not be taken at a disadvantage.

One paper reported that "Colonel Saunderson is

making a species of triumphal progress in the English centres of South Africa, being fêted everywhere;" but it was at Capetown, on his return, that he made his final and complete pronouncement, on January 7, 1898. Cape Colony, he said, was the one spot in all Her Majesty's dominions where Imperial feeling and views had not had effect. . . . He found racial separation existing and politics running, not simply upon ordinary political, but upon national lines. He looked upon that as disastrous. It had been a disaster to Ireland, and unless it was put down it would be a disaster to Africa. Turning then to the Afrikander Bond, he declared it was the story of the Irish National League over again, the only difference being that, as they were Protestants and not Roman Catholics, they did not hough cattle or shoot at their neighbours from behind hedges. Not without interruption he went on to press the analogy: as the National League had been financed from America, so the Bond was being financed from the Transvaal. As the Loyalist minority in Ireland had been organised to resist the Nationalists, so the British in the Colony must organise to resist the Bond. According to his custom, he read some "elegant extracts" from speeches made by members of the Bond, and created a great sensation by producing and reading a copy of the Bond rules, which had not been procured without difficulty. England, he went on, was threatened on many sides by the jealousies of European neighbours: at any moment the British in South Africa might have to defend themselves at a time when the mother country could spare little assistance. Meanwhile the Transvaal was piling up forts and armaments at the expense of British subjects who paid taxes and had no votes. This must lead to a convulsion sooner or later. Waxing warm as he proceeded, he next declared that President Krüger had outwitted England and Mr. Chamberlain. The British bore no grudge for their defeat at Majuba, but they knew the Boers hated them more than any other nation hated them, and they dared not sit still and watch in apathy these preparations for their own extinction. Little Englanders, he said—and it may be noted that the phrase was not a product of the subsequent war—Little Englanders had done much mischief. Even Governments had been guilty of regarding the Colonial Office as no more important than the Duchy of Lancaster, and sending there a third-class peer who knew no more about the needs and sentiments of the colonies than he himself knew of what a Chinese mandarin sang to his wife. In spite of what he had just said, he now held up Mr. Chamberlain as a minister of another type, who was to inaugurate a new system, and at whose hands they need never fear betrayal or neglect. Here he made a startling interpolation to deprecate any tendency towards stirring up racial animosity, which in the middle of such an uncompromising diatribe suggests the traditional self-contradiction of an Irishman; but on he went to eulogise Mr. Rhodes [1] as he had done in the House of Commons, and in an impassioned peroration he declared that, whilst Britain held the sea for them, it was her right to expect that they would hold South Africa for Britain.

This was throwing away the pretence of peace; it was stripping off the mask, and exhibiting the features of a resolute opponent. Needless to say, there was an outcry; Mr. Merriman denounced the speech as the most mischievous and ill-advised ever

[1] The Colonel was well acquainted with Mr. Rhodes, but did not meet him during this tour.

18

uttered in South Africa, stirring up race feud and embittering all the questions which it was the interest of the country to bring to a peaceful solution. The Colonel did not care; he had something to say, and he had said it. He was too old a dog to learn new tricks. For the past dozen years he had been making the same kind of speech in Ulster, and he was not likely to lapse suddenly into discreet and diplomatic banalities in order to obscure the imminent danger he beheld in South Africa. Nor was he without his reward. Supporters of the South African League were enthusiastic in their admiration and gratitude, and there was quite a brisk demand for the orator's photograph.

Two distinct motives were at work. He once made the suggestive confession to a friend that he believed he had a mission to expose the enemies of his country. This was an obvious opportunity. Moreover, it must be remembered that the men whom he was addressing were in an excited and impulsive frame of mind, and here was the very man to give them the kind of speech they wanted: he spoke "by request." They encouraged him, and he appealed to them, and each stirred up the other. We have just read that he "did not go far enough for the Reformers." It is easy, then, to estimate the pressure brought to bear on him to pitch his tone high, and the consequent temptation to "let himself go."

Mr. Merriman, however, was not the only one who found fault with the Colonel's speeches. There were others who doubted the wisdom of a prominent member of the British Parliament in laying so rough a hand on the sore places of the political system, and aggravating the inflamed condition of the community. It must be borne in mind that whatever the Colonel said gained point and emphasis from his dramatic[1] inspiration; and in this connection it is appropriate to describe his style as a speaker. It has been said that he possessed two of the orator's most precious gifts, a fine voice, and eyes that revealed the fervour of the mind. He would deliver his temperate passages in stately calm, his tall figure drawn to its full height, his hands often holding the lapels of his buttoned frock-coat. He could at times assume a grave and mournful tone, as when he once roused the House of Commons to shocked indignation by his sorrowful contemplation of the removal of Mr. Gladstone to another place, naïvely assuring those who shouted "Shame," that he meant the House of Lords, not Heaven. He had found the trick effective with a provincial audience,[2] and he amused himself by repeating it with some elaboration. As an oratorical ruse it was entirely successful, and is often quoted as his most characteristic achievement. He was full of playful resources; but when he came to the impassioned stage, he was another man. His eyes seemed to dilate and blaze with indignation; the body was swayed by the wrath within; the long arm was thrown out, not with clenched fist, as the illustrated papers had it, but with open palm, the nervous fingers ready, as it seemed, to close with a relentless clutch upon the object of his scorn. He articulated every word as if he uttered it with all his soul. The excitement of a strong spirit is contagious, and in this native force lay his power of compelling enthusiasm. When such a man, occupying such a position, made such a passionate appeal to an audience already restless enough, he

---

[1] The Colonel did not make a practice of visiting theatres : on rare occasions he went to see some particular actor, for the sake of his art.

[2] *Vide supra*, p. 125.

had gone a long way towards confirming them in their resolve to make force the final arbiter.

However, if the charge of imprudence has to be brought, against those who invited the Colonel to South Africa must it be levelled. It was certain that he would make speeches when he got there, and nobody who knew him could possibly doubt what line he would pursue. The man whose life had recently been spent in preaching the sacred duty of resistance to the menaced minority of Ireland, was not likely to preach contented acquiescence to his oppressed countrymen abroad.

But this does not complete the catalogue of his discourses during the journey. A fellow-passenger to the Cape, who was not an intimate friend, relates that—

" It was a rather impressive surprise to see and hear him preach more than one impromptu sermon in the fo'castle and either steerage or second-class deck on Sunday nights. . . . I realised on that voyage that [the effect of his political speeches] was due to the man's faith and firm conviction in the truth of what he said."

In this connection it would be avoiding the duty of a biographer to ignore his fierce allusion in his last speech to Roman Catholics. Although he always repudiated the spirit of bigotry, it must be admitted that he persistently spoke of Roman Catholics with pointed harshness. It was a fixed principle in his philosophy. He was certainly not a narrow-minded sectarian : his religious tenets were not confined within the narrow limits of an orthodox confession. He was liberal enough to recognise the right of every man to think for himself and worship his God in his own way and according to his faith. To him it was

THE COLONEL SPEAKING.

From the drawing by S. Begg.

so much a matter of reality and daily need that he attached less importance than most men to formularies and names. It was not therefore on spiritual or pedantic grounds that he regarded with aversion the practices and authority of Rome. But for one thing he was an Orangeman, and could therefore not be expected to be wholly uninfluenced by the traditional sentiments of the order. Furthermore, his life was devoted to political conflict, and, broadly speaking, his opponents were Roman Catholics. They had become identified in his mind with Home Rulers and Home Rule. Towards these he entertained feelings of hostility and mistrust which had become an obsession, and when he denounced Roman Catholics he was employing little more than a synonym for the Irish National League. The consequence was that he laid himself open to the charge of religious prejudice when he was often guilty of nothing but political prepossessions.

A strong character must inevitably rub sharply against some parts of the social surface. Saunderson did not trim his opinions to suit convention. He thought for himself, and said what he thought: consequently he was capable of shocking a good many people who said what other people thought, having no particular opinions of their own. Like many another independent character, he was notable even for his apparel. We have seen that his travelling attire consisted of " pyjamas and slippers, without stockings "; so in Buluwayo he preferred the blue flannels and bright red tie, in which he took his ease at home, to the more customary costume which his companions generally adopted.

We can only repeat that it was not to be imagined that the Colonel would go through these ceremonies

formal, uncritical, inconspicuous, and studiously discreet. In his speeches and action throughout, he did
but follow the natural bent of his character.

He departed early in January, and reached London
at the end of the month. To the Duke of Abercorn
he wrote a letter, evidently composed with care,
offering his thanks for the hospitality which had been
lavished by the Chartered Company, and paying
special compliments to Captain Lawley,[1] the acting
administrator of Matabeleland. To the Duke, as
Chairman of the Company, he made an encouraging
report upon the signs of progress and prosperity,
and enlarged on the important mission entrusted to
him and his colleagues in fortifying British authority
throughout South Africa.

Saunderson's warning that England might at any
moment be involved in a European war was no private
delusion. When Parliament opened on February 8,
1898, Lord Salisbury spoke with extreme solemnity
of the grave crisis through which the country was
passing. China was being raided by the Powers;
Russia was especially active, and conduct, which was
considered provocative, inflamed a large number of
reckless individuals in this country to a condition of
war-fever. Friction over the government of Crete left
an opening to a conflagration in the near East. We
were engaged in an unsatisfactory campaign on the
Indian frontier; we were about to advance on
Khartoum; in South Africa and in West Africa, where
we were at cross-purposes with France, we had cause
for apprehension. It was notorious that the Powers
of Europe, in conflict upon many issues, were united
in a desire for our destruction; meanwhile we were

---

[1] The Honourable Sir Arthur Lawley, G.C.I.E.. K.C.M.G., Governor
of Madras.

incurring fresh responsibilities and piling up our offences in the estimation of rivals who thought we already pervaded the world to an excessive extent. People were talking light-heartedly of our readiness to engage all mankind, if our interests were assailed. Meanwhile *The Spectator* asserted that it was really no exaggeration to say that we might at any hour receive a telegram which would show that the avoidance of hostilities had become almost an impossibility. If the war party had succeeded in forcing the Government to extremities in connection with Port Arthur, our position next year would have been desperate indeed. It is true that in the first case the brunt would have had to be borne by our Navy, which was not required for operations against the Boers; but that is a crude and superficial reservation. In the first place, we should have had neither time nor money to spare for the conduct of two wars; in the second place, it was the immunity of our Navy which gave us security whilst our Army was shut up in South Africa. Alexander Hamilton once declared that we must have crushed the American Revolution in time if our fleets had not been drawn away by the French entanglements into which American diplomacy thrust us.

One cannot exaggerate the gravity and extent of our peril had a false step in 1898 plunged us prematurely into the awful liabilities of war. Not only did we escape these contingent perils: the direct menace of a conflict later in the year, when the British and French found themselves suddenly in antagonism at Fashoda, likewise passed happily away.

Saunderson was at work early in the session. The debate on the Address included an amendment in favour of the establishment of a Roman Catholic

University in Ireland. It is needless to recapitulate the Colonel's objections to the proposal. Mr. Balfour had confessed himself in favour of it. Saunderson presently retorted that his right honourable friend was a very ingenious man, but that not even his ingenuity could devise a more expeditious method of destroying the Unionist majority. "The First Lord's name will be cheap in Ulster to-morrow," was the comment of one Tory peer from Ireland.

Early in the session Mr. Gerald Balfour introduced his Local Government Bill for Ireland. On the whole it had a peaceful reception. As a sop to landlords, it provided for a large grant in aid of rates. Not even this consoled some of the least tractable section of county magnates: "What is the use of that?" grumbled one of them, "it will only be deducted from our rents next time."

Saunderson's attitude was described in a speech to his constituents: if the majority were to have a free hand in taxing the minority, he said, it would be impossible to live long in the country with any clothes on one's back. . . . It proposed to give a man who paid no rates power to elect another man, who paid no rates, to spend money. If he had his way the Bill would never have been introduced, but he accepted it, and determined to do his best to make it as good a Bill as possible.

His great objection was to the election of non-ratepayers. A few days later in the House of Commons he complained that corner-boys might be elected. He was interrupted by an inquiry as to the nature of a corner-boy. The Colonel's definition was simplicity itself: "A man who stands at corners and generally drinks whisky." The Bill did not lead to any exciting incidents, and duly passed into law.

"*August* 3, 1898.—I have just said my last word on the Irish Bill : I am off with the Baroness to dine at Holly Lodge. London is too detestable for words : as hot as an oven."

There was another debate upon the question of financial relations; but it lacked vitality. The movement had lost impetus, and the coalition of the previous year had left Ireland where she was before.

There remains a speech worth noting which Saunderson made in Dublin in October :

"The Irish Church had received, as they thought, a very sad blow twenty-eight years ago when it was disestablished and disendowed and separated from the Church of England. Although he voted against the measure at the time, yet, if he could, he would now undo that vote : for he believed that the Irish Church at the present moment was stronger and more spiritual than it ever was before."

This was indeed a bold admission of one who in 1869 had mourned over the " poor Church tottering to its fall." [1] Here he was proclaiming its superiority in strength and sincerity to the English Establishment, which he declared was beset by dissensions within and enmity without.

At the same time an amusing correspondence passed between the Colonel and the Postmaster-General, the Duke of Norfolk, about some unimportant appointment in Armagh. It may easily be understood that the nomination of a Roman Catholic might have caused an outcry in some Orange quarters, and that the member would have been called upon to resist the machinations of a Roman Catholic minister. Nothing could be more dignified and just than the Duke's explanation that his action depended on the interests of the public service, not of his private religious

[1] *Vide supra*, p. 45.

282 THE RIGHT HONOURABLE [CHAP. XVII

connections ; nor does the Colonel appear to have had any intention of setting up a grievance. But it is a curious instance of how mountains may arise out of molehills, and how the religion of a village post-master may approach the region of Cabinet questions.

At the close of the year Saunderson received this letter :

"FOREIGN OFFICE,
"*December* 27, 1898.

"DEAR COLONEL SAUNDERSON,

"I hope that, as an old and very influential member of the House of Commons, you will not think it strange that I should have recommended your ad-mission to the Privy Council, a recommendation of which Her Majesty has graciously approved.

"I am glad that it has fallen to me to express the high appreciation with which your party, and much more than your party, regard your public services.

"Yours very truly,
"SALISBURY."

It was followed by letters of congratulation, which show that the Colonel's friends and admirers were to be found in many different classes of the community.

CHAPTER XVIII

1899

PARLIAMENT met on February 7, 1899. The Opposition had a new leader: Sir William Harcourt had resigned. It was known that the relations existing amongst Liberal ex-ministers were not entirely harmonious. In December Sir William Harcourt had written a manifesto to Mr. Morley, protesting his inability to retain his position and his innocence of having been the instigator of any personal antagonisms which might have arisen. Mr. Morley replied with an ample confirmation of this avowal, leaving the public to infer that Lord Rosebery had been the aggressor and Sir William the victim. It was tolerably well known, however, that amongst Sir William's colleagues there were some who would be less eager to stand forth as his ally than was Mr. Morley, and political opponents watched with mischievous amusement to see how far the quarrel was to be carried, and with interest to learn whether Lord Rosebery was to become the " predominant partner " once more. Mr. Asquith's selection as leader of the House of Commons was regarded as probable if this were to be the next move. But the political backers were putting their money on the wrong horse again: Sir Henry Campbell-Bannerman became leader, and the destinies of the Liberal party were definitely diverted into another channel. It will very soon be forgotten that during the ensuing years there was a distinct and active section of the party, known as the Liberal Imperialists, who looked up to Lord Rosebery as their future Prime Minister. Events, however, have taught us that when Sir Henry had once been installed as leader of the Liberal party he had come to stay.

Saunderson did not show any intention of appearing frequently in the House. He was now a "right honourable member"—a title of more credit and distinction than some others which are usually considered the prizes of political life; and he had duly gone through the antiquated ceremony which accompanies admission into the Privy Council:

"*February* 2, 1899.—I have just returned from Osborne. The ceremony went off very well: there was no difficulty about it. Afterwards we had lunch, which was pleasant, as I was starving. The Queen looked very well indeed."

He committed himself to one public pronouncement. The Emperor of Russia had conceived the project of assembling the nations of the world in conclave to consider the possibility of a general reduction of armaments. Saunderson at once dismissed this as a vision incapable of fulfilment: "The only thing that really carries weight at the present day is force," he said to one who came to elicit his opinion. "A nation is not respected because its objects are great and good; it is respected if its army and navy are big and strong. That is the outcome of civilisation." England, he pointed out, could not retain her present possessions and responsibilities without naval pre-eminence: "when we are asked to give up the command of the sea, England is not mad enough to entertain the idea. It is not even a remote possibility."

Candour here compels the admission that the Colonel was capable of dudgeon if he was thwarted in the course which he had elected to follow, or in the attainment of any object on which he had set his heart. He had occasion to remonstrate with the Lord-Lieutenant at this juncture because something which he himself had undertaken to get done had been left undone. He disliked being blamed, he said, and represented himself as placed in an uncomfortable predicament. There is a touch of pathos in Lord Cadogan's friendly rejoinder: " I envy you your dislike to blame falling on you. It rains on me; and it never rains but it pours, so I am accustomed to it."

There was the usual Irish amendment to the Address. Saunderson spoke in a cheerful vein. He admitted that Home Rule was at all events in abeyance, and poked fun at the Opposition leaders who were bent on reconciling their previous actions and professions with the scruples which prevented them from voting for the present declaration that the establishment of an independent Legislature for Ireland should be the first consideration for politicians. He contemplated with relief the disunion in the opposing army, and felt that for the moment he might lay aside his arms.

" *February* 17.—You will have seen that I spoke last night. They say my speech was a great success, so it is all right. At any rate the Radicals were furious."

During this debate an Irish member delivered himself of a bull which deserves preservation. Alluding with emotion to the recent death of a former Liberal minister,[1] he exclaimed, " Mr. Speaker, if I shut my

[1] Mr. Mundella.

eyes I can see him sitting there now."[1] Curiously
enough, a ludicrous slip of the tongue was made
next day by so accomplished a master of phrases as
Mr. Balfour: "We used to hear a good deal at one
time," he said, "about holding a stake in the country.
Sir, that steak (? argument) has been overdone."
Seldom has such uproarious laughter been heard in
the House of Commons; though it is probable that
none or few of the present generation can remember a
more boisterous outburst than that which Lord Randolph Churchill once provoked when he set out to make
fun of the very minister to whose death allusion has
just been made.   Him he quoted as having said, in the
course of a recent speech, "The other day I was
addressing my constituents in Paradise—Square."
The pause was the inspiration of an artist, and accurately gauged the taste of his audience for humour
of the rougher kind.   It must be admitted indeed that
there need not be too delicate a flavour about appeals
made to the sense of the ridiculous in the House of
Commons.   Thus in the April of this year (1899) when
Sir William Harcourt compared financial heresies
with woman's frailty, and added, "Sir, I have had
some experience in these matters," the delight was
as vehement as if he had uttered an exquisite witticism.
Nor was amusement much less keenly stimulated
when an English member accused an Irish member
of producing a "pregnant bull."

This does not mean that the parliamentary standard
is entirely depraved.   At one time classical quotation
was a necessary adornment of excellence.   That is
superannuated now : its use is regarded as pedantry.
Genuine wit and a deep vein of humour are probably

[1] This is perhaps not really a bull, but it was received as one by
the House.

more rare and less eagerly demanded than they were ;
but if another Sheridan or Disraeli could arise, or a
professed sayer of good things like Lord Erskine, he
would certainly not be as one crying in the wilderness.
A really good thing contributed to debate is still appreciated, and no fine flower of speech need blush
unappreciated.   Farce and low comedy are not in sole
request ; what in theatrical language is known as " the
legitimate " has not had to yield entirely to buffoonery.
The effect in the examples cited above was due to an
ordinary love of nonsense ; Lord Randolph's point
was witty, though it carried some sting of personality.
On the other hand, his son found immediate response
when he ventured on such ingenious audacity as his
" terminological inexactitudes " ; and, to take a random
recollection, another member scored a notable success
not long ago by a startling perversion of ideas : " You
may call the Mediterranean a home station if you like,"
he said ; " you may call Cairo Clapham Junction ; but
you won't get Tommy Atkins to believe you."

Saunderson's humour could claim to be on the
higher plane.   He had a natural capacity for drollery :
he had an original cast of mind and a lively imagination.   These pages must be taken as evidence and a
test ; the quick things he said, and, still more, the
comical ideas which he conceived, were cordially
applauded by the House of Commons, and were
certainly not the laborious efforts of a professional
funny man.

For the moment, however, he was contributing
nothing to the gaiety of parliamentary life.   He was
in one of his inactive moods.   The government of
London and its water-supply were the subjects with
which the session was chiefly occupied, and in
neither of these did he feel called upon to interfere.

In June he went to Kiel, sailing from Dover in the race for the German Emperor's cup with Mr. John Gretton, M.P., in his yacht *Betty*. Later in the year he was as intent as ever on the rivalries of Lough Erne. The following are amongst his reports :

"KIEL. *Betty*.

"*June* 23, 1899.—Here we are, safe and sound. We made a good race, and got second prize. . . . When we got within eighty miles of Heligoland it came on very strong, with a heavy short sea into which the *Betty* plunged up to her mast.

"To-day I expect we got the first prize in the handicap ; but there is a protest on the part of the Emperor's schooner about a buoy which we passed on the wrong side. No one explained the course, and none of us could read the German directions. John does not mind, so it does not matter. . . . The Emperor is going to present me to the Empress, to whom he says he has often spoken about me.

"*25th.*—This is a very fine bay and town, the Portsmouth of Germany.

"*26th.*—Yesterday I had a long talk with the Emperor. I saw him playing lawn-tennis at the club ; he spotted me and called me over and introduced me to the Empress. We then had half an hour's talk. . . . John and I dine with him to-night."

"CASTLE SAUNDERSON.

"*August* 29.—We sailed a most amusing race to-day. We made a good start and went away from the other boats. We rounded the Cow one mile ahead of *Squall ;* two miles of George.[1] The wind was fairly strong and the *Afrite* steered beautifully. . . . In the beat to wind from the Heron home, the *Squall* got a lift and headed us both. Then, on the way home, at the Owl I headed the fleet and looked like winning to a certainty. However I got into a light patch, and George got by me. I came in second, beating *Squall* by seven seconds. George is in great glee. It rained in torrents, and we forgot to bring our waterproofs. I feel very pleased at the way the *Afrite* went."

[1] Mr. Massy Beresford.

The summer passed tranquilly. The Government held their own at bye-elections, and domestic politics gave small scope for excitement. It was abroad that the storm-clouds were gathering—not unperceived indeed, but not greatly dreaded. It is worth while reviewing the story. A journal of events must always possess a certain value, not merely as a record of facts and dates, but as an index to the temper and opinions prevailing at the time.

The attention of the careless was first drawn with any earnestness to South Africa early in June, when it was known that Sir Alfred Milner[1] and Mr. Krüger had met in conference to try and settle outstanding differences, and had failed. People then began to talk of war, but to talk of it as an unfortunate necessity rather than a grave national danger. It is interesting, but not pleasant, to recall the unenlightened views which went to make up public opinion. Society was undismayed; no forebodings of serious trouble threw a shadow across the pleasant progress of existence. Some politicians became agitated: a coterie of Unionist members announced themselves as opposed to arbitrary measures. They argued that by the London Convention of 1884 we had surrendered our rights and title to authority in the Transvaal, and could not in honour attempt to re-assert them now; that, under pretext of claiming concessions to the legitimate political demands of British residents we were lending unwarrantable support to the pretensions of those adventurers, many of them German Jews, who were bent on exploiting the mines for their personal gain. The general tone was bellicose and defiant: yet some, who might be

[1] High Commissioner for South Africa. He became Lord Milner in 1901.

supposed to have good information, still discredited
the idea of hostilities. One who had good reason for
being acquainted with the Transvaal Government,
and was certainly intimate with all the leading men in
South Africa, declared in June that there was no
chance of fighting; President Krüger would hold out
until he saw our bayonets fixed, and then give
way. Even if his judgment was not profound, he
presumably repeated what was said amongst his
friends. The present generation need not be blamed
if they passed the matter off too lightly. They remembered, perhaps, the Ashanti war, the Afghan war,
and the Zulu war, and the various campaigns in Egypt
between 1882 and 1898. They were accustomed to
hear of little wars on the Indian frontier, or in some
region of Africa about the geography of which they
neither knew anything nor cared to learn. They remembered the last Boer war with vexation, but Majuba
had left no passion for revenge; it suggested little
more than a useful platform resource for the abuse
of Mr. Gladstone. The death of Gordon was a
grievous memory; otherwise news of a new outbreak
was wont to create curiosity rather than alarm;
public confidence had not been seriously shaken
for half a century. War-scares had been common
enough, but the lesson of experience had yet to be
learned.

The Government were confronted by a dilemma
which they did not successfully evade. If they made
a menacing display they would be accused of rendering
hostilities inevitable; if they refrained from military
preparations they ran the risk of losing an initial
advantage. In the light of our present knowledge we
can only contemplate with meekness and resignation
the fallibility of our foresight and our good intentions.

We know now that most of our wisest counsellors agreed in estimating 40,000 men as the utmost of our possible requirements. It is inevitable that men should be wise after the event, and many people can remember a warning of this or that general, or civilian observer, who predicted that the struggle was to be something far beyond our expectations. One thoughtful officer, having pondered long over the map of South Africa, arrived at the conclusion that with such extensive lines of communication, the country could never be penetrated with less than 170,000 troops. Having some military friends in Berlin, he wrote to inquire, as a matter of professional interest, what was the opinion of German experts. Their estimate reached 200,000. From first to last we had nearly half a million troops within the theatre of war, although it by no means follows that we always succeeded in overwhelming the enemy by actual numbers on the field of battle. We were not unprepared for the tenacity of the Boer in action, nor his mobility, nor his adroitness: the problems which rose to baffle and perplex us were those rather of strategy than tactics.

Late in September, about a fortnight before Mr. Krüger delivered his ultimatum, Saunderson expounded his views to a journalist; and they are worth recording, not only as showing how the situation presented itself to him personally, but as a fair illustration of the point of view common amongst men who knew something about South Africa, and were capable of forming an intelligent opinion upon a military proposition.

"Nobody who visited South Africa, as I did two years ago, could expect anything else," he said. " The whole of this movement is purely Dutch, and its object is supreme authority in South Africa. . . . We cannot afford to allow an independent Power hostile to us to be set up in the midst of our South African colonies, to be a source of perpetual irritation and danger. . . . Great Britain means to be supreme at all hazards. That is the meaning of the situation. . . . The danger, to my mind, is that we have not taken up a solid position at Laing's Nek. . . . If the Boers intend to fight they will probably make a dash for it. . . . Our advance into the Transvaal must be effected by way of Laing's Nek and, I imagine, through the Free State, which offers great facilities for the employment of cavalry. . . . It will be very important that we should get both ends of the tunnel which I have marked in this sketch, and prevent the Boers from blowing it up. To maintain our communications it is absolutely necessary that we should hold the railway which passes through that tunnel under Laing's Nek. . . . We should require 40,000 men at least to finish the war off properly. . . . Yes, war is inevitable. . . . When it does come, it will probably not last more than three months."

On December 6, at Belfast, he further explained his forecast, blaming the Government for not having sent troops sooner, and dilating on the hostile action of the Nationalists in adopting the cause of the Boers. Even now he ventured on the prediction that the war would terminate in four or five months. And within a fortnight the country was overwhelmed with astonishment and dismay : disasters had followed in quick succession.

It is only fair to say that the Colonel's optimism was shared by one eminent man whose local and military experience was both far more extensive, and who on the same day was disposing of the future with equal confidence.

It is not necessary to follow the progress of operations; they only concern us in so far as they affected the course of politics and public feeling at home. The revulsion from comparative indifference to extreme anxiety and gloom was sudden and complete. Men's hearts were failing them. Instead of "giving the Boers a jolly good hiding," they began to talk of the loss of South Africa. After all, we had lost America, said they, and we had survived. So soon after the glorious days of Chatham we had undergone that indignity, yet we had easily recovered. It was impossible that America could have remained a British dependency for ever: probably it was impossible that we could retain the African states for ever. We should be none the worse; in many ways it would be a good riddance. So they argued, seeking consolation where no comfort was.

At the same time young men of all classes hastened to become soldiers. Those who held commissions in the Yeomanry, Militia, and Volunteers, were eager for active service; those who had never given an hour's thought to the necessity of soldiering, either offered to go out as they were, or joined one of the auxiliary forces at home. London dandies went out as yeomanry troopers; owners of all the world's pleasures and possessions sought a place in their county contingent of Yeomanry or Volunteers, or willingly went with their embodied Militia. One sybarite, so the story goes, created a sensation by appearing on the veldt in an improvised corps, with the explanation that he knew nothing about fighting, but had found that it was no longer possible to appear anywhere in England without having to give your reasons in writing for not being at the war.

The nation was to be congratulated on the spirit which was thus made manifest; on the whole it was to be congratulated on the firmness with which it faced its ordeal. Not so much to be admired was the universal resolve to find a scape-goat.

The War Office was sore beset. It had to meet demands beyond all measure in excess of anything that had been imagined or suggested, such as no Secretary of State could have sought to anticipate without being scouted as a madman. Invective was poured out on the heads of two devoted ministers. They could not make bricks without straw, and they could not produce trained men where none existed; but if they failed in respect of quality, at all events they contrived to find quantity, and to transport them to the scene of action; and in spite of immense difficulties, they succeeded in maintaining the necessary provisions of food and equipment for the growing numbers in the field. Finally their efforts were rewarded with success; we did not have to make an ignominious surrender; we succeeded in wearing out the enemy.

Meanwhile an army scheme had been produced to meet the hot fit of enthusiasm, only to be rejected as extravagant in a cooler mood of criticism. And it was one of the strangest incidents of the strange story that when peace was finally reached, the terms of settlement seemed to please everybody; they were neither too lenient for the stalwarts nor too severe for the party of concession, though these had seldom been in agreement at any previous stage of the proceedings. But now, instead of praise or satisfaction, the public thought of nothing but a searching inquisition into the shortcomings of each individual and every department concerned. None could truly claim to be wise after the event; none could say, "I told you so," yet they must ease their minds by blaming somebody. Criticism throughout had been legitimate; in matters of detail there were many grounds for differences of opinion and fault-finding; but, regarding the situation from every point of view, it was surely obvious that the shortcomings were due to our system and ourselves, and could not be laid entirely at the door of any Cabinet, Department, or Minister. There had been no flagrant dereliction of duty nor wanton neglect of national interests. But people were angry, and inclined to be ashamed, and they did not rise above the human infirmity of airing their grievances at somebody else's expense. We now return from this anticipation of events.

At the beginning of October 1899, President Krüger had delivered his ultimatum: unless we ceased our military preparations, they would be considered an act of war; so that the last hope of peace was dispelled. On October 17 Parliament met in a sombre mood; only Lord Salisbury seemed disposed to retain a ray of cheerfulness. His allusion to Mr. Krüger as "an amiable but very sensitive old gentleman," and a passing reference to "hysterical school-girls," seem in retrospect inappropriate phrases for application to the people who were to give us so much trouble. The other speeches were sedate, and generally on a high plane. On the 19th Mr. Chamberlain spoke for two and three-quarter hours, and made perhaps his finest oratorical display—a moving, dignified, and eloquent speech, not unworthy of the occasion, nor of the peculiar position of responsibility in which he stood. It was a short and formal session; and Parliament was prorogued. The War Office was, at all events, to be spared incessant nagging and cross-examination, and the public were left to endure as best they could the jeremiads of the Press and the lamentations of their neighbours.

At Christmas-time Saunderson was summoned from Castle Saunderson to London, where his eldest son was seriously ill. He himself fell a victim to another attack of influenza, and was obliged to go first to Dover, and later on to a villa at Stanmore, lent by his friend Mr. D'Arcy. When Parliament met he was in his place.

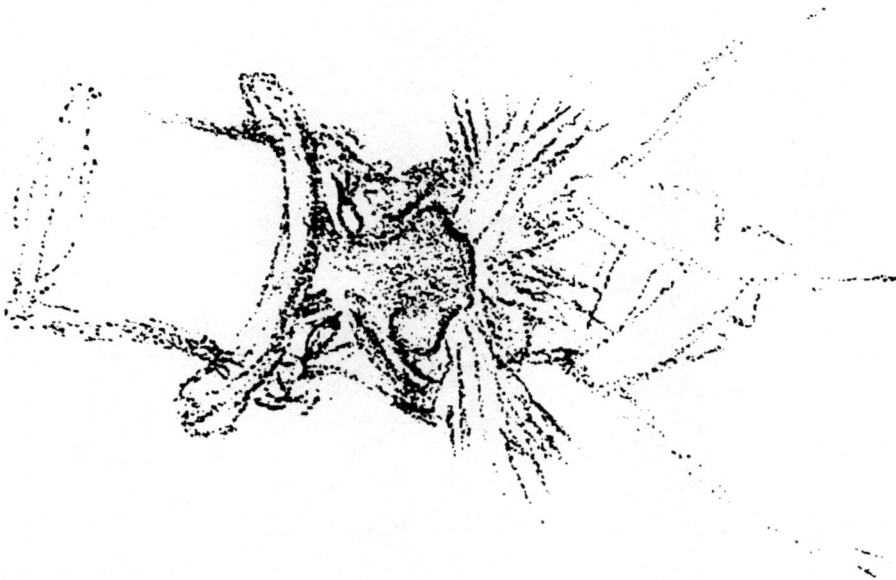

M. BLOWITZ.

(E.S.)

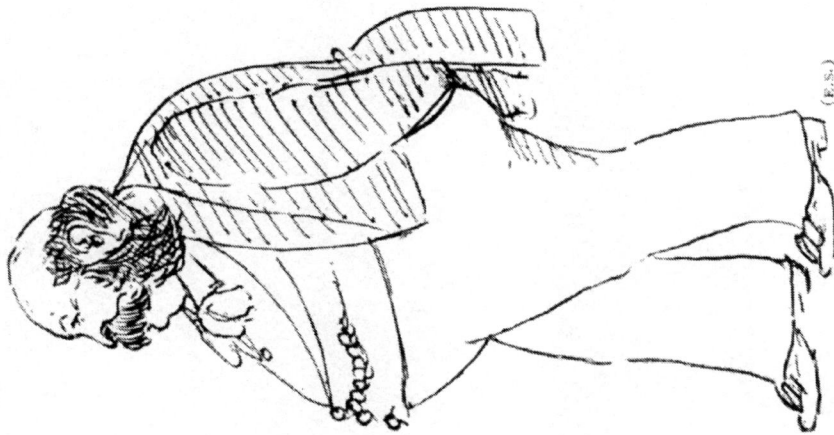

SIR RICHARD TEMPLE, BART., M.P.

(R.S.)

CHAPTER XIX

1900—1901

WHEN Parliament met on January 30, 1900, there was little enough to make members merry. The condition of the garrisons in Ladysmith, Kimberley, and Mafeking seemed precarious to the last degree. One Unionist was heard to ask, "Does any one still think it possible that Ladysmith can be saved? I am delighted to hear it." Saunderson, like a wise man, determined to get what satisfaction he could out of the situation, and set himself to make the most of the language which had been used by the Nationalist members, whose sympathy with the Boers was openly avowed.

On February 2 he made a speech which, as one paper said, recalled the McFadden episode of earlier days. The British Government, he said, were menaced from two directions: they had the Boers to face; meanwhile they would be assailed from behind by the Irish, who never attacked in front. There was immediate uproar. Mr. W. Redmond, one of the loudest of the objectors, enlivened the proceedings with a new bull: "If I had said anything of the kind, I should not have been allowed to." The Speaker ruled that nothing had been said detrimental to the honour of any member of the House, and reminded Irish members that they had frequently said hard things of Englishmen. But it would not do. Mr.

Dillon protested that the Colonel's language was cowardly and insolent, which the Speaker observed was hardly the best way of getting a ready retraction.

Matters were not improved by Saunderson's explanation that he intended no slur upon the valour of his countrymen; he was only going back to historical records in Ireland. Mr. Balfour was obliged to intervene with some amicable suggestions, upon which Saunderson uttered the magic words " I withdraw," and the storm subsided. In fact light humour quickly took the place of rage and fury. The Colonel was twitted, as might have been foreseen, with not having volunteered with his armed men of Ulster, and not being at the war. He pleaded advancing years. "You are not as old as Lord Roberts," came the retort. " If her Majesty will make me a Field-Marshal I will go at once," was the quick rejoinder; and he proceeded to inquire why his interlocutor, who was in the flower of his youth, had not practised what he preached. The Government, he promised, would gladly assist as many Nationalists as were willing to go to the front, and would never press them to hasten back.

"I can serve the cause of liberty and the Boers a great deal better in this House," was the candid response.

Much capital was made of the Colonel's accusation, and he thought it prudent to write to the Press. He repudiated the suggestion that he had impugned the courage of the Irish people : nobody boasted of that with greater pride than he. What he had been describing were the political methods of the Nationalist party; he had quoted a speech as an illustration in which this passage had occurred : " The Boers are taking the stuffing out of the British army in South

Africa : when the stuffing has been taken out, then will be the time for the Irish people to step in." He pleaded this and similar speeches in justification of his assertion that the Nationalists intended, not to tackle Great Britain in front, but to stab her in the back.

So fine a confusion of metaphors might mean anything, but the Colonel could fairly argue that it showed a malicious desire to take England at a disadvantage.

To make his sentiments quite clear, he presently wrote to the officers commanding the two battalions of the Dublin Fusiliers at the war to express his profound admiration of the gallantry and valour which they had exhibited in action ; and he had the satisfaction of learning that these letters had been published in battalion orders.

Late in May he offered some forcible remarks to the House of Commons on the administration of the land laws in Ireland. The Irish landlords naturally did not like the Act of 1881, he said, but they were not foolish enough to suppose that the House would ever go back on it. There was urgent need of an Appeal Court for cases of revision of rent : at present immense interests were absolutely at the mercy of an irresponsible tribunal against which there was only an illusory appeal. He heard a great deal about the tyranny and injustice of President Krüger towards the Uitlanders, but that was nothing compared with the case of the Irish landlords.

Already the reports of dissolution were in the air. It was known that there could be no long delay, and members of Parliament were once more intent upon their prospects in their constituencies rather than upon the business of the House of Commons.

"*June* 7, 1900.—I should not be surprised if we had a dissolution in July, which will alter all plans."

This he writes from Castle Saunderson, where he seems to have been spending his time with great satisfaction.

"CASTLE S.

"*June* 2, 1900.—I never saw anything like the clematis on the cloisters. It looks as if some one had poured tons of cream on the top of the tower and it had poured over in a stream and covered the length of the balcony. It is quite astounding. The Rhodys are splendid. . . . Everything is growing like mad. It looks lovely. . . . We sit out after dinner and have our coffee."

A week later he was speaking at Portadown in the bold language of Imperialism. On us, he said, had been bestowed the greatest honour attaching to the human race—we had been the great instrument in the hand of God for proclaiming the Gospel to the world. . . . Imperialism was born in Ireland. . . . The Home Rule question not only affected Ireland, it affected the whole empire. . . . The Nationalist members of Parliament, who took the oath at the table of the House of Commons, had to his mind absolutely violated that oath by making speeches in Ireland, inciting the country to animosity against Great Britain and sympathising with her foes. He censured the Government for not having peremptorily forbidden the warlike preparations of the Boers, but singled out for eulogy Mr. Chamberlain, "by far the most distinguished man in the House of Commons"—a personal predilection which was to be repeated in his later speeches.

In July he was back in Parliament, and came to the support of his friend, Mr. Burdett-Coutts, who had created considerable sensation by animadverting most severely on the hospital arrangements in South Africa, whence he had lately returned. A Commission of Inquiry was to be appointed. What they wanted, said Saunderson, was to find out the truth expeditiously. He had no opinions to put forward; but he was well assured that what his honourable friend said he had seen, he had indeed seen. The Colonel was not afraid of standing by a man who had taken on himself the unpopular duty of saying disagreeable things to his leaders. He became deeply interested in the controversy which had been raised, and which resulted in the reform of the Army medical service.

But his most notable performance during the summer was the adoption of a large soft hat for daily wear, the season being excessively hot. The attention paid to this whim, by no means an original innovation, was in itself a sign that political life was flagging. The Parliament was moribund, and, apart from the war interest, there was no sign of animation.[1]

In August he was at home again, presenting an ambulance at his own cost to the Portadown District Nursing Society, a gift which presumably could not be brought within the purview of the Corrupt Practices Act, in spite of the near approach of the election.

On this occasion he was not to be unopposed. A section of the constituents induced Mr. Orr, a local gentleman of character and position, to contest the seat. Mr. Orr was, like the Colonel, a Unionist, a

---

[1] During the summer the public mind was further exercised by the "Boxer" rising in China. The European Legations in Pekin were besieged, and one London paper was found to publish a forged description of the fall of the British Legation, and the slaughter of its inmates. An expedition, composed of contingents of all nations, suppressed the movement. Some one wittily said that we had to deal with another lot of Boers with the addition of x, the unknown quantity.

Conservative, and a Protestant, so that the object of the manœuvre is obscure until we learn that he was prepared to stand as a stalwart advocate of compulsory purchase.

In a very long speech at Lurgan on September 29 the Colonel presented his apologia to the electors. In excusing the failure of his efforts to obtain satisfaction in the matter of financial relations, he claimed to have secured, at all events, £800,000 in relief of local taxation. Had the state of the world been peaceful, he would have preferred to leave politics and retire to home life ; but the empire was menaced from every side, and no man who felt capable of lending aid was justified in seeking repose. The landlords' position he defended, and compulsory sale he condemned in familiar language. Next he justified himself in having voted against the Church Discipline Bill of the previous year. It was a bad Bill, he said, and instead of destroying Ritualism would have destroyed the Church. Again he extolled Mr. Chamberlain as "the first man in the House of Commons," and made the bold promise that his right honourable friend was going to ameliorate the condition of the working classes by carrying through a comprehensive scheme of old-age pensions. At the end came local colour in the shape of legislation for weavers, and the procuring of a Government grant for the drainage of Lough Neagh.

So far he was disposed to protest on principle against the intrusion into the field of Mr. Orr, who only dissented from the official programme on one point, and that one of pernicious doctrine ; otherwise he had no wish to speak harshly of his opponent, and was content that they should stand before the electors on their relative merits and records.

As the contest proceeded, however, his patience was strained. He did not for a time carry his attack beyond his original protest. He pointed out that his friend, Mr. Macartney, was being treated in a similar manner in South Antrim, and he insisted on it that there was greater need of men who had fought and could fight for the Union, than of men who advocated extravagant panaceas such as compulsory sale. His speeches were more or less identical, with repeated eulogies of Mr. Chamberlain, and a recommendation to the effect that if the Boers refused to surrender they should be proclaimed rebels, and all their property handed over to the loyalist settlers.

Meanwhile Mr. Orr was passing through an agitating ordeal. One of his meetings is described as a scene of wild tumult, accompanied by a free fight and the firing of " quite a number of revolver shots "—apparently blank. On another occasion the tables were turned on him, and his meeting was transformed into one in support of Colonel Saunderson, whilst the mob and the police waged war outside. Naturally this could not be endured with meekness, and Mr. Orr's friends became pugnacious. At his next meeting, therefore, the Colonel had to complain that he had been branded as a Ritualist and a pro-Boer, and had been accused of voting for the disestablishment of the Irish Church. The last allegation was false in fact. As for the others, it was trying to his temper to be credited with principles which his soul abhorred : " He had been fighting against Ritualism in the English Church for the last thirty years," he said. We have already learnt that he voted against a Church Discipline Bill in 1899, but at the opening of that session, when the public mind was keenly interested in the question, he had spoken plainly

of his detestation of any innovation savouring
of the practices of Rome; and indeed his uncompromising hostility to the Church of Rome had,
as we know, brought him into trouble on previous
occasions.

So with pro-Boerism. For the man who had once
incurred censure for making fighting speeches in
South Africa to be blamed now for want of patriotism,
was to be beaten with too many rods. But when it
came to being told that he was a poor speaker, the
Colonel's spirit rebelled. Mr. Orr was alleged, rightly
or wrongly, to take to his meetings a written speech,
to be read—if a hearing could be secured—and then
handed to the Press. The Colonel felt constrained
to boast a greater proficiency in oratory than this;
the difference between them was, said he, that Mr.
Orr pulled his speech out of his pocket whilst he
pulled his speech out of his head. He had previously
had occasion to allude to refusal on the part of an
audience to listen to Mr. Orr. "He can't speak,"
shouted an enthusiast. "At all events he can read,"
retorted the Colonel. The result, however, was not
jeopardised by these onslaughts, and the Colonel
was returned for the fifth time, his majority being
1,111.

After the election he visited his triumphant constituents, and at Lurgan he took an opportunity of
welcoming the new Chief Secretary, Mr. Wyndham,
whose intellect and ability he acknowledged handsomely:

"These virtues, however, were not enough for the
government of Ireland; the essential quality was
backbone. It was to the display of this formation
in Mr. Balfour, where many had doubted its existence,
that his success had been due. He could not conceive
a better man for the post than Mr. Wyndham, provided

he exhibited the rigid qualities which had distinguished his former chief."

Mr. Wyndham had been private secretary to Mr. Balfour during his tenancy of the Chief Secretary's Lodge, and seemed marked out by every consideration for promotion to his new office. Lord Cadogan remained at the Castle.

Amongst other Cabinet changes the most important was the departure from the Foreign Office of Lord Salisbury, who became Privy Seal. In defiance of public opinion, he chose as his successor Lord Lansdowne, who was enduring all the odium of our South African troubles. Even sedate Unionists pronounced against this sign of confidence in a man who had been tried and found wanting. Within a couple of years the new Foreign Secretary was being lauded by his former critics. To the fatal heritage of the War Office succeeded Mr. Brodrick, than whom no man was ever called upon to undertake a more thankless task. Mr. Goschen retired, and Lord Selborne became the First Lord of the Admiralty. A Liberal Unionist of the first rank retired in the person of Lord James of Hereford.

With the Cabinet thus reconstructed, Parliament met on December 4, and was prorogued on the 17th. The incident which most nearly affected Irish politics during this interval was the meeting of the National Convention at Dublin on the 11th, when Mr. Healy was solemnly expelled from the ranks of the Irish parliamentary party, together with one or two of his colleagues. Mr. Redmond presided, and Mr. Dillon took the opportunity of moving a vote of sympathy with the Boers, which was carried unanimously.

Saunderson might well regard the position complacently. His opponents were bent on a policy of self-destruction. They were driving out of their ranks their ablest men; they were opening the door to further secessions and the intrusion of renewed strife. By persistently proclaiming their devotion to the cause of the enemies of England they were extinguishing whatever flame of Home Rule ardour might still be glowing in the breasts of Englishmen. As one distinguished Liberal put it, " Not content with killing Home Rule, they are never tired of hammering nails into its coffin."

At the end of the year Saunderson was contemplating a lecture to his constituents upon the history of the House of Commons, and on New Year's Day he received a letter from the Speaker, to whom he had written in search of information. Whether Mr. Gully's learned advice made the undertaking appear too formidable, or whether some other impediment occurred, is not evident; but there is no record of the lecture having been given. Mr. Gully's postscript is worth transcribing : " I never like to prophesy about parliamentary weather; all we can be sure of is, that there will be days of sunshine and days of storm—and many dull days." It had been his duty to direct a good many storms in which Saunderson was at the centre of disturbance. Also they had been together, on many a day of sunshine, round the golf-links. He was one of those who had extended a personal friendship beyond the confines of Parliament, and his judgment of the Colonel stands recorded that "in the House of Commons he made plenty of opponents, but no enemies."

The year 1901 was to open with accumulated sorrows. On January 19 the public became suddenly aware that Queen Victoria was seriously ill. Two days later they perceived, with consternation, that her condition was desperate : on the 22nd she expired. So closely guarded had the secret been that the nation was wholly unprepared. Of late years Her Majesty had occupied a position comparable only to that of an oriental monarch, who is regarded as a being set apart. That the Queen should cease to exist was as remote a proposition as the failure of the sun to rise. It was a rare event to converse with anybody who remembered any other occupant of the throne : the Queen had become a part, and a cherished part, of the life of individuals, and not of the Constitution only. In a moment, as it seemed, the inspiring motive of all British pride and veneration was taken away.

The ceremonies attending the passage of the coffin from Osborne to Windsor were noble in the solemn dignity of mourning. On February 1 the first stage was made through lines of war-ships in the Solent water. In advance went some destroyers, like funeral mutes : then came the yacht, carrying the Queen's dead body, a single figure standing motionless in the bows. The choice of this modest vessel in pre-ference to a battle-ship was singularly wise : so simple was the effect that one could imagine Her Majesty going in her familiar pony-carriage to gaze upon her fleet. Guns banged ; ships' bands were faintly heard playing funeral anthems ; the German Emperor's yacht and other yachts followed ; and, as they passed and vanished into Portsmouth harbour, the sun went down in a splendid blaze of light.

Next day the coffin was taken through the streets of London, with full military honours, to Paddington Station. Vast multitudes, in silence and sombre garb, exhibited a subdued and sorrowful spirit, which was probably without parallel in history for sincerity and for extent. Quitting thus her capital, hidden from the eyes of those who had last seen the Queen driving, in the zenith of her fame, from her palace to St. Paul's, reverently attended, and lovingly mourned by this huge and orderly concourse of her people, her journey culminated at Windsor in an undesigned incident supremely dramatic. The artillery-horses attached to the gun-carriage had become restive from cold, and it seemed as if the coffin might suffer mishap. In a moment a team of bluejackets were at hand, and, harnessing themselves, they drew the carriage home. It seemed most fit that sailors, the symbol of her country's power, should render her the last service upon earth. Somebody said that, even in death, the Queen could not help\doing the right thing.

Each stage of the proceedings, indeed, was marked with impressive incidents. From Paddington the coffin was conveyed in a saloon carriage adapted to the occasion. The imperial crown rested in its place; four Life Guardsmen bent above their sword-hilts. The line was cleared, and no trains passed. At each station the railway staff stood at attention : every field and open place was thronged with gazing country-folks, who stood bare-headed and quite still. Those who witnessed the night-watch in the Castle, speak of it as solemn and affecting beyond description; and one who was present throughout this long series of events declares that nothing was more striking than the profound emotion displayed by the private soldiers at their various posts and duties.

The actual interment at Windsor on Monday,

February 4, was, to a certain extent, a private ceremony, but Saunderson was one of those who attended.

"*January* 31, 1901.—I wish you were with me to see the last of the poor Queen. The streets are wonderfully gloomy; every one in black. I am very glad I came. . . .

"*February* 2.—I have had to change all my plans, as I have been commanded to attend the funeral at Windsor, and to lunch afterwards with the King."

CHAPTER XX

1901—1902

PARLIAMENT met on January 25, 1901, to receive the King's message, and was then prorogued, to commence the new session on February 14.

This was opened by the King in state, and the novelty of the scene brought together another great concourse of people, bent now upon enjoying an inspiriting scene, despite the intense cold. Inside the House curiosity was no less eager than in the streets. So impetuous was the rush of members from the House of Commons, when summoned to the presence of their new sovereign, that the tumult ensued to which allusion has already been made.[1] Saunderson came to work full of energy and spirit, and during the ensuing months made some of his liveliest speeches. In the debate on the Address, Mr. Redmond moved an amendment in favour of compulsory purchase. "He was perfectly aware that all the tenants of Ireland were in favour of compulsory purchase," said Saunderson, when his turn came; "but they would be still more in favour of a Bill giving them the land for nothing."

Mr. T. W. Russell, who had not been retained under the new allocation of Government appointments, had been making fiery speeches in Ireland, and assuring his audiences that they would be read with rapt attention in England.

[1] Page 29, note.

" His honourable friend believed," said Saunderson, " that England, Scotland, and Wales would breakfast next morning on muffins and T. W. Russell. . . . Fancy the enthusiasm of John Bull on being asked to fork out £120,000,000! . . . This was to be a free gift, given by the British people (Nationalist cries of 'No'). Well, a loan then. If anybody would give him a loan of £20,000 he should be very much obliged: it would not be a gift, but it would be next door to it. . . . He had been asked what was his own solution of the land question. He had always been in favour of gradually placing the tenants in the position of owners of the land they tilled. A large addition to the present amount of money set apart for buying out the landlords would be, in his idea, the ultimate and best solution. It might be against the interest of the class to which he belonged, but he believed it would be to the best interest of Ireland and the country at large."

Saunderson was a consistent supporter of all legislation which aimed at the promotion of Temperance. In March a private member's Bill came on for second reading in which a good deal of interest was taken. Its object was to prohibit the sale of all intoxicants to children, and Saunderson, in supporting it, contrived to amuse the House. One member had insinuated that it would be a vexation to golfing members if they could not send their caddies for whiskies-and-sodas during a round. The Colonel tartly rejoined that he never wanted whisky-and-soda when he was playing golf; not even when he found himself in a bunker. Another gentleman had objected that he would henceforth be forbidden to provide his boy with a glass of beer when they bicycled together. The Colonel slyly suggested that perhaps his grievance was that in future his son would not be in a position to provide refreshment for the entertainment of the father.

His disapproval of Ritualism he made manifest by

presiding in Yorkshire at one of the meetings of the League [1] recently founded by Lady Wimborne.   He objected, he said, to clergymen who took the pay of the Church of England and taught the doctrine of Rome.

" I am no bigot," he declared.   " Although a Protestant and an Orangeman, I get on very peacefully with my fellow-countrymen on the other side of the Channel, although I don't get on with them in the House of Commons."

In April he threw further light upon his relations with his Roman Catholic fellow-countrymen by a speech in the House upon a motion in favour of a state-aided Roman Catholic University in Ireland. He denied that any member of that religion need be at a disadvantage by reason of going to Trinity College.   Mr. Redmond had been there, and " it could not be pretended that the Protestant atmosphere had exercised a deleterious effect upon his faith or morals." What he objected to was the influence of the clergy. He would object to a Protestant University under clerical control :

" There were priests in all denominations, and he disliked them all equally. . . . If the House wanted to know what kind of citizens Roman Catholic education in Ireland turned out it had not far to look.   There were about eighty specimens of it below the gangway opposite.   He did not say bad specimens, for that would be uncivil to members opposite ; and he did not say good specimens, because he thought that would be insulting to the Irish people.   They openly avowed that they hated the British Empire (Nationalist cheers, and a voice, ' And they will do it again '). Whoever struck at Great Britain was their friend. . . . Was this assembly going to increase the output of this product ? "

---

[1] Ladies' League for the Defence of the Reformed Faith of the Church of England.

In May he made what was nothing but the speech of a fine old high-and-dry Tory. The motion before the House was for the placing of a time-limit on all speeches : Saunderson objected.

"Without parliamentary speaking," he said, "he did not believe we should have any institutions left in the country. He looked upon eloquence in the House of Commons as a pneumatic brake on over-legislation. . . . The less legislation they had the better. . . . The Irish members, whose eloquence no one could deny, had the faculty given to them—he did not know by whom—of speaking on every subject, whether they knew anything about it or not ; and the less they knew about it the more eloquent they were. The Irish members might lay this flattering unction to their souls, that every speech they made, helped to maintain the permanence of the institutions they desired to destroy."

As an Orangeman he was called upon to take a strong line in connection with the proposed alteration in the King's Coronation oath. The existing terms were condemned as offensive to His Majesty's innumerable Roman Catholic subjects. The Ulster Unionist members met and passed a Resolution that "In the Protestant interests of the country it is inexpedient to alter in any way the Declaration provided for the Sovereign by the Bill of Rights." In July Saunderson stoutly maintained this proposition at an Orange meeting in Belfast, and he was not less emphatic at a public meeting in St. James's Hall, where his allusion to Lord Salisbury's Bill elicited a cry of "Traitor."

The measure was duly passed through the House of Lords, but the Roman Catholic Peers denounced it as inadequate, and rejected the proposed alternative as so gratuitously offensive that it was only received in the House of Commons to be dropped. Mr. Balfour announced that, in view of the hostility with which it had been received, no steps would be taken to ensure its further progress.

At the Orange anniversary meeting in Belfast on July 12 he inclined rather to sing his old song, enlarging upon the mischief threatened by the United Irish League; but his programme throughout the year consisted more of declamations against surrender of Protestant interests to Roman Catholic pretensions: a tendency which he further denounced in a long letter to *The Times* on August 5.

Meanwhile tentative overtures for peace in South Africa had proved ineffective; we had been on the verge of a serious rupture with Russia concerning the occupation of land at Tientsin; and a scare had been suddenly raised about the state of our Mediterranean fleet, which was about to be attacked, according to the panic-mongers, on some unexplained pretext, by France. Consequently the condition of the public mind was still unquiet and unhappy.

A week before Parliament rose, on August 10, a great Unionist demonstration was held at Blenheim, where Mr. Balfour and Mr. Chamberlain both spoke. A fine spirit of confidence and vivacity was exhibited, and the party made a brave display. Saunderson was amongst the numerous eminent politicians who were the Duke of Marlborough's guests, but his ambitions, for the moment, were humble. He was not one of the speakers, and he did not sin to the extent of coveting his neighbour's house. What he enjoyed most appears to have been a game of golf.

"BLENHEIM PALACE.

"*August* 10, 1901.—The meeting has been a great success; the speaking very good. . . . This is a most enormous house. I don't think I should care to live in it. However, of its kind, it is splendid."

In the autumn he received a letter from the venerable Primate, the Archbishop of Armagh, in reply to an invitation. With this had gone one of his own drawings, and a transcript of some verses which he had found in his library, a translation by an unknown hand from an Italian poem.

" The Archbishop of Armagh (Dr. Alexander) to Colonel Saunderson

"THE PALACE, ARMAGH.
"*October* 22, 1901.

"MY DEAR COLONEL,
    "Thanks for your Oom Paul; what a sinister old fellow he looks! I have kept both portraits as specimens of your ready hand and penetrating art. . . .
    "I should like to preach in your church, and, if I did so, would take care to stick to the real eternal things about which there would be no difference between us. *But*—how uncertain is one's tenure of life at seventy-seven! and how many reasons for thinking, if not saying, 'If God wills!'
    "I was much touched by your kindness at Beauvoir. I was a comparatively young man in 1869, and the Synods of the following years. If I ever attempted to tackle you, I am sure you left 'Edward Saunderson his mark' upon me. But I ought not to have done it. Always most truly yours,
                    "WILLIAM ARMAGH.

"Thanks for the verses; a fine conception finely expressed."

The verses were as follows:

"I envy thee, thou Rose," exclaimed the Thorn,
"With all thy beauties opening to the light,
Sweet to the sense and lovely to the sight;
Whilst me no charms of hue or flowers adorn."

"I envy thee, thou Thorn," the Rose replied,
"For when on earth, the King of Glory chose
No laurel wreath, no coronal of Rose,
Nor radiant crown lustrous with sparkling gem ;
When on His brow the sacred diadem
Was placed, thine was the shame but yet the pride
A crown of thorns circled the Crucified."

Saunderson's religious convictions were fashioned, as we have seen, by his own thoughts and intuitions. He never surrendered an independence of judgment nor accepted formularies without consideration. Consequently it was inevitable that he must at times have found himself in conflict with authority. The following note written by the Archbishop after Saunderson's death throws an interesting light upon the position which the Colonel occupied in the Synod :

"In our first days of perhaps exuberant liberty after Disestablishment, the gift of eloquence—so marked in Grattan's Parliament—was renewed. After nearly forty years I can certainly say that Edward Saunderson was the most notable of all in that goodly company. I am far from saying that he was always *right*—what speaker always is ? But he was transparently clear ; always full of happy illustration—I will add, something rarer still. A speaker who gains a mastery over a large and enthusiastic audience cannot usually succeed without a certain satirical element which clothes itself in fun. Speaking for myself, as a young Bishop I was not slow in catching the President's eye. At some point or other of Edward Saunderson's speech he was sure to turn upon me, and his answer clothed itself in the spontaneous and delighted laughter of his hearers. This perhaps might be a little hard for flesh and blood, but there was something almost *miraculous* about it. At the present moment, after so many years, there are words, even of Bishops, which as they ring in my ears I find it hard to forgive ; but Saunderson's are not, and never were, hard to forgive."

A chapter of Saunderson's life—perhaps the least

satisfactory to narrate—had its origin in this year, and, at the risk of anticipating events, it will be best to proceed without interruption. Early in 1901 Saunderson had been elected Grand Master of the Orange Institution of Belfast in succession to the late Lord Farnham.[1]

At the close of the session of 1901 the Government's Factory and Workshops Acts Amendment Bill came back from Grand Committee, where it had been considered, for Report stage in the House. As it then stood, provision was made incidentally for inspection of laundries attached to Roman Catholic convents. To this the Irish Roman Catholic members took exception, and it was understood that, unless the point was conceded in their favour, they would compel the abandonment of the Bill by dint of opposition.

On August 13 therefore Mr. Ritchie, the Home Secretary, moved to omit Clause 103, a proposal which Sir John Stirling Maxwell, a Conservative member, denounced as "a monument of surrender where no surrender was necessary." In the division which followed Saunderson and his friends supported the Government, preferring to counteract their policy by different methods. Later in the same day, therefore, upon Schedule 7 of the Bill, at the Report stage, Mr. Macartney moved to omit certain paragraphs of a subsection of the Act of 1895 which was to be incorporated in the new measure. This would have had the effect of cancelling the exemption recently accorded to the laundries. In support of this Saunderson spoke strongly, and with Mr. Macartney told in the division against the Government. They were

---

[1] Somerset Maxwell (tenth Baron, died 1900), frequently mentioned in these pages.

defeated by 180 to 51. Eventually they voted for the third reading.

The next scene does not occur till nearly a year later. On July 12, 1902, the Orange anniversary was celebrated at Castlereagh, near Belfast. The gathering was very large, and the weather was very wet. Here we may pause for a moment to remark one of those traits wherein, as it has been suggested, the Colonel bore some resemblance to Parnell.

There is a story told of Parnell that he once undertook to deliver a lecture on Irish history. The appointed hour was eight. He dined at seven, and, having finished at his ease, he asked his host to take him to the library and show him some books about Ireland. In answer to the astonished inquiries which this proposal evoked, he explained that he knew nothing of Irish history, and must read it up. The host pointed out that the audience were waiting: Parnell replied that they must continue to wait; and he proceeded to make sufficient extracts from certain volumes to answer his purpose. Mr. O'Brien tells this anecdote in his book as an illustration of Parnell's indifference to the petty trammels of convention, and of the independence and power of detachment of a strong man.

To-day Saunderson did something of the same kind. The meeting was fixed for one o'clock. The crowd assembled, but the rain continued to descend, and the Colonel lingered over his lunch in comfortable seclusion. When he eventually reached the platform he found—to use words which he afterwards employed —that the crowd had assembled round it; very few of them had on Orange sashes: the meeting was continually interrupted in the rudest and most outrageous way, and was in the end practically broken up, after he himself had been publicly insulted. The insult was attributed to Mr. Sloan, who is described as " of the Belfast Protestant Association, wearing the insignia of his office as a W.M. of the Orange Institution." Having been hoisted on to the platform, and having exchanged a few introductory recriminations with one of the officials, Mr. Sloan proceeded as follows :

" I want to know, is it a fact that you, Colonel Saunderson, the Grand Master of the Orange Institution of Belfast, voted against the clause for the inspection of convent laundries going into the Laundry Bill ?

" Colonel Saunderson : It is absolutely untrue.

" Mr. Sloan : Then if that is absolutely untrue, the Press that are present are liars."[1]

This was a declaration of war from an enemy whom even the Colonel found himself unable to bring into subjection.

In August died his faithful friend and ally, Mr. Johnston of Ballykilbeg, and the seat became vacant in South Belfast. As official Orange candidate there was put forward Mr. Dunbar Buller. Against him there appeared the redoubtable representative of the Belfast Protestant Association. Saunderson exerted his influence as Grand Master to confirm the adoption of Mr. Buller, but Mr. Sloan had a powerful following of insurrectionary Orangemen, and in addition, so it was believed, the working men of the constituency, to say nothing of Nationalists. The Colonel visited

---

[1] It ought to be explained that the proceedings of August 13, just now narrated, had not been well reported. The House had sat very late, and there was some excuse for people who had no acquaintance with parliamentary procedure, if they did not clearly understand what had taken place from the short summary which had appeared in the Press.

Belfast, but could do nothing, and left this mournful message behind him : "Any Orangeman who votes for Sloan is voting for the destruction of the machinery of the Orange organisation, which is absolutely necessary to its continued existence." Notwithstanding which, Mr. Sloan was elected with a majority of 826.

It is not to be supposed that the Colonel accepted this rebuff to his authority with complacency. Nor were his vexations at an end. During the autumn he found his meetings attended by Mr. Sloan's friends, and the unbroken enthusiasm, with which he was familiar, gave way to a system of interruption.

However, he confronted the situation boldly. At Portadown, on October 15, he confessed that he had accepted the Grand Mastership reluctantly and only in obedience to the unanimous request of the Orangemen of Belfast :

"On July 12 he had been publicly insulted by a member of the Order, and it was impossible to maintain discipline in any army if soldiers were to be permitted to come out of the ranks and call the Colonel a liar on parade. Mr. Sloan's proper course had been to bring any charge he had to make before his District Grand Lodge. It was not on personal grounds that he felt indignant ; he was concerned for the dignity of the office which he held."

A week later, at Lurgan, he put it that " he did not care a straw about Mr. Sloan, as a man, calling him a liar ; what he did care for was that Mr. Sloan, as an Orangeman, called his Grand Master a liar."

At this meeting he set about exposing the fallacies of Mr. Sloan's professions. He and his friends, it appeared, were not going to rest content until they had banished every Roman Catholic, including the Pope, off the face of the earth. The Colonel described Mr. Sloan's threatened invasion of Rome at the head of an army of corner-boys, and his capture of the Vatican—all of which heroic promises he set aside as "unmitigated bosh." What he feared was that, by entering the House of Commons pledged to the profession of these extreme principles, he would subject the Institution to the charge of fanaticism and extravagance, from which it had hitherto been immune. He could not disguise the fact that the mutiny in the ranks had given him a considerable pain.

On October 29 Mr. Sloan was solemnly charged before Grand Lodge in Belfast with insubordinate conduct on the occasion of July 12. The Colonel was present; Mr. Sloan was not; and a decision was deferred until after the autumn session of Parliament, which was then in progress. On November 13 there was another meeting; neither the Colonel nor Mr. Sloan attended, and there was a further adjournment. When the session was over Mr. Sloan announced his readiness to meet his accusers and make his defence; but still no decisive action was taken.

At the end of November Saunderson decided to resign. On January 1, 1903, he was requested by the County Grand Lodge to reconsider his decision; but what he had said he had said, and a week later it was announced that he had ceased to be Grand Master. He had accepted office under the self-imposed condition that he should keep in touch with all the lodges within his district, and he was discovering that the faithful discharge of his parliamentary duties was in itself a sufficient tax upon his health and energy. The new situation which had arisen demanded increased application, and he felt

21

that he was no longer able to "ride in the whirlwind and direct the storm."

Mr. Sloan had established his *imperium in imperio*; he had set going a movement within the Order which had gained momentum, and was not to be checked without great efforts.

The Colonel, after all, was sixty-six years old; he lived at some distance from Belfast; he might fairly claim to have done his day's work in and for Ulster; it is no ground for astonishment, still less for blame, if he began to grow weary, and to feel that if new battles had to be fought, the leadership might be left to younger hands than his.

Many there were who deprecated his decision; but it was irrevocable, and the days of his Grand Mastership were numbered.

The sequel to these events may here be related. On January 21, 1903, Mr. Sloan was charged before the Orange Grand Lodge of Belfast with having been guilty of conduct towards the Grand Master on July 12 which was unbecoming an Orangeman. The charge was considered proved, and he was suspended from membership for two years. He appealed to the Grand Lodge of Ireland.

On January 31 Colonel Saunderson wrote a letter pointing out that the issue had nothing to do with his action in the House of Commons; it was entirely a question of discipline in the Order. This proposition was confirmed in a statement published by Grand Secretary of the Grand Lodge of Belfast.

In March, thanks to the good offices of Mr. Lonsdale, M.P., a reconciliation was effected. Mr. Sloan wrote a letter admitting that he had not properly understood the transactions in the House of Commons of August 13, 1901, and that he now recognised the sincerity of the Colonel's efforts with regard to the laundries. On March 28 the Colonel wrote to the Grand Lodge urging them to stay further proceedings against Mr. Sloan. On January 4, however, the Grand Lodge of Ireland confirmed the judgment of the Grand Lodge of Belfast; whereupon Mr. Sloan formally instituted the Independent Orange Society, in which act of secession he was accompanied by his personal adherents.

CHAPTER XXI

1902

SAUNDERSON took no prominent part in the House of Commons during 1902. He was much away; moreover, the year was chiefly devoted to the Education Bill, in which he was not greatly concerned. An Irish Land Bill was introduced, but it was withdrawn in October, to make way for the great measure of next year. So exacting indeed were the claims of the Education Bill on the time of the House that an autumn session was required. Parliament, having met in January, adjourned on August 8, met again on October 16, and was prorogued on December 18.

The year was unusually eventful. In March a reverse befell Lord Methuen in South Africa, and the delivery of the news in the House of Commons was received with uproarious delight by some of the leading Nationalist members; but it was their last chance of satisfaction. On Sunday, June 1, came the information that peace had at last been arranged; and so modestly did it come, so little excitement did it provoke, that people in London actually learnt it by chance in the course of conversation at dinner. The Mafeking spirit made no appearance.

In July Lord Salisbury resigned, and Mr. Balfour became Prime Minister. In August the postponed ceremonies of coronation were happily fulfilled, to the admiration of a sceptical public, who had been unable to believe that the King could so speedily recover from his alarming illness of June.

In August, also, Lord Cadogan left Ireland and the Cabinet. Mr. Wyndham was promoted to the latter vacancy, and the Viceroyalty was conferred upon Lord Dudley. Lord Cadogan had already extended his rule for the accommodation of Government arrangements. Now that Lord Salisbury had resigned, and Sir Michael Hicks-Beach had followed his example, Lord Cadogan presumably thought himself justified in seizing the opportunity of making his exit from active political life.

In January the Colonel made a long speech at Lurgan, which was principally composed of criticisms on the policy of compulsory sale. He repeated his desire to see occupiers become owners, but the process must be assisted by voluntary agreement; to fix an arbitrary selling price for land was no better than to compel a shopkeeper to sell his goods at a Government valuation. Again, he wanted to know whether the labourers would rest contented when they beheld the tenant farmers being put into possession of the land upon unduly favourable terms. With great satisfaction, he recounted the gallant behaviour of a man named Quinlan, who had confronted a meeting of the United Irish League in Dublin, and denounced their policy from their own platform. "If you bought out the landlords you would have the same thing again, only multiplied," Mr. Quinlan had said: after which he had been compelled to retire precipitately, according to the newspapers, followed by much imprecation. Saunderson made his wonted contribution to the debate on the Address; but early in the session he was obliged to go to Wiesbaden with Mrs. Saunderson, whose eyes were a cause of anxiety. To his son John he writes on March 29 :

" I blame myself for not bringing her [here] a year ago. . . . I intend going through a course for rheumatism which may unstiffen me and give me something to do. Words can't describe how I hate this place ; I need hardly say I don't mind if it does your mother any good."

Then this ominous and pathetic comment :

" There is no golf here."

On April 12 he relieved the tedium of existence by writing a long letter to *The Times* about the United Irish League which, by the confession of Nationalists, was "the good old Land League over again." Reviving once more his old phrase, he writes :

" Years ago I stated in the House of Commons that Mr. Parnell 'had his hand on the throttle-valve of crime, and could turn it on or off as he chose.' The present leaders of the Nationalist party occupy the same position, and have the same power. Crime with violence is not at present needed. Boycotting and intimidation are sufficient for the moment, and have succeeded in forcing a large portion of the population in the western portions of Ireland to bow their necks to the yoke of the League. . . . Years ago we spent the best part of a session[1] in forging a weapon capable of coping with the present state of affairs. The question is, how long will the Government refrain from using it ? "

On May 18 he writes to his son John, dwelling with delight on games of golf which they are to play together on his return ; then he goes on :

" The wise people of Wiesbaden have settled in their minds that I am no less a person than Lord Roberts ! Since the night I dined with the Emperor and went with him to the opera, and sat in state in uniform on his right hand, they are quite sure. So

[1] 1887.

I am regarded with a mixture of hatred and admiration. There has been a paragraph in the paper each morning about me. The day before yesterday it said I might call myself Lord Saunderson if I chose; but I was Lord Roberts all the same." [1]

Amongst numerous presents which from time to time he received from the German Emperor was a photograph of his Majesty riding with his escort, sent as a souvenir of their meeting at Wiesbaden. The Colonel always declared that it was owing to this royal recognition which was bestowed upon him in the street that rumour credited him with being Lord Roberts.

If the Colonel could send the Emperor the skilful work of his own hands in the shape of yachts' models, the Emperor was by no means at a loss for fair exchange, and returned plentiful proofs of his own accomplishments as a versatile artist.

Meanwhile Saunderson had paid a visit to Berlin.

" BRITISH EMBASSY, BERLIN.

"*April* 22, 1902.—I am in great state here, but I fear I shall not see the Emperor, as he starts to-morrow morning and is on the rampage all day. . . . Lascelles [2] is a first-rate man in every way and mad about golf. . . .

"*3rd.*—I was fortunate enough to be able to see the Emperor; he was engaged all day, and had to dine with the Empress at the Austrian Embassy. He sent to say he would see me after 6.30. So I got into my frock coat and . . . arrived at the Palace. I had considerable difficulty in effecting an entrance; at last, however, I managed to get into the private part of the Palace and was shown up into a huge room, where I met the tallest officer in the German Army. I had to wait until past seven. . . . I was then shown

[1] For the information of strangers it may be noted that the Colonel bore no physical resemblance whatever to the Field-Marshal.

[2] Sir Frank Lascelles, G.C.B., British Ambassador.

into a small room. . . . He was very kind, and we had a long talk, when in came the Empress and their little girl, a very nice, bright child. I found the Empress extremely nice and pleasant; she remembered meeting me at Kiel. I started by kissing her hand. . . . The Emperor says his daughter rules them with a rod of iron. . . . He was delighted with the photo I sent him. . . .

"We had a great excitement just before I went to the Palace. I was sitting with Lady Edward[1] when there was a crash in the next room; then another smash in the room beyond. This was caused by a scoundrel throwing two stones, about the size of the one that hit me in Lurgan,[2] through the windows; thus smashing in four big plate-glass panes. He was instantly arrested; he was out of work, and wanted to be sent to prison; so now he ought to be happy. It was lucky he did not send the stone through our room, as it would probably have hit Lady Edward. . . . After lunch I go to play a game of golf with Lascelles. . . . He is a delightful man. . . . The Unter den Linden did not appeal to me, as the trees are little things. I always thought they were huge."

In July Saunderson was back in London. It occurred to some journalist in search of "copy" that he was one of the very few surviving members of the Parliament of 1865. Consequently an interview was sought, and it is not without interest to record the impressions of different public men which were then confessed. Palmerston he described as the Chamberlain of his day, the embodiment of the John Bull spirit and national feeling. Mr. Bright was the most striking of all speakers; he gave utterance to the finest English the Colonel had ever heard in the House of Commons. Outside, Spurgeon was almost as striking in the excellence of his language. Disraeli, in his opinion, was the most interesting speaker; Gladstone

---

[1] Lady Edward Cavendish, sister of Sir F. Lascelles.
[2] This formidable missile has been preserved.

the most powerful—which presumably means in contrast with one another. The House generally sympathised with Disraeli, who was the most popular member of Parliament that ever lived. He was the embodiment of parliamentary feeling. Lord John Russell was a very able man, but had never impressed the Colonel: he did not capture the imagination of the country as Lord Palmerston did. Finally, he regarded Mr. Chamberlain as far and away the best orator in the existing House of Commons; as a parliamentary debater he would place him on a level with any speaker he had ever heard.

He admitted at once that the character of Parliament had greatly changed. The standard of oratory had declined; the modern clothes and hats revealed a weakening in the hold of venerable traditions. But the ways of the nation were changing, and those of Parliament did but reflect the spirit of the age.

On July 23 Saunderson spoke in the House of Commons upon the Chief Secretary's vote. Mr. Redmond had initiated a comprehensive debate. Two prominent topics were the disturbances on Lord de Freyne's estate, where a no-rent agitation was in full progress; and the vexed question of Sheridan, an ex-sergeant of the Royal Irish Constabulary, who had been dismissed from the force on the ground of having invented outrages for the purpose of distinguishing himself by thwarting them. The Nationalists declared that he was only one specimen of a system of " spies, informers, agents-provocateurs, and perjurers," and demanded a searching investigation and reformation on the part of the Government.

With regard to these matters the Colonel averred that the former was only an illustration of the arbitrary methods and deliberate tyranny of the United Irish

League. As to the latter he made the compendious remark that—

"he looked upon Sheridan as a scoundrel, and was only sorry that he had not been hanged; but that was not a sufficient ground for impugning the government of Ireland by England."

Turning to his friend Mr. T. W. Russell, he observed that—

"the honourable gentleman had suddenly fallen in love with the members for Cork and Mayo (Mr. O'Brien and Mr. Dillon). That of course was a matter of taste. But he was surprised to read in a speech of the honourable member that the opinion he had formerly entertained of the Nationalist members was entirely wrong, and that the years he had spent in attacking them would have been better employed in slanging landlords."

On another occasion he advocated the parliamentary grant to Lord Kitchener, whose services he fervently extolled.

We have now reached the summer of 1902. It would have been well if we could have put an end here to the Colonel's political record. Throughout the best and most memorable years of his career, those succeeding 1885, we have seen him fighting courageously for the Union; showing a bold and manly front to all Home Rulers, and, although at issue sometimes with the Unionist Government in this or that respect, yet upon the whole in hearty accord with the English leaders. For the few years that remained, it was his unhappy fate to be involved in constant conflict with the friends of his own political household, and to watch with angry apprehension, not only the machinations of the United Irish League, but the policy of the Unionist Irish Government. These events are so

recent, and the controversies arising out of them were
so painful and so acute, that they shall be lightly
handled here.   As far as possible, the merits of the
case, and the action of individuals, will be left undis-
cussed.   But a statement of admitted facts is necessary
in order to make Saunderson's position intelligible.
We have seen that in the latter part of 1902 Lord
Dudley became Viceroy, and that Mr. Wyndham, the
Chief Secretary, entered the Cabinet.   No exception
could be taken to the appointment of Lord Dudley.
We have already seen that Saunderson accorded a
hearty welcome to Mr. Wyndham, when he first went
to Dublin.   But there was a third change in the Irish
Government.

The vacant Under-Secretaryship was presently
bestowed upon Sir Antony MacDonnell, who had
already gained distinction as an Indian administrator.
Now it was known that Sir Antony was a Roman
Catholic ; it was understood that he was not an
anti-Home Ruler of the most convinced and uncompromising type.   These pages have been written in
vain if it need be added that such credentials were
little likely to commend themselves to a man who
held such opinions about Roman Catholics in politics,
and about the sanctity of the Union, as did Colonel
Saunderson.

Before these changes took place Saunderson and
his friends had already found a grievance against the
Irish Government.   The Orangemen of Rostrevor had
intended to hold a demonstration on July 12.   It had
been represented that this would inflame the resentment of the local Roman Catholics, and the meeting
was proclaimed.   Another demonstration was, however, held without interference at Warrenpoint, a short
distance away.   In his speech on July 12 Saunderson

professed himself dissatisfied with these proceedings; they were unjust and illogical. At the same time he admitted that the highest Orange authorities had acquiesced in the proposal, and that its adoption need not be construed into want of sympathy on the part of the Government. Whether this may be regarded as the first rift within the lute or not, it was a trifling matter compared with the subsequent cleavage. Let us refresh our memories by carrying the story to its close.

In August, 1902, Captain Shawe Taylor, as a private individual, came before the public with a proposal to convene a joint meeting of landlords and of tenants' representatives, to examine into the possibility of adopting a common policy. Saunderson's refusal was emphatic. He published a letter, explaining that the principles of Mr. Redmond, Mr. Dillon, Mr. O'Brien, and Mr. Davitt, were explicit and uncompromising; so were his own. No good result could possibly come from a conference, and he would be no party to such a project. In this decision he was supported by the Duke of Abercorn and Lord Barrymore, amongst others. There were, however, landlords of another temper.

On October 10 the landowners' convention held a meeting. Lord Mayo moved a resolution in favour of a conference, and was defeated by seventy-seven to fourteen votes. A motion was, however, carried that a welcome would be extended to any expression of opinion coming from the tenants. Amongst those who agreed with Lord Mayo were the following peers: Dunraven, Meath, Donoughmore, Powerscourt, Rossmore, Monteagle, and Castletown. They formed a committee, and proceeded to nominate the following delegates to represent them at the conference: Lord

Dunraven, Lord Mayo, Colonel Hutchinson Poë, and Colonel Nugent Everard. The tenants' representatives were Mr. Redmond, Mr. O'Brien, the Lord Mayor of Dublin (Mr. Harrington), and Mr. T. W. Russell.

It is a remarkable fact that Irishmen are never more tractable and effective than when they are collaborating with their bitterest opponents. As in the case of the Recess Committee, as in the case of the Financial Relations Committee, so now the deliberations were expeditious, harmonious, and fruitful.

The Conference did not meet until December 20. Lord Dunraven was elected chairman, and on January 3, 1903, he was able to produce his report. Despite the presence of such a stout protagonist of compulsory sale as Mr. Russell, a compromise was reached on the basis of the voluntary extinction of dual ownership. On January 7 the landlords' convention gave the report its blessing, and commended its recommendations to the attention of the Government in view of their forthcoming Bill.

Next session Mr. Wyndham introduced and passed his great Land Purchase Act. It is true that at the end of the year the stalwart Nationalists set out to hinder its operation by urging tenants to insist on their own terms; but Mr. O'Brien, for one, would be no party to this attempt, and, as a protest, he resigned his seat for Cork and stood again. He was returned unopposed.

In the following year, 1904, a great and critical advance was made. In August the Land Conference became the Irish Reform Association, under the presidency of Lord Dunraven. On September 23 the fruits of their labours were offered to the world;

and the word "devolution" was added to political nomenclature.

Probably the proposal which secured most attention was that which advocated the establishment of an Irish Financial Council, with funds and authority to deal with Irish expenditure. On September 27 Mr. Wyndham wrote to *The Times* to make it clear at once that this scheme was impracticable apart from any objections it might incur in principle, and that it would receive no encouragement from him.

But this was not enough. The Ulster members were roused ; they detected in this movement Home Rule creeping in under a disguise, and at once decided that they would on the whole prefer the original avowed plan to what they deemed an insidious and treacherous substitute. Furthermore, they beheld clearly the working of the Under-Secretary, whom they had suspected from the first, and now unequivocally condemned. The situation was strained to breaking point ; there must be a rupture somewhere. Either the Cabinet must remove all suspicion of complicity from themselves and their colleague, and disavow the heresies of their servant in Ireland, or the Ulster Unionists must sever their connection with the Government. They were satisfied that Sir Antony MacDonnell was at the bottom of the devolution scheme, and they would have nothing to do with a Government which employed such agents.

The issue between them may be epitomised by quoting one sentence from a subsequent speech of Saunderson's, which was followed by a letter to *The Times*. "Sir Antony MacDonnell drew up the scheme," he asserted at Lurgan a year later, and he stated "on irrefutable authority, that it was under the direct orders of Mr. Wyndham." After which he had to write :

"Mr. Wyndham informs me that there is no foundation for the statement I made on what I believed to be accurate information. . . . I accept his denial, and regret that I should have been led to employ those words. At the same time, I cannot think that Mr. Wyndham will be disposed to say that Sir A. MacDonnell drew up the devolution scheme without his knowledge."

It is probably fair to say that the Chief Secretary was accused of connivance rather than initiation. At all events, he was held responsible for a share in the transactions. Something must be done to relieve the pressure. The solution was the resignation of Mr. Wyndham in March, 1905, on the ground that he could no longer hold his office with advantage to the public service.

It is right to add that many people considered it illogical that Sir Antony MacDonnell should be allowed to remain whilst Mr. Wyndham was sacrificed in the interests of peace. So much may be stated as to the opinions which were expressed, without discussing their propriety or justice. And in order to avoid suspicion of prejudice or bias, a summary of the case shall be taken from the unimpassioned pages of *The Annual Register* :

"Mr. Wyndham's chief offence, in the eyes of his relentless opponents, lay in the confidence which he had reposed in Sir Antony MacDonnell, as Under-Secretary at Dublin Castle, and in his failure to prevent that official from influencing the course of administration in a sense too favourable to Nationalist aspirations, and from participating with Lord Dunraven and the Lord-Lieutenant, Lord Dudley, in conversations which issued in the devolution proposals of 1904." [1]

This may claim to be an impartial statement of facts. That they influenced and embittered Saunderson's latter days must be admitted; but the time has not yet come for surveying them as history or for confidently distributing praise or blame.

It will be a relief to go back to 1902 and turn attention to Colonel Saunderson at home. I was at Castle Saunderson in August, as I had been in the year preceding. Again the Colonel shall be presented through the medium of some private notes taken at the time:

"We had a great talk on Sunday night. His conviction of salvation through personal faith in Christ is complete. He illustrated this by the fate of passengers who take tickets for a ship and, trusting themselves to the Captain, feel that, no matter what they may do, they will arrive safely at the other end. I suggested that they might wantonly imperil the safety of the vessel. He said they would not be such fools. His religion is very comfortable, and perfectly sincere. . . . He protects himself by saying, 'It is not what I say; I don't judge any one; I am only quoting Jesus Christ and St. Paul.'"

I had added that he would not allow his children to be baptized because he could not believe that sprinkling water over an unconscious child could save it from hell; but I find that this is an exaggeration. He did not indeed accept the ministration of baptism without reserve: consequently his children went through the ceremony with the omission of the words "This child is regenerate."

I recollect quoting to him on this occasion a couplet

---

[1] *Annual Register*, 1905, p. 245.

translating Voltaire's "Si Dieu n'existait pas, il faudrait l'inventer":

"'Did God not fashion me?' the sceptic cries in doubt,
'Then I must fashion Him: I cannot live without.'"

He said "I like that," and repeated it more than once. Then added suddenly, "What a thing it is to be a poet!"

The entry goes on: "He had some good stories. A man once asked Thackeray to lend him five shillings, which he would convert into £20,000. Asked how, he explained that he knew a young lady with £20,000 who he knew would marry him if he asked her, but he had pawned his teeth and wanted five shillings to redeem them in order to propose effectively."

For the rest, he was in excellent spirits, and as happy as ever with his sailing and golf. He was also a good deal interested in the bog-garden which Mrs. Saunderson had created, making paths, ordering water-courses, planting and tending, until a wilderness had blossomed into a bright unconventional enclosure. My impression is that this was the only place where I ever saw him content to sit still and do nothing.

These extracts from a description written by a distinguished botanist may be of interest to garden-lovers:

"At Castle Saunderson there is by far the most extensive and beautiful bog-garden I have ever seen. Several acres of pools and canals running amongst islands and peninsulas of bog earth capped with Ghent and other azaleas now turning crimson and gold, torch lilies, Arundo, Pampas Rhus, Euonymus, Berberis, Japanese plants, and many other shrubs and herbaceous plants. . . . The paths are soft and springy, like Persian rugs, and there are simple seats and shelters, reached by little log bridges, from which a survey of the whole expanse can be made. Here and there sheltered bits and mossy nooks are jewelled or enamelled with Shottias, Sarracenias and other bog-loving rarities, while along a soft and moist wood-path under trees in the vicinity the dainty little *Sibthorpia Europœa* spreads itself happily over a considerable area.

As we have seen, Parliament met again on October 16, 1902 : the succeeding weeks were occupied with the Education Bill, which was one of the most hotly contested measures of late years, and, whatever may have been its faults or merits, afforded, by common consent, a rare exhibition of parliamentary skill on the part of Mr. Balfour. Saunderson attended when the spirit moved him. It must be understood that he considered that his position and seniority in the House of Commons absolved him from the punctual and constant attendance which is the duty and the heavy burden of the ordinary member of the party, and which becomes instinct and a second nature in some loyal veterans. Saunderson was sociable and accessible ; he was never ungenial, and he was fond of talking to people he liked. But he was by no means effusive, and was not one of those whose greatest happiness is to get an audience for interminable talk. He would walk across the lobby with long smooth strides, not looking about for some one to accost; rather preoccupied and solemn, as if he was here for business, not pleasure. He naturally frequented the smoking-room, because he liked tobacco and disliked answering letters. In the summer he was fond of spending his time on the terrace, which in hot weather is undoubtedly the coolest and pleasantest place in London. He did not shirk the House; he held it in sincere esteem,

THE BOG-GARDEN.

and found constant interest there; but he had never been a party hack, and he did not pretend that the Whips could count on him as a permanent voting asset.

On November 27 he spoke at some length on the Education Bill. Apparently he was drawn into the discussion by something that had been said about the interests of laymen in religious education, and he at once repeated his familiar complaint that, amongst Roman Catholics, clerical influence was supreme. Then followed a striking passage:

"He spoke in the name of Irish Protestants in this matter, and Protestant was a word which he had not heard often enough in this debate to please him. If an intelligent Pagan had been sitting up in the gallery and had listened to the course of the debate, he would have been led to believe that there were a vast number of different religions represented in the House. He should say, at the outside, there were only three religions represented there. There were, first of all, in overwhelming majority, the Protestants, then Roman Catholics, then the Jews. There were certainly some Unitarians, but he did not know what religion they belonged to. But the intelligent Pagan would make a great mistake if he imagined that the gentlemen who spoke as Presbyterians, as Methodists, as Churchmen, or as Quakers belonged to different religions. One word covered them all, and that was the word Protestant. Therefore, whatever affected in his estimation the welfare of the Protestant religion was of deep interest to the Protestant Irishmen. He had approved very much of the Kenyon-Slaney[1] Amendment until he heard it explained by the Attorney-General. . . . He had always been thrown into a state of mental confusion by hearing two distinguished lawyers speaking on the same subject against each other. . . .Which was right? Possibly

[1] Colonel Kenyon-Slaney's Amendment had been to secure to voluntary schools religious instruction in accordance with the Trust Deeds and under the control of the managers. A different clause was now under discussion.

neither. . . . Any one who had considered the present position of the Church of England, must come to the conclusion that the teaching of some of the clergy was diametrically opposed to Protestantism and to the principles of the Reformation. He believed that his Roman Catholic fellow-subjects had just as much right to have their religion respected as he had himself, but he had no respect at all for the man who took Protestant pay and taught Roman Catholic doctrine, and he believed the noble lord, the member for Greenwich,[1] made a great mistake if he thought that Protestant feeling had died away in the country. . . . It had been argued that only the priest had any right to teach the Christian truth. That might be the doctrine of the Anglicans—a word he hated—it used to be Church of England—Anglican was a new word, brought in of late years; but it was that Anglican movement which to his mind had rendered this clause an absolute necessity, unless they wanted the Protestantism (a word he was not ashamed of) of their children . . . to be upset by dishonest priests."

With the passing of the Bill the year came to an end.

[1] Lord Hugh Cecil.

CHAPTER XXII

1903—1904

THE personal event of most memorable importance in 1903 was the death of Lord Salisbury.[1] He had retired from office; consequently it cannot be said to have come as an irreparable loss to the party : the blow had fallen when he resigned. But with him there passed away an Englishman of the first rank, a statesman of the old order, a noble type of the great patrician.

Lord Salisbury was known to the world as an august Prime Minister. Some remembered that he had once been something of a fire-brand in politics and a free-lance in journalism. Many were puzzled and amused by the cynical wit which often broke out in his gravest utterances, and had been classified as "blazing indiscretions." He lived aloof, and made no pretence of familiar intercourse with his followers. None of them were given a chance of cornering him in the Carlton Club. To most people he was the embodiment of cold and proud reserve. To those whom accident brought in his way he was the least formidable of men ; simple and urbane, easy to talk to, overflowing with humour, an entirely lovable man. His apparent chilliness was the result of a kind of modesty or shyness which showed itself in many curious ways. Once when he

[1] August 22.

341

had to occupy an hour in London on his way to Windsor, he was seized with the happy idea of seeking refuge with a novel in the Junior Carlton Club: " I shan't be in any one's way there," he said. The day was cold, and he had on a thin coat. When he was asked why he did not wear a famous cloak which he used at Hatfield, he quietly answered, " Those Maids of Honour do laugh at me so."

He was amazingly wise, and entirely courageous : he had the spirit of the master, and whilst he led he governed. He was considerate, not weak. When Saunderson went to " give him a piece of his mind," then "two strong men stood face to face," but not even before the Colonel was Lord Salisbury likely to quail. On the other hand, all the private communications that he had occasion to make to him revealed unfailing courtesy and care and attention ; and Saunderson " knew him at home," as schoolboys say, on happy and friendly terms. The Colonel was of an age and in a position to appreciate the gravity of the event : one of the few pre-eminent figures in the world was taken away, and he could not count on living to see the void supplied.

It was an eventful year for Ireland. During the debate on the Address Mr. Redmond moved an amendment expressing a hope that in the land purchase proposals which had been foreshadowed advantage would be taken of the unexampled opportunity produced by the Land Conference to put an end to agrarian strife in Ireland.

When Saunderson spoke he explained his reasons for declining to take part in the conference, but he frankly admitted that he had judged too harshly : valuable recommendations had been produced. Still more surprising, the landlords of Ireland had been given a flattering certificate of character. He could not refrain from pointing out that the tenants had received no less satisfactory a testimonial in respect of their capacity for repaying advances, which was not consistent with the familiar plea that they were frequently incapable of paying any rent at all.

Mr. Wyndham introduced his Bill on March 25. Its main principles were these : to put an end to dual ownership, and establish a peasant proprietary; to employ public credit to secure this national boon; to make a free grant. The last concession was to amount to £12,000,000, to take the form of a bonus to the landlord to facilitate purchase where the price would otherwise be uninviting. The recommendations of the Land Conference were freely discussed. A novel system of zones was introduced for limiting and regulating reductions of rent as a basis of bargain between the tenant on the one hand and the State, as the landlord's financier, on the other. There was no attempt at compulsion. The Bill was welcomed by all sections of Irishmen. The tenants' advocates could not object to so large a slice of the loaf for which they had always clamoured. The approval of the landlords was to be accounted for by Saunderson's avowal that this was the first of all the Land Bills with which he had had to do which had not meant the plundering of the class to which he belonged. The Bill was read a second time on May 7, and after a considerable Committee stage, it passed its third reading on July 21.

Saunderson was away during the second reading debate, but he spoke freely in Committee. On June 17 he had to criticise some of Mr. T. W. Russell's speeches which suggested that he was going back on the Conference report. Mr. Russell at once retorted that if the proposals of the report were put into a Bill he would vote for it. The Colonel next brought up a case on which the honourable gentleman had based some arguments—an instance, according to Saunderson, of an absentee tenant and a resident landlord: the tenant's wife had been left in charge of two acres, a hen, and a cow. He took this to be the feminine of a cock-and-bull story. Again he blessed the Bill.

Outside the House he made a speech on June 25 in which he repeated his approval, and declared that the Irish people were anxious to see it passed, but that there was "an outside party amongst the Home Rulers" who had a mind to wreck it. Once more he laid it down that if it was to the interest of the State to secure agrarian peace in Ireland, the State should not refuse to pay something. Nevertheless, he was represented as having said to a reporter, a few days later, that he was not satisfied with the development of affairs. There had been too much surrender; the zones had been almost swept away.

On the third reading he paid a compliment to the Chief Secretary on the ability and good temper which he had exhibited in carrying his measure. He admitted that it gave the landlord a prospect of selling without being driven out of his home. The only danger ahead lay in the likelihood of the tenant being reluctant to purchase at existing valuations, in view of the further reductions which the Land Commissioners might be relied upon to make.

In the House of Lords an amendment was carried against the Government on the question of zones: this was rejected on return to the House of Commons.

Other amendments were accepted, and when the
Bill went again to the Peers it passed into law
without further impediment. The session closed on
August 14.

It ought to be recorded that when the Home
Office vote was under discussion in June, the Colonel
and Mr. Sloan had stood forth in alliance to demand
from the Government a promise of legislation on the
subject of convent laundries. If no immediate result
was produced, at all events whatever misapprehen-
sions concerning Saunderson's action might still
linger in Ireland ought, after this, to have been dis-
sipated. Furthermore, it should be said that he gave
himself considerable trouble during the year in urging
upon the Chief Secretary the needs and claims of his
constituents in connection with a system of drainage
for Lough Neagh and the river Bann.

It has been said that the personal event of greatest
interest during the year 1903 was the death of Lord
Salisbury. A political event of infinite importance
has now to be noted.

Unpardonable would it be to enter here upon a
dissertation upon Tariff Reform. In pursuance of
the principle adopted in the previous chapter, little
more than bare facts shall be recorded. On May 15
Mr. Chamberlain, who had lately returned from a
tour in South Africa, made a speech at Birmingham
in which he laid down two propositions : one, that
it behoved us to cement the union between our
Colonies and ourselves by some system of preferential
fiscal treatment ; the other, that we should no longer
be bound by any technical definition of Free Trade.
It must be remembered that there had never been
lacking a widespread demand in the country for
an alteration in our fiscal system. During the

general election of 1885 many Conservative candidates had committed themselves to an urgent advocacy of some change under the title, as a rule, of "fair trade." Resolutions with this tendency had frequently been adopted at Conservative conferences. Periodically the question had been argued at great length in the Press, and the reformers were known to include many men of position both in and out of politics. But the movement had never gained strength. The advocates in Parliament were regarded as men with an amiable hobby; those in the Press were looked upon as visionaries and cranks. In 1893, at the end of a prolonged correspondence, *The Times* summed up the case in its leading article thus :[1]

"Scratch the Fair Trader, and you will find the Protectionist. . . . It is a bad thing in itself to attempt to encounter hostile tariffs by countervailing duties, and even if it were a good thing it would be impracticable. . . .'I maintain,' said Sir Robert Peel in 1849, ' that the best way to compete with hostile tariffs is to encourage free imports.' . . . If we are to fight the battle of Free Trade over again, those words and those arguments will once more do noble service in the cause of right reason and national prosperity, and we cannot give our new Protectionist friends a better piece of advice than to ponder them patiently and refute them if they can."

It will be remembered that even Lord Salisbury had gone so far in his speech at Hastings in May, 1892, that during the ensuing general election the cry of the little loaf was successfully raised against his party in Mr. Walter Long's constituency and elsewhere. But the foregoing facts are recalled to show that an alteration of our fiscal system had

[1] September 24.

never been seriously considered as within the range of practical politics.[1]

Now, what a change! Mr. Chamberlain spoke, and in a moment the scene was transformed. The character and the fortunes of a party were to be violently wrenched, and the political situation modified in innumerable ways.

After an interval of great excitement, Mr. Chamberlain resigned in September in order to prosecute his object free from the restrictions of office. Not satisfied with the repudiation offered to his proposals by the Prime Minister, Lord George Hamilton and Mr. Ritchie retired with diametrically opposite intentions. They were speedily followed by Lord Balfour of Burleigh, and eventually by the Duke of Devonshire. The circumstances attending these events were the topic of eager curiosity: it will be time enough to discuss them when the memoirs of the day come to be published.

It must be recorded, however, that in accepting Mr. Chamberlain's resignation Mr. Balfour set forth that whilst they aimed at the same ideals, the means they would employ were not at present identical: he himself thought it premature to advocate a tax on food; but he had nothing but good wishes for the new enterprise. To explain exactly what Mr. Balfour meant or did would be to enter on an embittered controversy which has raged ever since, and has not been disposed of yet. Many there were who would have quoted against him from Holy Scripture, " He that biddeth him God speed is partaker of his evil deeds."

[1] A prominent member of the Unionist party was once heard to declare that the leaders would never adopt this policy; it would mean twenty years' exclusion from office; moreover, it must inevitably drive Mr. Chamberlain back into the arms of the Liberals. Not even experts are infallible political prophets.

But it was generally accepted as a fact that Mr. Balfour had taken his position on ground upon which all men without extreme predilections could unite. Some were irreverent enough to speak of sitting on the fence. One uneasy politician said he felt rather as if he were sitting on barbed wire; another, with better spirit, avowed his intention of nailing his colours to the fence. No amount of ultimate knowledge will ever decide the problem of what the Prime Minister should have done. Either way disaster lay. Nothing now could arrest the Tariff Reform movement; nothing, it is to be believed, could have satisfied the Duke and his friends. Immediate surrender of office was one solution; earnest endeavour to find a *via media* was another. Mr. Balfour chose the latter, and with amazing adroitness kept his Government in power until it seemed expedient to go once more to the country. The defeat which overwhelmed it then will be attributed by Free Traders to the heresies of Protection, and by Tariff Reformers to weakness in not boldly proclaiming the new faith. As Saunderson said in a speech lately quoted, "Which is right? Possibly neither."

It could not be doubted that Saunderson would welcome the new propaganda. It is true that he had never gone so far as to accept the principle of a tax on food, but in view of his election address of 1885[1] he might with justice claim that he had long ago advocated Colonial preference and a modification of free imports:

"He intended to back up Mr. Chamberlain with all the power at his command," he said at Ballinary in November. "He believed that Mr. Chamberlain and Mr. Balfour were absolutely at one in their views.

[1] Page 87, note.

Mr. Balfour went one length, and Mr. Chamberlain went a bit farther, but they were both working for the same cause. . . . There would be no duty on Colonial corn and consequently the cry of the cheap [dear?] loaf fell to the ground. . . . If a two-shilling duty was put on—and he fancied that was about the figure—he believed the price of bread in North Armagh would remain exactly as it was now. . . . They had a member of the party who was undoubtedly above all others in the estimation of the empire, yet he was outside the Cabinet. He did not think he would be outside it very long. He should like to see —and he knew he was speaking the opinion of many men who sat on the same side of the House as himself—Mr. Chamberlain Prime Minister, and Mr. Balfour Foreign Secretary."

This is not without interest as illustrating the point of view adopted by those who unreservedly associated themselves with what was known as the policy of the whole hog. At the end of this speech he announced that—

" he had felt it his duty to inform the Government that if they brought in a Bill to establish a Roman Catholic University or a Roman Catholic College in a university endowed by the State, he and his colleagues would no longer accept the Government Whip and would look upon themselves as outside the party."

He could not help watching the Irish Administration with a suspicious eye.

The year 1904 does not afford a very happy retrospect. In the debate on the Address Saunderson's annual, contribution was lively enough. He began with a fling at a Nationalist member who for the moment was the object of his severe displeasure. He had never been able to understand, he said, why the honourable gentleman's constituents elected him. Now he knew: they hated the House of Commons,

"The suggestion you make is that Sir Antony MacDonnell accepted the statements of the Rev. Mr. O'Shea and over-rode the decision of the police authorities. The facts are that the clergyman in question asked the Under-Secretary to have Constable Anderson removed to another station. In consequence of that application the Under-Secretary acquired from the Constabulary authorities what were the facts, and learned from ... that a general complaint of ... made against the constable by ... the constable had been, on a summary inquiry, exonerated by the Inspector-General; that he had been again charged with specific acts of misconduct, and that this second charge was to be made the subject of a Court of Inquiry. On hearing how matters stood the Under-Secretary gave no instructions and made no suggestions on the case. The Court of Inquiry was formed on the initiative of the police authorities themselves, and not at all at his suggestion. Sir Antony MacDonnell took no further interest in the matter, and did not again even hear of it until the report of the Court of Inquiry and the decision of the Inspector-General, approving of the Court's finding and recommending the constable's dismissal, came before him in the ordinary course of official procedure. He concurred in the recommendation of the Inspector-General, and properly, since it would be subversive of discipline for the Government to retry without evidence a case determined on the examination and cross-examination of witnesses.

"The subsequent reinstatement of the constable was in no sense a reversal either of the finding arrived at by the Court on the evidence before it or of the decision of the Inspector-General based on that finding. It was due to the fact that evidence in the constable's favour, not produced by the defence before the Court of Inquiry, came afterwards to the knowledge of the Government."

Mr. Wyndham, therefore, gallantly defended his subordinate, who, as he pointed out, had no opportunity of defending himself.

But Saunderson was not appeased. At the Orange demonstration on July 12 he recapitulated his charges, and on August 3 he laid them before the House of Commons. It was, he declared, an Irish Dreyfus case, and with noble rage he denounced the accusers for involving the woman in the accusations brought against the man. "It had been the constant boast and glory of Irishmen, and Moore had enshrined this in his poems, that their women were chaste; and now, to serve a semi-political purpose, the honour of a woman was impugned." Mr. Wyndham could do no more than repeat the defence of his department.

The incident must be recorded, but it need not be unduly emphasised; and it must not be taken as a personal duel between the Colonel and the Chief Secretary. The Colonel had, as we have seen, gone out of his way more than once to praise the Chief Secretary, first on the occasion of his appointment, again in recognition of his skill in managing the Land Purchase Bill. It was elsewhere that he looked for the source of mischief. On July 12, he explicitly declared that Mr. Wyndham's conduct in the Anderson case redounded to his credit, but " his friend had a bad adviser and bad influence at his side." Nothing could reconcile him to the new spirit which, in his conviction, animated the life of the Castle.

His other grievance was in connection with the drainage of the Bann and Lough Neagh. This was not a formal action taken to satisfy local prejudices. He pleaded in the House of Commons, with sincerity, for the poor tenantry who paid drainage rates, and every year saw their houses invaded by the flood. The Irish Office had promised redress, but their proposed grant was inadequate. Such an offer, said the Colonel, was "as if he were to meet a poor friend and offer to stand him a good dinner on the condition that the friend paid one half of the bill." Later on he wrote to the Press to say that he and one of his colleagues had formally represented the question of the Bann drainage as the first to be considered in the interests of Ulster, and in view of the poor response that had been made, he confessed that his patience was exhausted.

We have to remember that here the Colonel was

pressing a particular claim, in which he was interested, upon a department which had many claims to meet, and not unlimited money to spend. It must be borne in mind also that the House of Commons is full of members who have cases of urgency to lay before Government with little prospect of securing satisfaction. The merits of the Bann drainage controversy need not be further discussed, nor any judgment be positively given. All that is required is to indicate the attitude which circumstances were inducing Saunderson to adopt.

He was not without other causes of vexation. In March there had been rival Unionist candidates at the bye-election in the St. Stephens Green division of Dublin; and when he endeavoured to influence the choice of the Association, he found he had put his head into a nest of hornets. Nor had the dissensions bred by the late election in South Belfast failed to occasion moments of difficulty and irritation. His speeches in Ireland reflected his state of mind. They contained few jokes and much earnest language. In April, at Portadown, he promised his audience that he and his colleagues meant to "squeeze justice out of the Unionist Government" in the matter of drainage. As to relaxing their vigilance against the dangers of Home Rule,[1] he pointed out that so long as there were eighty Home Rule members in the House of Commons, Home Rule could never be set aside as dead. He spoke reproachfully of the revolt in the Orange Institution, and finally declared that if he perceived the faintest indication that his constituents thought the time had come when he should

---

[1] In denouncing devolution proposals later in the year at Cavan, he declared that " he would a thousand times sooner have Mr. Redmond than Lord Dunraven."

make way for a younger man, he would willingly retire.

On July 12 he was equally austere. Incidentally he alluded to the Licensing Bill which was passing through the House of Commons, and made a distinct pronouncement upon compensation. He would deal with license-holders as the Government proposed to act towards Irish land agents. The landlords were left to compensate them: so ought brewers to be called upon to compensate publicans. He then lamented that successive Lord-Lieutenants and Chief Secretaries, with the notable exception of Mr. Balfour, had always yielded to the temptation of securing peace in their time by trying to pacify a class of Irishmen, whom nothing would pacify, at the sacrifice of those who were loyal to the Government. Besides the case of Anderson, he had to complain of the injustice done to a Protestant medical officer who had been passed over in favour of a Roman Catholic subordinate in a case of promotion, in spite of the protest which the Colonel had himself addressed to the Castle.

The pleasantest passage in this speech was his admission that " Mr. Sloan—whose conduct with regard to Orangeism he deplored absolutely—had proved an excellent member of the party" in the House of Commons. It may well be ascribed to the Colonel as a virtue that he had hastened to make peace with the new member who had set him at defiance and succeeded in winning South Belfast. Saunderson in old days had not shrunk from "gingering" Lord Iddesleigh, from giving Lord Salisbury "a piece of his mind," nor from defying Lord Randolph Churchill at the height of his power. He was not likely now to be cowed by any independent private member. But he had the unity of the party

at heart, and in the interests of peace and of strength
he had been willing to forgive and forget whatever
wrong he might consider he had suffered.

It will be a relief, after this gloomy reading, to
glance at his private occupations.   The following
extracts are from letters to his youngest son :

" *To his son John*

" *May* 8, 1904.—You will have seen in *The Times*
that I had no success at Sandwich.   I ought to have

THE COLONEL : "BY HIMSELF"

won easily, but threw away my chance by going down
in a motor eighty miles without goggles on, which
played the mischief with my eyes.   I began to pull
up towards the end, and if I had only made an easy
put at the fifteenth hole I think I should have won.
. . . I was only one hole to the bad on the round."

" 5, DEANERY STREET, PARK LANE,
" *July* 6, 1904.

" MY DEAREST JOHNIT,
" I have at last seen Taylor play.   He was in
very fine form: two less than Vardon.   I had a long
talk with him. . . . He will gladly arrange to play

round with us. . . . I never knew what golf was until
I saw the crack play. . . . Did you see my head in
Punch?—I drew the original."

The Colonel had often been portrayed in the journal
of Toby, M.P. On this occasion the illustration was
adapted from a drawing of himself done by his own
hand.

"*August* 25, 1904.—I have just come in from the
finest sail I ever sailed on the Lake. . . . George [1] said
yesterday, ' What I want is a strong wind and heavy
sea.' Well, to-day he had his desire: it blew like fury
from the south. We all carried whole mainsails and
spinakers. We got the start. Running down the
Lake to the Cow buoy the whole fore part of the boat
was submerged. We ran the fleet, and in the heavy sea
left the *Mistral* on the reach coming back. I was very
anxious to see how the boat would go to wind in the
heavy jump. I jumped away from George and won
by 3 min. 4 secs. Well done, *Sprite*!"

But his troubles were not yet over. In October he
had an attack of pneumonia. His recovery was not
altogether satisfactory, but he was able to move from
Castle Saunderson to Rostrevor. Here he became
much worse, and it was evident that there was lurking mischief. He was taken to Newcastle, and a
consultation revealed the existence of an abscess on
the lungs.

It was decided that an operation was necessary,
but here a difficulty presented itself: the condition
of his heart seemed to prohibit the use of anæsthetics.
The only alternative was to submit to the knife
without it, and this the Colonel consented to do.

He had suffered much, and suffered patiently. At
Rostrevor there had been some blunder in the arrangements made for his removal to Newcastle, and

[1] Mr. George Massy Beresford.

the journey had to be performed with as little danger
and discomfort as possible in an open motor. Now
a worse ordeal confronted him. The Colonel prepared
for this with composure; he rather resented what he
thought fussy attention to his comfort; but was careful to brush his hair with precision before he mounted
the table. It is conclusive evidence of his physical
and moral bravery that he then endured not only
the pain but the shock of what followed without
complaining at the time and without boasting afterwards.

The operation completed, he was put into bed; and
when Dr. Tait, whose skill had achieved an entirely
successful result, came to see his patient, he found
him contentedly listening to one of the psalms which
he had begged Mrs. Saunderson to read to him.

As soon as his condition permitted, he was conveyed
to the house of his son-in-law and daughter, Major
and Mrs. Head, at Ferry Quarter, Strangford, for
a long rest; and here, during convalescence, he made
some of the best sketches to be found in his many
books. He amused himself by sitting up in bed and
painting the shipping that passed to and fro beneath
his windows. On February 3, 1905, he writes as follows
to his son John:

"FERRY QUARTER.

"*February* 3, 1905.—I am still kept to the house
doing the rest cure. It has done me a world of good.
The Saunderson whose name you saw was my
cousin . . . He was frightfully ugly, but great fun. . . .
It is an interesting time in the world's history to be
alive in. I am sending you a book which I like very
much; it puts into very good language what I have
been speaking about off and on for 35 years." [1]

There was some consolation, at all events, to be

[1] "The Living Christ and the Four Gospels," by R. W. Dale, LL.D.

derived from the congratulations which poured in upon him when his recovery was assured. One, from a gentleman in high official position outside politics, will serve as an example:

"One never knows the truth about a man till he is very ill. You would be grateful if you could have heard how you were spoken of. Every one of your friends felt a keen personal anxiety, and your enemies were hardly distinguishable from your friends. . . . This is your reward for your honest, manly life—universal admiration."

CHAPTER XXIII

1905—1906

THE consequence of Saunderson's illness was that he could take no part in Parliament during the early months of 1905 ; and this, for purposes of biography, cannot be regretted. The tension between the Ulster party and the Government was at its highest pressure. The session began on February 14 ; there was an animated debate upon the circumstances of Sir Antony MacDonnell's appointment ; and a great deal of talk amongst politicians. On March 7 Mr. Wyndham resigned. The absence of the Colonel happily removes the necessity of adding to what has been said about these troubles. It need only be recorded that he kept in touch with affairs, and placed entire confidence in his colleagues. In a recent speech he had declared his obligations to the three most active of these : Mr. Lonsdale, M.P. for Mid Armagh, who since Mr. Johnston's death had acted as secretary to the party in the House of Commons, Mr. Craig, M.P. for South Antrim, and Mr. W. Moore, K.C., M.P. for North Antrim.

Having finished his rest cure, Colonel Saunderson went with his wife to Arcachon, on the sea coast, thirty miles from Bordeaux, where he appears to have spent his time contentedly, sailing, playing golf, and examining the neighbourhood. He gives an account of himself in the following letter:

"*To his son John*

"ARCACHON, *April* 7, 1905.

"I am just in from a sail. . . . I go out for two hours before lunch. After lunch we go to the golf ground. After tea I knock about a bit. I find I can hit a ball as well or as badly as ever. I wish you were here. . . . Rather a queer thing happened yesterday. We were sitting at the golf club when we heard a tremendous blowing of horns. This was a wild boar which had been hunted and came to bay just outside the links. Fancy the excitement at Eltham if such a thing occurred. Brighton has been a bad blow to the Government.[1] It shows what is to be expected at the next election. If I am still alive I must look to troublous times again. Home Rule again to the front. Old C.B. is pleased (*Picture*)."

Saunderson might well take a despondent view of the prospects of the party. They were drifting on to the rocks, and nothing could save them from disaster. It was a wonder to most people that the Government had endured until now. Unionist members had long been predicting that they would not see another session. Still they survived. Members of the Opposition confessed that they were eagerly and confidently looking forward to an exchange of places, but that the Prime Minister was too clever for them, and they despaired of manœuvring him out of his position until he chose to evacuate it.

If bye-elections were to be taken as reliable tests, the signs were threatening indeed. In 1902, when there was a vacancy for a Junior Lord of the Treasury, Mr. H. W. Forster had been appointed, and on seeking re-election in Kent, his majority of 4,812 was reduced

---

[1] Mr. Gerald Loder, who had been appointed a Junior Lord of the Treasury, sought re-election and was defeated.

to 891. Now Mr. Loder, who had sat for Brighton since 1889, and was supposed to have a safe seat, was actually defeated.

There were constant debates on the Tariff question. The more strenuous advocates were loudly crying

alive I must work to troublous times again – Home Rule again to the front –

"Old C.B. is pleased –

"Forward!" whilst those who entirely disapproved or were only half-hearted, were as determined to cry "Back!" Mr. Balfour's position was difficult enough, but it had become an established fashion to assume that he was purposely enigmatic; friend and foe agreed in looking for fresh obscurities rather than light in his speeches, and refused to attach the obvious interpretation to anything that he said. It was not surprising that the public, who had no clear convictions, should grow weary of what appeared to be a vacillating Government and a distracted party.

On March 28 there was another motion condemning the principle of retaliation. Mr. Balfour announced his intention of wasting no more time over these factitious debates; he proposed to absent himself, and advised his friends to do the same. This they accordingly did, with the exception of one or two who foresaw a chance of being allowed to address the House; and several others who had every intention of supporting the motion. The Opposition mustered in great strength, and contrived to make the Government cut a sorry figure in the estimation of plain men. In fact the party were demoralised: they knew it, and they were aware that the country knew it. The Aliens Bill might get them a little popularity; it was welcomed in the constituencies; but the latest Army scheme woke no enthusiasm; the Irish administration had bred suspicion; and the employment of Chinese labour in the South African mines was already inflaming indignation. The majority of the Unionists who intended to stand again might well raise the chorus of *morituri te salutant* to the Speaker.

Saunderson returned to the House of Commons on June 1. His reappearance was the signal for a general cheer, in which his Nationalist foes joined cordially. Nevertheless, before the evening was over, he was attacking them with his old spirit in the discussion of an Irish resolution:

"It was asserted that the Crimes Act interfered with the liberty of the Irish people, but that was

because of the peculiar ideas of liberty entertained
by some Irishmen. His idea of liberty was the
freedom of every man to pursue his avocations within
the law. It was because the League interfered with
this freedom and sought to impose its doctrines on
the will of others by intimidation that the Act was
passed."

Next day he wrote to his son John :

" You will have seen that I received a great reception when I entered the House. I wish your mother
had been there to hear. The Home Rulers cheered
tremendously. I must admit that I was much touched
by this token of friendship from both sides of the
House. You will have seen that I spoke at the
evening sitting. They say I made a very good speech,
so I suppose I did."

A week later he offered, on behalf of his Irish
friends, a tribute of respect to Mr. Gully, who was
retiring from the Chair.[1]

" I think," he said, "that Irish members are gifted
with the power of understanding what a Speaker
ought to be."

Then, embracing in his purview his Irish opponents:

" They have in my estimation been endowed with
the faculty of eliciting and bringing to the surface
those great qualities which are necessary in any
great Speaker."

As the summer went on the public were further
annoyed by the report upon the mis-management in
the disposal of surplus war stores in South Africa,
and by disturbed relations which led to the resignation of the Viceroy of India ; and the credit of the
Government fell lower and lower. In July they
introduced a re-distribution scheme. The Prime
Minister proposed to carry it in the form of a resolution ; this was objected to by the Opposition and

[1] Mr. J. W. Lowther was elected Speaker without opposition.

ruled out of order by the Speaker. It was thereupon withdrawn, and a Bill promised for next year. This would have the effect of postponing the general election election into a remote future—a prospect of which most people were sceptical. The consequence of all this was that the Government, by publishing these proposals, offended many constituencies without gratifying any, and were left in an undignified position after all. Trade continued bad, and the stars in their courses seemed to fight against them.

On July 18 there was a meeting of the party at the Foreign Office, when the leader urged his friends to attend constantly in order that business might be satisfactorily concluded; and he was warmly cheered. Next night the Government found themselves left in the lurch, and suffered defeat by 199 to 196 on the Land Purchase Commission vote in the Irish estimates. There was a great demonstration, and grave inquiries were made as to their intention of resigning. The Prime Minister promised to make a statement on Monday. On the 24th little surprise was caused by Mr. Balfour's announcement, prefaced by ample array of precedent, that he and his friends saw no reason why they should retire from office on such a trifling provocation.

Those who were anxious to prolong their days urged the necessity of retaining the Unionists in power whilst the war between Russia and Japan still continued, and affairs abroad were full of menace and unrest; but this argument had been exhausted in connection with the pending settlement of affairs after the war in South Africa. Moreover, it would presumably entail the repeal of the Septennial Act if no Government were to be removed from office so long as the surface of the world was at all ruffled.

It was, however, an open secret that the Cabinet had no intention of resigning, if they could avoid it, until they had brought to a happy issue the negotiations then in progress for a new treaty with Japan. Through all these vicissitudes Saunderson was a regular attendant. He was in a happier frame of mind with regard to the Irish Government. The new Chief Secretary was Mr. Walter Long. It was understood that he had left the Local Government Board with reluctance; but, having undertaken his formidable task, he set to with a will. He was able to make a fresh start and dispel the cloud of mystery and misunderstanding which had so long hung over the Irish Office. He brought unlimited courage and resolution to bear upon the problems before him, and contrived, during the nine months of his tenure of office, to establish an abiding place in the confidence of those who had lately been dismayed. The Colonel found in him a man after his own heart, and he took occasion to say so in the House of Commons on July 24.

There lingered a vague idea that the Ulster members were implacable, but this reconciliation, at all events, was sincere. On August 7 some members of Parliament dined with me, in preparation for an all-night sitting. Amongst those who came were the Colonel and the Chief Secretary, and I can, at all events, testify to the warmth of their personal relations.

I hope I offend no one when I say that, even in the presence of members of the Government, I considered the Colonel my guest of honour. I asked him to sit next to me, and it was the last occasion on which we had a long and intimate talk. I was not in Ireland that autumn; next year I was out of Parliament, and saw him seldom. That evening we talked of many interests past and present, and he was as inspiriting as ever. But he bore undeniable traces of his recent illness; and as we went back to the House of Commons I could not help observing to one of my companions that he had aged appreciably. Nevertheless, one trifling incident showed that the masterful spirit had not grown infirm. We dined at a club, and coffee was brought at once, because we were pressed for time. The Colonel jumped up and insisted on this being sent downstairs, because it was a terrible thing to have coffee without a cigarette. Downstairs we accordingly went.

And so the Government came safely through their ordeal. Thanks to consummate leadership, the doomed army was brought into temporary refuge; but their reputation was sadly damaged.

At the end of November there was a ray of hope when Sir Henry Campbell-Bannerman made a speech of a Home Rule tendency, and Lord Rosebery immediately announced that he " would not serve under the banner of Home Rule." A split in the Liberal party and a revival of Home Rule promised invaluable succour at such a crisis. But this feeble glimmer flickered out. On December 5 Mr. Balfour resigned. Sir Henry Campbell-Bannerman formed a Government, including Lord Rosebery's most prominent allies. Lord Rosebery had taken pains to make it known that he did not desire to return to office: and he did not return. Parliament was dissolved, and the floods descended on the Unionist party. In Manchester Mr. Balfour's majority of 2,450 was turned into a minority of 2,000. Mr. Chaplin, the monarch of Lincolnshire, was defeated. In Kent Sir William Hart Dyke was driven out, after forty years' service. The rout was absolute.

It is wiser to avoid saying any more concerning the effect of Tariff Reform upon this election. It was, at all events, an unsettling element. The imputation of religious tyranny in connection with the Education Bill had had some effect. Chinese Labour was the most effective cry. Some people no doubt objected on principle to the introduction of Asiatic labour into what ought to be a white man's country. Others managed to persuade themselves that it meant slavery under the British flag. Others, again, saw in it nothing but a good expedient for catching votes. Early in the year it had been the fate of speakers at Unionist meetings in the country to be met with objurgations on the ground that Chinamen were coming here to take away the livelihood of the agricultural labourers: the juxtaposition of plough-tails and pigtails was an obvious opening for effective declamation. When the elections came the Chinaman made great play upon the hoardings. It is an unsolved problem what turns votes on these occasions. Speeches affect some, but not a critical number; the popularity of a candidate counts for much; local interests must not be ignored; but, to judge from the crowds which continually gazed upon the Chinese cartoons in January, 1906, there is little doubt that the posters on this occasion were largely responsible for the amazing result.

But in any case defeat was inevitable. The breeze from the Home Rule quarter flagged and fell, and there was no other wind to fill the Unionist sails. A wretched remnant of one hundred and fifty-seven came back to Parliament to confront four hundred and twenty-nine Liberal and Labour members, exclusive of eighty-three Nationalists. The exact complexion of the fifty so-called Labour members need not be classified. Suffice it to say that the seed sown in 1867 had at last borne fruit : the Labour organisations throughout the country had set about electing their own representatives, and a new element had been introduced into our political system.

Saunderson was returned unopposed. He had first entered Parliament forty years ago in the old days of Whig and Tory, whilst Palmerston was yet alive; before Home Rule was a watchword, or a Labour Party had entered into the mind of man. He had lived to see the old order changed almost beyond recognition, and he was surely entitled, had he chosen, to bid politics farewell.[1] But at Portadown, on January 12, he told the electors that to his mind the present election was the most important, so far as the destinies of Great Britain were concerned, that he had ever taken part in since 1885, and, God willing, he would carry on the fight in which he had been engaged for the past twenty years.[2] He had to deplore a breach in his party ; at Belfast a Unionist meeting had been broken up by a band of men who supported another Unionist candidate : " To organise a faction of this kind within the party was to betray the Union. They saw the Home Rule coach coming up the road, and the driver was John Redmond. Recent speeches showed them that a bargain between him and Sir Henry Campbell-Bannerman had been amicably settled and, so far as Ireland was concerned, Sir Henry would be

[1] A paragraph appeared in some of the papers late in 1905 reporting that Saunderson was to be raised to the Peerage. This would have surprised nobody ; but the bestowal of political honours is not always in accordance with expectation, and it would serve no good purpose to argue here that the revival of the title of Castleton would have been a suitable acknowledgment of such long and vigorous parliamentary service.

[2] On February 19, he wrote to Mr. W. J. Allen, " So long as God gives me work to do and I can do it, I shall remain at my post."

absolutely and entirely in the hands of Mr. Redmond."
Nor did he conclude a very long speech without proclaiming that Mr. Long was "by far the best man he
had ever known in Ireland."[1]

It cannot be said that the Unionist party took their
defeat very handsomely. The general inclination was
rather to fix the blame than to find a remedy. On the
eve of the opening of Parliament a meeting was held
at Lansdowne House[2] for which the way had been
prepared by the publication of a letter from Mr.
Balfour to Mr. Chamberlain. In this an earnest
attempt was made to remove existing difficulties and
differences, and, from the speeches at the meeting
which followed it might have been hoped that this
had been successful ; but within an hour, all those who
had attended were interpreting the new understanding
according to their several and divergent desires, and
the fiscal dilemma still awaited its solution.

Saunderson was asked, at the last moment, to say
something as an old and distinguished member of the
party ; and this duty he discharged with credit. But
it was not an exhilarating occasion, nor was it within
the power of man to instil a spirit of blessed content
or sanguine expectation.

On February 19 the Houses met, and on the opening
day Saunderson and the new Chief Secretary, Mr.
Bryce, exchanged friendly notes, in view of a quiet
conversation upon Bann drainage and other Irish
matters. On the 21st Saunderson moved an amendment to the Address expressing the alarm inspired
in His Majesty's most loyal subjects by the promise

---

[1] In a private letter he had written, " I have been staying with Walter
Long. He is a brick, and if he had a year or two more in Ireland he
would make a wonderful change."

[2] February 14.

of interference with the system of government in Ireland :

" Believing that your Majesty's present advisers, by their past declarations, have committed themselves to a policy which will endanger the liberty and property of the loyalist minority, promote discord and civil strife, and impair the integrity of the United Kingdom."

It was the last of his set speeches against Home Rule, and there is something sad in reading such a familiar passage as this :

" But whatever he [the minister] did, he was confronted in Ireland by an Opposition which was absolutely united in opposing his aims, and which he must find in the end too strong for him, if an attempt were made in the future to hand over the Irish loyalists of all denominations to a power which their forefathers would not serve and which the Unionist party of to-day would never consent to obey."

The party was perhaps not so absolutely united as it used to be. Mr. Sloan had elected to keep a free hand in his political action ; and Mr. T. W. Russell had passed over to the other side. Mr. Moore had lost his seat and was temporarily absent, destined, as it turned out, to succeed the speaker in the repre-sentation of North Armagh.

After this Colonel and Mrs. Saunderson again went to Arcachon. He was in excellent spirits, and took part in the passing amusements, including a picnic, where he insisted upon acting as cook. But he was presently seized with a serious heart attack, to which his family were obliged to attach grave importance.[1]

[1] Amongst other disquieting symptoms, the Colonel was seized with an attack of faintness one day in Grosvenor Square, and had to be tended by a policeman. His first words on recovery were, "The Irish members would like to see me now!"

He went later to Pau and Biarritz; and at the last of these he met Lord Dudley. With the ex-Viceroy he had a great deal of confidential intercourse. The two men liked one another. Lord Dudley, free from the restrictions of office, was anxious to set certain matters in their true proportions. Saunderson was deterred by no malice or prejudice from regarding them dispassionately; and he afterwards desired it to be known that these conversations had done much good, and that he was anxious that full justice should be done to a man whose path had been beset by many and great difficulties.

With the approach of summer Saunderson returned to London. He spoke occasionally during the session. On July 26 he seconded a motion, brought forward by Mr. Lonsdale, to reduce the Chief Secretary's salary, in order to call attention to the general administration of Ireland; in doing so he dwelt chiefly upon the eviction proceedings upon Lord Clanricarde's estate, and the violent resistance to the authorities offered by one tenant, Martin Ward. His last effort in the House was to claim justice for a landlord who, he declared, was the unfailing resource of the Nationalists when they were in search of a grievance. Into this solemn protest he instinctively introduced a whimsical turn:

" Lord Clanricarde's estate in Galway," he said, " was one of the lowest rented in the county, and when his tenants went into Court to get a fair rent fixed, their rents were raised. Ward had no intention of going, and he skilfully fortified his house with manure bags."

His point was that the Government had secured peace by promising legislation; he disclaimed having made any party attack; his desire was to let the

Government see the danger of the course they were pursuing.

It will be remembered that he had been busy this year upon a new yacht, the *Witch*, and in August he was as deeply immersed as ever in the races on the Lake. On August 21 he writes a long letter to his youngest son full of technical criticism and showing unabated ardour.

Again, on the 29th, he writes a graphic description of a race in which he appears to have been hard pressed for some time by Lord Dudley's boat; but in the end "We won by ¼ hour. Cyril Ward gave up miles behind." The ex-Viceroy and his brother had now become active members of the Lough Erne Yacht Club, and the younger of the two, a resident on the Lake.

"You remember the problem I had to solve," the Colonel adds; "viz. to build a boat that could tackle *Vanessa* and *Breeze* in light weather, and go pretty well in strong. So far as the light weather is concerned the *Witch* is a wonderful solution; it remains to be seen how she will go in a blow. You will be delighted with her. We do not use our centreboard— we keep it up all the time."

In September he wrote to *The Times* urging the necessity of removing any lurking suspicions which there might be of complicity on the part of the late Government with the Devolution proposals, and declaring his unalterable determination to resist any step in the direction of Home Rule. A final letter appeared in *The Times* the day before his death, in which he said that the result of county government in Ireland had been to remove all Protestants and Unionists, himself included, from local administration and to instal Roman Catholics and Nationalists instead.

THE LAST RACE.

This letter was written on Wednesday, October 17. On Thursday, 18, he sailed in a race, and, as it happened, was photographed on the Lake with some Arcachon friends, his daughter-in-law, Mrs. Armar Saunderson, and his daughter, Mrs. Head. It was the last of a lifetime of happy days on Lough Erne.

Mrs. Saunderson was kept in her room, not well enough to go out. In the evening the Colonel went to her and said that he had had a sudden bleeding at the nose. However, he recovered and went down to the smoking-room.

On Friday morning he read for some time to Mrs. Saunderson, and exhibited no bad symptoms. Later in the day he became seriously ill, with violent coughing; and congestion of the lungs declared itself. He then confessed to having felt a good deal of pain for some days ; but he had concealed the fact for fear he should be kept off the Lake.

On Saturday morning he was well enough to be impatient for the post. " I suppose it is conceit," he said, " but I want to see my letter in *The Times* " ; and his last wish was gratified. Towards night it was seen that his case was desperate. The powers of endurance were overstrained : very early on Sunday morning, October 21, happily exempt from long and grievous suffering, he quietly died.

It was no small comfort to the stricken widow that amongst the first of the messages of condolence to arrive was a generous telegram from Mr. John Redmond, the leader of the Nationalist party. Of the innumerable communications which followed, none was more kind than the letter of Sir Henry Campbell-Bannerman.

A fortnight before his death, as he came out of

church on Sunday, he pointed to a large oak-tree near the door, saying, "That is where I am to be buried," and proceeded to give minute instructions. He had little reason to imagine that these would have to be so speedily obeyed; but on October 24 his coffin was carried there upon a gun-carriage, supplied by the battery of Royal Field Artillery at Belturbet; and beneath the shadow of the chosen tree his dead body was deposited. Masses of flowers surrounded the grave; upon the coffin there lay his racing flag and Mrs. Saunderson's cross of red salvias. A contingent of his old battalion was paraded. There was a full concourse of his political and private friends, of his tenants and neighbours. Roman Catholic priests were there; even the Nationalist members supplied a representative. So great a volume of sorrowing messages poured in that all Ireland, for the moment, seemed to be united in community of sorrow.

The Bishop of Ossory,[1] a devoted personal friend, delivered a beautiful address, too long to be quoted at length and too good to be spoilt by condensation; from which, none the less, a few phrases must be borrowed, because none can better tell what should be told.

His intense personal affection, said the Bishop, had its origin thirty-two years ago:

"Ever since then I have learned to reverence, admire, and love him—a little more than yesterday, a little less than to-morrow. . . . His strong convictions were based upon the passionate belief, which was part of his very soul, that he was fighting for the prosperity, happiness, and peace of the land of his birth—the land he loved best on earth. . . . To the beloved partner of his life's work, who was, if I may so say,

[1] Bishop of Down, 1907.

a trusted comrade as well as a devoted wife; to his sons and daughter . . . we offer the strong assurance . . . that in their lawful pride in Edward Saunderson we claim, as his fellow-countrymen of every creed and class, the right to share. . . . And just as in his political speeches he often startled friend and foe by some bold antithesis for which he seemed to have no basis, or which it seemed impossible to explain, so in religious matters his utterly unconventional presentation of Divine truth often startled the listener, till you realised that his faith was deep grounded, as the roots of yonder oak, on Jesus Christ."

The Primate had already paid his tribute at a meeting of the Armagh Diocesan Synod; but, employing the gift which had long made him familiar to Englishmen as a poet, he sent this memorial to *The Times*:

THE RIGHT HONOURABLE COLONEL EDWARD SAUNDERSON, M.P.

In Memoriam

Him to whom Heaven such varied utterance gave,
The Christian " Hail and Farewell " said at last
Amid the dropping leaves and gathering mists,
Yesterday morn we left within his grave—
We who are children of a mighty past,
Sons of unconquerable colonists.

There are too many orators just now
Fresh from the horn-books of the insolent,
Of rhetoric redundant, dull of eye.
Thine was the rhetoric of books unsent,
God's finger laid upon the tongue and brow,
One touch whereof is immortality!

The logic fired by humour and by wit,
The splendid wrath that centres in a jest,
And wakens its interminable laughter—
And lo! a sequent wisdom taught thereafter,
And one more folly stripp'd and manifest,
And the world wiser for the joy of it.

Far more than this. They called him "Puritan."
Who is not partly so is incomplete,
Hath not the home that lies beyond the stars,
Marches not panoplied to the noblest wars,
No preparation made to shoe his feet,
No eyes of the lit heart its foes to scan.

And we stern Northerners are such in fate.
This is beat into us by the falling rains,
By the sad roaring of the Psalmist-waves,
By overbearing hands Italianate,
By our simplicity of sacred strains,
By the sweet texts upon our mothers' graves.

We like to see our chosen soldiers face
The battle singing, and our statesmen wake
The foe with bitter gibes as Samson might.
Well did our man in Parliament fill his place,
Facing their numbers like his own fierce lake.
We think of him walking with Christ in white.

And now is left of all that manifold speech
Nothing that makes for any strife or hate,
Nothing that is not pure and clean and good,
Nothing that does not calm and elevate,
Nothing that is not meet our land to reach
Out of the distance and the altitude.

WILLIAM ARMAGH.

October 24, 1906.

The Bishop of Ossory had reminded his hearers that, a fortnight before he died, the Colonel had preached from the text, " Come unto Me all ye that are weary, and I will give you rest." Perhaps his strength was failing him, and he was not unwilling to lie down and rest. Surely he was not afraid to die; but, to those who loved him, the passing was sorrowful indeed. There was an instant consciousness of one of those losses that matter in this world. " The dear old Colonel is gone!" was an exclamation from a deep fount. Perhaps no words can explain the feeling more shrewdly than the comment of the dead man's friend, Mr. Burdett-Coutts: " Ed. was the kind of fellow that gets hold of one."

These pages have indeed been written to little purpose if it is necessary now to dilate upon his character: they pretend, no matter how unskilfully, to make that manifest. Yet one or two reflections may be added.

It is natural that in the story of so bold and adventurous a man the salient points should indicate a spirit of assertiveness. Yet it is easy enough to prove that Saunderson was not one who cared only for the praise of men. To take a single instance: it was he who undertook the labours of organisation when the first great Unionist demonstration was held in the old Haymarket Opera House in April, 1886. Lord Cowper, an ex-Liberal Viceroy, presided; Mr. Forster, an ex-Liberal Chief Secretary, spoke, and Lord Hartington; Mr. Rylands, a veteran Radical; Mr. Goschen, and Lord Salisbury; Mr. W. H. Smith, and others of both parties. Here surely was an opportunity for Saunderson to claim recognition and make himself conspicuous had he been so minded; but he was content to sit and rejoice in silence. The day's work was of good omen for Ireland, and that was enough for him.

Of his religion enough has been said. His sermons were deemed worthy of preservation, and a little volume of three, to which the Bishop of Down has written a preface, will ensure that the lover of the Gospel will not be forgotten in the party politician. It may be permitted to suggest that a fitting sermon might be preached about himself upon the text of Romans iii. 23, 24, "For all have sinned, and come short of glory; being justified freely by His grace through the redemption that is in Christ Jesus."

Nor did he rely exclusively on faith without works. To take again one example: he was sufficiently bent

upon doing his duty towards his neighbour to take
the trouble one winter's night to descend into Deanery
Street and offer some remedy to the watchman of
road repairs whose painful coughing had been heard
in the bedroom upstairs.   He endeavoured to be
as good as his word.

So far as personal accomplishments are concerned
little remains to be said.   As an orator he had not the
genius which one associates with an Irish origin in
the case of Sheridan, or Burke, or Richard Lalor
Sheil; but even if he fell short of the highest form
of eloquence, he remains one of the most effective and
forcible speakers of his own generation.

It has been said that he had no love of details.   He
was essentially a man of action, and apt to be impatient
of too much lingering by the way.   He made no
pretence to scholarship, but he was fond of reading,
and loved fiction: he knew his Walter Scott.   Poetry
appealed to him in certain forms; and such pieces
as he liked he at once committed to memory.   He
never attempted authorship beyond his pamphlet and
his little volume of sermons; but he had a curious
habit of writing fragments of essays on scraps of paper
in pencil, without obvious motive or any appearance
of design.   He lived heartily; was loyal and attached
to his friends; was kindly affectioned towards all men,
and encouraged those with whom he came in contact
to show themselves at their best.

It is evident that he had something of the dreamer
in him.   His views and principles were the outcome
of long and silent thought, and there were times when
he liked to have no other companion than his wife.

But, whether he was in his liveliest mood, or in the
humour for solemn self-examination, he undoubtedly
impressed all those who came near him in a remark-

able manner, and left them sadly conscious of some extinction of vitality when they knew that they should see his face no more.

In Ireland his name will not be forgotten; and the statue, which is to be raised at Portadown to commemorate his faith and works, will serve as an ensample to future generations of loyal Ulstermen.

Panegyric and excess of eulogy serve no man's memory; but one need not fear to say that those who knew Edward Saunderson will remember him all their days; and that when he died, the world in which he lived was the poorer for his loss.

INDEX

Printed by Hazell, Watson & Viney, Ld., London and Aylesbury.

THE LETTERS OF QUEEN VICTORIA.

A Selection from Her Majesty's Correspondence, 1837—1861. Published by authority of His Majesty the King. Edited by Arthur Christopher Benson, M.A., C.V.O., and Viscount Esher, G.C.V.O., K.C.B. With numerous Photogravures. Medium 8vo. Three Volumes. £3 3s. net.

LIFE AND LETTERS OF JOHN THADEUS

DELANE, Editor of *The Times*, containing hitherto unpublished Letters of Palmerston, Disraeli, and other Statesmen, and numerous Anecdotes of the Court and London Society in the Reign of Queen Victoria. By Arthur Irwin Dasent. With Illustrations. 2 Vols. Demy 8vo, 32s. net.

CORRESPONDENCE OF GEORGE CAN-

NING AND SOME INTIMATE FRIENDS. Containing hitherto Unpublished Letters, *Jeux d'Esprit*, etc., of George Canning, the Honble. Charles Bagot, the Rev. J. Sneyd, the Marquess Wellesley, Lord Binning, William Wellesley Pole, Lord Lyttelton, George and Charles Ellis, Bootle Wilbraham, John Hooker Frere, Stratford Canning, and many others. Edited by Josceline Bagot. With Portraits. 2 Vols. Demy 8vo.

OUR FIRST AMBASSADOR TO CHINA.

THE LIFE AND CORRESPONDENCE OF

GEORGE, FIRST EARL MACARTNEY, 1737—1806, Governor of Grenada, Envoy Extraordinary at St. Petersburg, Chief Secretary for Ireland, Governor of Madras, Ambassador Extraordinary to Pekin, Governor of the Cape of Good Hope, etc. By Mrs. Helen H. Robbins. With Portraits and other Illustrations. Demy 8vo. 16s. net.

THE REMINISCENCES OF THE LATE

ALBERT PELL, sometime M.P. for South Leicestershire. Edited, with a Memoir, by Thomas Mackay. With an Appreciation by the Right Hon. James Bryce. With Illustrations. Demy 8vo. 15s. net.

FOURTEEN YEARS IN PARLIAMENT,

1892—1906. By A. S. T. Griffith-Boscawen, formerly M.P. for the Tonbridge Division of Kent. Demy 8vo. 10s. 6d. net.

SIR ROBERT PEEL. Based on his Correspondence and Private Documents. Edited by Charles Stuart Parker. With a Summary of Sir Robert Peel's Life and Character by his Grandson, the Hon. George Peel. 3 Vols. Vol. I.—From his Birth to 1827. With Portraits. 8vo. 16s. Vols. II. and III.—From 1827 to his Death in 1852. With Portraits. 8vo. 32s.

"A work of first importance to English history."—*Daily News*.

"Mr. Parker has done his work with admirable fidelity and judgment."—*The Times*.

"They replace the gossip of Croker and Greville with authentic data, and tell in themselves a tale more eloquent than that of all the previous writers of the time."—*Daily Chronicle*.

THE DUKE OF ARGYLL, 1823-1900. Edited by the Dowager Duchess of Argyll. With Portraits and other Illustrations. 2 Vols. Medium 8vo. 36s. net.

"It is full of vivid reminiscence of persons who have filled large places in the history of their country, of science, and of literature. For the general reader the charm of these volumes will be found in the personal reminiscences, and the refreshing irregularity in which chapters upon high affairs of State are interspersed with notes of travel, natural history, literature, and general society."—*Morning Post*.

LIFE OF THE MARQUIS OF DUFFERIN AND AVA. By Sir Alfred Lyall, P.C. Third Impression. With Portraits, etc. Demy 8vo. 2 Vols. 36s. net.

"A masterpiece of biographical art; the writer never obtrudes his own personality, devoting sound judgment and consummate skill to moulding in just proportions the figure and lineaments of his subject."—*Punch*.

THE HATZFELDT LETTERS. Letters of Count Paul Hatzfeldt to His Wife, written from the Headquarters of the King of Prussia, 1870-71. Translated from the French by J. L. Bashford, M.A. With Illustrations. Demy 8vo. 15s. net.

"Will be one of the most widely read volumes of the present season, because it reveals a personality of infinite attraction. . . . We have nothing but praise for this most attractive book."—*Morning Post*.

THE LIFE AND LETTERS OF GEORG JOACHIM GOSCHEN, 1752-1828. By Viscount Goschen. With Portrait and Illustrations. Demy 8vo. 36s. net.

This is not merely a biography of a distinguished publisher and printer, but is practically a history of German literature during the latter half of the eighteenth century (including many previously unpublished letters from Goethe, Schiller, Wieland, Klopstock, etc.), and of the political struggles of Germany in the Napoleonic Era.

THE LIFE AND LETTERS OF SIR

JAMES GRAHAM, 1792-1861, First Lord of the Admiralty in the Ministries of Lord Grey and Lord Aberdeen, and Home Secretary in the Administration of Sir Robert Peel. Edited by C. S. Parker, Editor of "Life of Sir Robert Peel." With Portraits and other Illustrations. 2 Vols. Demy 8vo. 24s. net.

SIDNEY HERBERT. Lord Herbert of Lea. A

Memoir. By Lord Stanmore. 2 Vols. With Portraits and other Illustrations. Demy 8vo. 24s. net.

"An admirable record of a noble and all too brief career."—*Pall Mall Gazette.*

"Will rank high among political biographies. . . . Will be read as a matter of course by all students of political history. It is a most valuable contribution to the chronicles of the Government of fifty years ago, and it is also a wonderful picture of the desperately hard life of a minister of the Crown. The book is most instructive and most salutary."—*Daily Telegraph.*

FURTHER MEMOIRS OF THE WHIG

PARTY, 1807-1821. With some Miscellaneous Reminiscences. By Henry Richard Vassall, 3rd Lord Holland. Edited by the Earl of Ilchester, Editor of the "Letters of Lady Sarah Lennox." With Portraits. Demy 8vo. 18s. net.

"Lord Holland's writings form one of the most admirable running comments upon an interesting period of history that a politician has ever left behind him. These Memoirs are admirably written, and they abound in wise sayings, keen observations of character, and many flashes of wit and epigram."—*Westminster Gazette.*

THE LIFE OF ISABELLA BIRD (Mrs.

Bishop). By Miss Anna M. Stoddart. Third Impression. With Portraits, Maps, and other Illustrations. Demy 8vo. 18s. net.

"Have you ever been taken into a studio by an artist to look at the portrait of a friend, and been delighted and surprised by the likeness? This is exactly what will happen to the friends of Mrs. Bishop who read Miss Stoddart's life of her. . . . Miss Stoddart has portrayed for us, as few could have done, the untirable and brilliant mind of the feeble body, the loving and broadening soul, and the wide and philanthropic charity of Isabella Bird Bishop."—*Blackwood's Magazine.*

LETTERS OF RICHARD FORD, 1797-
1858. Edited by Rowland E. Prothero, M.V.O.,
Author of "The Psalms in Human Life," etc., etc. With
Portraits and other Illustrations. Demy 8vo. 10s. 6d. net.

"Full of interesting reading about many people and far travels."—*Daily Chronicle.*

"It is altogether a welcome and fascinating windfall, or rather treasure-trove."—*Outlook.*

DIARIES AND CORRESPONDENCE OF
SIR CHARLES JAMES FOX BUNBURY, Baronet,
1809–1886. Edited by his Sister-in-Law, Mrs. Henry
Lyell. With Portraits. 2 Vols. Demy 8vo. 30s. net.

Sir Charles Bunbury was a distinguished member of Society and an accomplished botanist and geologist during the middle and later part of the nineteenth century. These volumes contain his Diaries and Letters to his family, together with much of his Correspondence with Sir Charles Lyell, reminiscences of eminent men of his day, of his life in London, of his travels, etc.

MOLTKE IN HIS HOME. By Friedrich
August Dressler. Authorised Translation by Mrs. C. E.
Barrett-Lennard, with an Introduction by General Lord
Methuen. With Illustrations. Demy 8vo. 6s. net.

This does not attempt to give a biography of the great Field-Marshal, but contains a series of sketches and incidents of his life, and of the characteristics and surroundings of one of the greatest soldiers of the nineteenth century.

MEMOIRS OF THE LORD OF JOIN-
VILLE. By Mrs. Josiah Wedgwood. Square demy
8vo. 9s. net.

"This is one of the most delightful works we have come across for a long time. The translation is spirited and excellent, and the preface and notes are just what a reader wants, and no more than he wants, for intelligent enjoyment of one of the great stories of all times."—*The Spectator.*

A PIETIST OF THE NAPOLEONIC
WARS AND AFTER. The Life of the Countess Reden.
From Diaries, Letters, etc., hitherto unpublished. By
Eleonore Princess Reuss. Authorised Translation by
Mrs. Charles Edward Barrett-Lennard and M. W. Hoper.
With an Introductory Note by Robert S. Rait. With
Portraits and other Illustrations. Demy 8vo. 15s. net.

LONDON: JOHN MURRAY, ALBEMARLE STREET.

9 781287 499749